CW01163340

Mediation and Hierarchy of
Knowledge on Communication

*To Yves Jeanneret, who wove Ariadne's thread through my research*

SCIENCES

*Scientific Knowledge Management*,
Field Director – Renaud Fabre

*Knowledge Exploration and Analysis*,
Subject Head – Daniel Egret

# Mediation and Hierarchy of Knowledge on Communication

*The Case of Professional Training*

Aude Seurrat

iSTE                    WILEY

First published 2025 in Great Britain and the United States by ISTE Ltd and John Wiley & Sons, Inc.

Apart from any fair dealing for the purposes of research or private study, or criticism or review, as permitted under the Copyright, Designs and Patents Act 1988, this publication may only be reproduced, stored or transmitted, in any form or by any means, with the prior permission in writing of the publishers, or in the case of reprographic reproduction in accordance with the terms and licenses issued by the CLA. Enquiries concerning reproduction outside these terms should be sent to the publishers at the undermentioned address:

ISTE Ltd  
27-37 St George's Road  
London SW19 4EU  
UK  

www.iste.co.uk

John Wiley & Sons, Inc.  
111 River Street  
Hoboken, NJ 07030  
USA  

www.wiley.com

© ISTE Ltd 2025

The rights of Aude Seurrat to be identified as the author of this work have been asserted by her in accordance with the Copyright, Designs and Patents Act 1988.

Any opinions, findings, and conclusions or recommendations expressed in this material are those of the author(s), contributor(s) or editor(s) and do not necessarily reflect the views of ISTE Group.

Library of Congress Control Number: 2024950063

British Library Cataloguing-in-Publication Data
A CIP record for this book is available from the British Library
ISBN 978-1-78945-211-2

ERC code:
SH3 The Social World and Its Interactions
 SH3_9 Social aspects of teaching and learning, curriculum studies, education and educational policies
 SH3_10 Communication and information, networks, media

# Contents

**Foreword** . . . . . . . . . . . . . . . . . . . . . . . . . . . . . . . . . . . . . . . . vii
Pierre MŒGLIN

**Acknowledgements** . . . . . . . . . . . . . . . . . . . . . . . . . . . . . . . . . xiii

**Introduction** . . . . . . . . . . . . . . . . . . . . . . . . . . . . . . . . . . . . . . xv

**Chapter 1. The Promises of Communication
Training Programs** . . . . . . . . . . . . . . . . . . . . . . . . . . . . . . . . . . 1

1.1. Diversity of structures, diversity of authoritative discourses . . . . . . . 1
1.2. Segmentation of communication fields . . . . . . . . . . . . . . . . . . . 18
1.3. Mediation and the performative ideal: the promises of
guaranteed learning . . . . . . . . . . . . . . . . . . . . . . . . . . . . . . . . . 26
1.4. Instrumented mediation: the digital seen as an
educational panacea . . . . . . . . . . . . . . . . . . . . . . . . . . . . . . . . . 37
1.5. The explicit request for communication "tools"
and "techniques" . . . . . . . . . . . . . . . . . . . . . . . . . . . . . . . . . . . 49

**Chapter 2. Mastery Over Communication: Professionalization
and the Injunction to Efficacy** . . . . . . . . . . . . . . . . . . . . . . . . . . 57

2.1. The figures of facilitators and the legitimization of
communication expertise . . . . . . . . . . . . . . . . . . . . . . . . . . . . . . 57
2.2. "Mastering" communication to gain professional efficacy . . . . . . . . 69
2.3. Reinforcing the professionalism of communicators . . . . . . . . . . . . 79
2.4. The argument of the paradigm shift and
communication conceptions . . . . . . . . . . . . . . . . . . . . . . . . . . . . 89

## Chapter 3. Procedures and Standards for "Communicating Properly" ............ 99

3.1. Toolboxes and communicational claims.................. 99
3.2. Prescription and planning to "master" communication .......... 107
3.3. "Best practices" and the circulation of standards............. 115
3.4. Prescribing and standardizing "creativity"?................. 120
3.5. Debates on standards and the reflexivity of social actors ......... 128

## Chapter 4. Exemplification, Modeling and Memorization of Instrumented Bodies of Knowledge in Communication.......... 137

4.1. Casuist mediation: the presumed efficacy of practical wisdom ..... 137
4.2. The order of "scholarly" discourses in professional training ....... 146
4.3. The quest for certainty and the scientific relationship with knowledge ........................................ 152
4.4. The neuroscience, experimental psychology and management science triptych ...................................... 156
4.5. Theory and memorization: understanding versus mastering? ...... 165

## Chapter 5. Communication in the Face of Evaluation: Efficacy and Extension of the Managerial Model ............ 177

5.1. Evaluation and institutionalization of values ................ 177
5.2. Evaluation and (willing) (temporary) suspension of reflexivity ..... 185
5.3. Metrics and quantitativist reduction .................... 193
5.4. Knowledge about communication and managerial regime ........ 198

## Conclusion............................................ 203

## References........................................... 211

## Index ............................................... 229

# Foreword

**Pierre MŒGLIN**
*LabSic, Université Sorbonne Paris Nord, France*

How does communication reach those who practice it in firms and organizations in general? This is the question which sparked the idea for this book.

The question is twofold: on the one hand, it concerns what knowledge in communication does to communicators who follow short-term internships; on the other hand, it focuses on what this same knowledge does to occasional communicators in the context of general public internships, where it is introduced as a transversal skill. Those internships provide training in speaking, media training and the fundamentals of communication, among other topics.

Aude Seurrat is better placed than anyone to address this question. In fact, she can tackle it from three different perspectives.

A university professor in Information and Communication Sciences, she co-directs a renowned research unit, CEDITEC (*Centre d'étude des discours, images, textes, écrits, communication*). Mastering the most rigorous scientific methods, not only does she have privileged access to cutting-edge research concepts in the human and social sciences, but she also maintains the essential distance for understanding the organizational strategies and logics which underlie the environments she studies.

A recognized expert and specialist in the management of bodies of knowledge, she is well aware of the ideals and practices of corporate communicators. In particular, she knows the fears and obsessions of a corporation whose legitimacy is regularly called into question by occupations relying on other bodies of knowledge, such as management, marketing and advertising. These competing occupations have seniority on their side, as well as certain toolboxes whose usefulness is no longer discussed. This could be one of the reasons why, as a countermeasure, communication facilitators place so much emphasis on performance and profitability imperatives, including "personal development" and "personal efficacy" training programs, destined for nonprofessional communication practitioners.

Fully up to date on training practices and a seasoned teacher herself, Seurrat knows the educational offer in communication better than anyone; she is no less aware of the pedagogic challenges raised by the logic of educational industrialization. A logic which – as seen in other fields, but even more blatantly – subjects facilitators and trainees to the imperative of instrumental rationality. Here, it is essentially the private educational offer that is in question, despite the boundaries between the public and private spheres being porous. What happens in professional training is of great interest to university training programs and vice versa.

The project involves studying short (one-day or several days) communication training programs. The hypothesis is that in the "best practices" and "cases" presented therein, lies the precious concentrate of all the normative ideologies of corporate communication and communication in general. More than others, those training programs give the profession the opportunity to assert and strengthen its professionality.

In retrospect, the hypothesis turns out to be particularly fruitful. And this to such an extent that we were surprised to discover that other researchers – including those who have studied training manuals, the discourse of professionals and long-term training – have not made this point before.

Still, what was needed was a method. The method used by Seurrat is based on three pillars: the study of the prospectuses of provider organizations and their teaching aids, the analysis of in-depth interviews with facilitators, and participant and ethnographic surveys. Whenever necessary, she also had recourse to scientific literature and the writings of experts.

In that sense, it was crucial to avoid two fatal errors: the superficial approach and the overhanging viewpoint.

The first one would have led Seurrat to stick to cookie-cutter appraisals, derived from the examination of a few promotional brochures and supplemented by the analysis of a small number of testimonies taken at random. The second one would have led her to give in to the temptation of value judgment. Temptation would have been all the stronger in this case, because, when they showcase their expertise (in a highly competitive market), facilitators do not hesitate to invoke the "best authors", scholars included.

Seurrat made the right choice to avoid those two errors. She took the prospectuses seriously, she studied the arguments and the content presentation, she worked in the field and followed training programs in person, whenever authorized to do so. For a long time, she patiently held meetings with facilitators and interrogated them. Most importantly, she left aside all prejudice, without ever losing her critical spirit.

The result is up to par. While she stresses the unrealism of promises and the irrationality of injunctions, she also reveals that instructions often give in to evaluative quantophrenia, to the tyranny of return on investment (ROI) and the imposition of performance standards. On the other hand, she emphasizes that facilitators themselves do not all believe in the usefulness of instrumentalized communication. She even points out that, for some of them, "knowledge is not a control instrument, but on the contrary, the place of humility where we experience the complexity of the world".

One of the great qualities of her book is that it raises awareness about the existing gap between the concern for immediate operationality and the need for reflexivity, a sine qua non condition to avoid reproducing obsolete professional practices. Another quality is that she considers and accounts for a diversity of situations and the complexity of contexts. Despite being only a few in number, the training organizations studied by the author cover a wide spectrum, ranging from powerful agencies and large research and consulting firms to tiny and artisanal structures, as well as two *grandes écoles*.

Seurrat is no less attentive to the heterogeneity of facilitators. These differ even more from one another considering that not all of them are professional facilitators. Actually, only a certain number of them are professionals who provide training. According to the author, each has their own rhetoric, tricks, promises of results and success indicators. Each also displays their own legitimating arguments, which vary from person to person, and from structure to structure. Nevertheless, all face the same problem: making sure that relevant goals are achieved despite the short time allocated for training.

In this regard, the pages devoted to the use of the reference to the "paradigm change" are particularly enlightening. Aware of the fact that it is not possible to acquire new skills within a short time frame, facilitators choose to prioritize the conversion of the ways of thinking. Two themes, supposed to act as electroshocks for trainees, are brought to the fore: the theme of the transition from the information society to the communication society, and the "digital revolution".

It is nonetheless impossible to ignore the dubious and reductive character of the opposition between information and communication. This scheme artificially presents information as the keystone of a top-down, mechanical and impoverished transmission regime. In contrast, communication gives the impression of being the collaborative vector of symmetrical and participatory exchanges. In reality, neither information nor communication corresponds to what this scheme claims. A fortiori, there is something artificial in the staging of their confrontation.

No less questionable is the use of the theme of the "digital revolution". In no way should we underestimate the importance of social networks and the weight of influencers. But, as Seurrat clearly states, what is at stake is the primacy granted (in the name of digital technology) to the idealization of relationships and to a "conversational model" which overlooks the political and economic dimensions of communication mediations.

The concluding pages, "Elements for a Sociopolitics of the Bodies of Knowledge on Communication", should be read as a tribute to Yves Jeanneret. Following in the footsteps of her master, Seurrat opposes the imperative of effective action and world domination with the goal of understanding the frameworks of action. Therefore, each practitioner is free to enter into these frameworks, become more or less detached from them, or help them to evolve. The teaching of business communication does not involve training professional protesters, it is true. Even less does it have to plant "time bombs", as one trainer stated. On the other hand, it must avoid the short-term vision of instrumentalized communication subject to technocratism and the productivism of managerial normativity.

This is the challenge that the book we are about to read addresses: neither does it give in to the triumphalism of omniscient gurus, nor to the dismay of practitioners destabilized by the rapid changes companies are now subject to. On the contrary, it cleverly shows that the requirement for the professionalization of training programs does not dispense with the critical analysis of the mechanisms of social production of the bodies of knowledge and power. This concerns the efficacy of training programs as much as the facilitators' honor.

# Acknowledgements

This work, which is largely the result of my HDR accreditation to supervise research, was nourished by exchanges with various colleagues and friends whom I would like to thank here.

Yves Jeanneret, my late thesis director, will always be a source of inspiration and someone who I deeply cherish.

I express my sincere appreciation towards Pierre Mœglin, who kindly agreed to write the foreword of this book and has played a prominent role in my career path as a researcher, as well as Karine Berthelot-Guiet who accompanied this accreditation work.

I would also like to express my esteem and friendship to Sarah Labelle, Joëlle Le Marec, Emmanuël Souchier, Claire Oger, Laurent Petit, Karine Grandpierre, Judith Mayer, Thomas Grignon, Sabine Bosler, Marlène Loicq, Julie Bouchard, Vincent Bullich and Lucie Alexis.

I thank my laboratory for its support throughout the editing process, my colleagues at CEDITEC, with whom I have stimulating and friendly discussions, and Françoise Dufour for her attentive proofreading.

This editing process was initiated after a meeting with Renaud Fabre, who gave me the opportunity to rework and publish this text, and with whom I have had fascinating exchanges ever since.

Last, but not least, I would like to thank my husband, Fabrice, who for almost 20 years has consistently shown interest in my work, and my daughters, Alice and Inès, who fill my every day with unparalled joy.

# Introduction

The aim of this book is to analyze the forms of knowledge selection, hierarchization and mediation of bodies of knowledge in "communication" during professional training. A body of knowledge (BOK or BoK) refers to the comprehensive set of concepts, terms and activities that define a particular professional domain. It serves as a framework for guiding practitioners within that field, encapsulating the essential knowledge and practices necessary for effective performance. For this, we will investigate the link between two types of ideologies: the performative efficacy promised by training programs, and communication seen as a logistic to be managed and optimized to achieve mastery. The choice of professional training in communication is related to the hypothesis that training is a place where communication ideologies and standards crystallize. Starting with professional training will allow us to question the functions attributed to the BOK in communication within organizations, because professional training corresponds to an adaptation logic to the demands of such organizations. The question that will pervade this book is: How does the efficacy imperative affect the mediation of BOK in communication in ongoing professional training? The question is to determine to what extent the promise of efficacy is linked to behaviorist, logistical, instrumental and managerial conceptions of communication, as well as scientistic expectations[1] (Jurdant 2009, p. 5) towards said bodies of knowledge. This problem makes it possible to understand contemporary forms of communication engineering, "the way in

---

1. In *Les problèmes théoriques de la vulgarisation scientifique*, Baudouin Jurdant explains that scientism is a certain type of social relationship towards bodies of knowledge. Scientism is an ideologically constructed attitude which, in response to social demand, involves believing that a certain "knowledge of the truth" is possible.

*Mediation and Hierarchy of Knowledge on Communication*,
Aude SEURRAT. © ISTE Ltd 2025.

which various social actors take over all of these processes to produce power and value" (Jeanneret 2014, p. 32).

This book aims to bring to light the construction of communication conceptions in the field of professional communication training. It will therefore be marked by a reflection on this discipline, its challenges, its modes of social visibility and its relations with the socio-economic world. Working on the elaboration of professional BOK in communication leads to questions on the relations between academic knowledge and knowledge deemed relevant and efficient for professional practice. The concept of knowledge (*savoir*) can designate bodies of knowledge with highly varying statuses. Depending on the approaches, some will produce certain categorizations: theoretical, procedural, experiential, informal bodies of knowledge, etc. The goal is not to discuss these forms of categorization, nor to produce any new ones, but to see what, within professional training, constitutes action-related bodies of knowledge (Barbier 1996, p. 16). As Foucault has pointed out, "knowledge is that of which one can speak in a discursive practice, and which is specified by that fact" (Foucault 1969, p. 182). This means that "there are bodies of knowledge that are independent of the sciences (which are neither their historical prototypes, nor their practical by-products), but there is no knowledge without a particular discursive practice; and any discursive practice may be defined by the knowledge that it forms" (Foucault 1969, p. 183).

What types of knowledge are considered "useful", "practical", "operational" in professional communication training? These questions are related to the modes of instrumentalization of BOK in professional training and, more generally, to the quest for certainty (Dewey 1929) in the knowledge transmitted. On the other hand, short professional training programs – and not only those devoted to communication – place particular emphasis on the development and sharing of "best practices" drawn from the concrete experience of facilitators or trainees. This helps us understand casuistry (Passeron and Revel 2005) as a knowledge mediation communication process derived from concrete experience and compiled as exemplary cases. While professional training is not the only framework in which the development of cases actively participates in the circulation of communication standards, it is a privileged field of practice for investigating this question.

This book is at the crossroads of research on organizational communication, knowledge mediation and the industrialization of training.

However, as Bonnet (2015) has emphasized, the mediation field of organizational knowledge is still a relatively underexplored area of research.

> Knowledge mediation is a process which is not naturally associated with the objects of research inherent in the field of organizational communication. Closer to (or even interdisciplinary with) Educational Sciences, it is nonetheless at the heart of the info-communicational challenges of collective entrepreneurial, associative or administrative action (Bonnet and Galibert 2016, p. 5).

For Bonnet and Galibert, this perspective should "go beyond a functionalist vision of information management, knowledge management or organizational learning" (Bonnet and Galibert 2016, p. 5), as done by management sciences to understand the forms and challenges of the processes underlying organizational knowledge mediation. This project aims to contribute to structuring this area of research and highlighting the interest of this type of approach applied to the field of organizations. For Jeanneret, "this approach to communication based on the claims it substantiates proves particularly crucial for those seeking to conduct a constructed reading of the way in which the procedures, skills and occupations that make communication a professional reality, are established and transformed" (Jeanneret 2014, p. 249).

As shown in Lépine and David (2014)[2], the relations between professional practices and communication training show to what extent it is complex to desire to establish a foundation of common skills for communication occupations, which are highly diverse and ever-evolving

> Far from being superimposed on epistemology, the communicational approach becomes the center of the interrogation on the production, recognition, and publicization of bodies of knowledge and, conversely, their repression. It is not surprising that in such theoretical frameworks, the reflection focuses more on the sciences than on science: it now opens a new investigation into what can be called an anthropology of

---

2. The articles compiled in this publication were chosen from all the contributions presented at the international symposium *Entre réflexif et prescriptif: Analyse des dispositifs d'apprentissage et de formation des communicateurs*, held as part of the *81st ACFAS Congress – Savoirs sans frontières* in Montreal on May 9 and 10, 2013 under the scientific responsibility of Marc D. David and Valérie Lépine.

the bodies of knowledge, raising the question of the legitimization of knowledge with a broader scope than the sole category of scientificity (Jeanneret 2004, p. 21).

Research begins with a first choice: to focus on training organizations, and this is for several reasons. The first is that in France, as in most countries in Europe and North America, professional training is mainly provided by organizations offering training internships. It is relevant to question the ways in which these organizations position themselves, establish their expertise, divide communication into "products", promote their offer and claim mastery over communication processes. The second is that training organizations themselves have been the subject of little research, despite being key actors in lifelong professional training. According to Delamotte, "if we agree to recognize an industrial type of mutation in the social representations underpinning the practice and development of the field of training, it is also appropriate to construct an observation around the main actor in industrialization, namely the training organization" (Delamotte 1993).

When studying the training programs proposed in France, these share similar content with other training organizations in various countries. To begin with, part of the training organizations studied deploy their offer at an international scale. We were able to show that the contents of these training programs are quite similar from one organization to another, and based on the same models (such as SWOT or the Deming wheel), designed in the United States and promoted by numerous agencies or communications consulting firms around the world.

Professional training in communication involves diverse structures (general organizations, specialized organizations, *grandes écoles*, associations, independent units) and the offer is quite heterogeneous. From this observation arises a bias in research: not delimiting the field of research a priori (based on a certain definition of "communication"), but taking into account what training organizations designate as "communication" training programs. By analyzing the segmentation and construction of short professional educational offers in communication, we will see that communication has close relations to marketing, management and personal development. However, this question of the permeability of boundaries seems particularly interesting to understand the conceptions of communication at work and the standards referring to them.

This work is the result of a triple methodological approach: an analysis of corpora of catalogs from training organizations and their teaching aids, an interview survey and an ethnographic survey[3]. In order to analyze the rhetoric of training organizations, their educational offers in communication, their segmentation and positioning, I studied a corpus of 2017–2018 catalogs from eight educational structures and updated the analysis by establishing a comparison with 2023–2024 offers. The analysis of these catalogs accounts for the plurality of arguments for legitimizing educational structures and the construction of promises relating to offers where communication is considered as a transversal skill and in those dedicated to communication professionals. The understanding of the positioning of training program providers, their methods for elaborating offers, as well as the specificities of communication training programs, are also analyzed based on interviews conducted with professional training program actors[4]. Finally, the ethnography of professional communication training practices is at the heart of this research work. It aims to observe the way in which BOK in "communication" are hierarchized, legitimized, transmitted and put into practice within different communication training program courses. As Petit (2013) did in his publication to obtain his accreditation to supervise research (HDR), I will argue that the "cases" studied for this book are research constructs which shed light on different questions.

For the ethnographic survey, given their extent and variety, I chose to observe two main types of educational offers: training programs in strategic communication and planning, and training programs in public speaking. Apart from the fact that these two types of offers have the highest demand (qualified as *"Best"* by training organizations), they make it possible to understand two frameworks for deploying the mediation of BOK in communication: the one intended for communication professionals (where BOK in communication are associated with "professional" skills), and the one targeting a far wider audience (where BOK in communication are

---

3. In this book, the remarks obtained from interviews and those resulting from observation are differentiated because, in the first case, they are comments elicited by the researcher in an interview situation, whereas in the second case, comments were collected from a real-life scenario, targeting a group of participants within the frame of their training program.
4. Ten 90-minute semi-structured interviews were conducted with different actors from professional training: structure director, line manager, monitoring director, trainer.

associated with "transversal" skills[5]). I will argue that there are remarkable differences between the economy of BOK in "communication" during the communicators'[6] training phase and BOK in communication during training in "communication techniques"[7]. Furthermore, the real challenge is to analyze them jointly, to identify the common conceptions of communication and associated standards which are engaged.

My position was that of an observing participant (Flamant 2005, pp. 137–152), a researcher who does not attempt to erase her role in communication situations, but on the contrary, wishes to think of it as having a structuring character in how the bodies of knowledge explored by research are elaborated. For Soulé, this expression stresses "the primacy of interactional and intersubjective involvement over the claim to objective observation" (Soulé 2007, p. 131) and evidences the transition from the observation of the "other" to the observation of human relations – I would say, communication situations the researcher helps to configure. This research posture, which assumes its subjectivity, goes against certain idealized conceptions of the researcher as blurred behind the research object. Among other things, this makes me think of the "shadowing" method. Introduced by McDonald, professor of psycho-sociology at Aberdeen, the research modality known as "shadowing" involves following a person "like their shadow", and postulates that, over time, the person will forget about us, producing "a detached distance from the informants, thereby reducing the influence of our presence" (McDonald 2005, p. 32). On the contrary, I believe that this method contributes to avoiding the mediations through which the survey is tackled and deprives the researcher of the knowledge which is precisely the fruit of this reflection. Far from being in the background and even less, "a shadow", I became involved in the debates within the training programs and triggered some of them. Combined with the participant observation of training programs, I created a corpus of teaching aids (sheets, slideshows, booklets, downloadable documents, quizzes, etc.). The method for compiling the corpus focuses on communication situations

---

5. Eight training programs were observed over 18 days. We looked into two media training programs (on an exploratory basis, which will only be engaged occasionally), three public speaking training programs and three training programs on strategic communication and planning.
6. Training programs in communication planning, press relations, community management or communication audit.
7. Training programs in media training, public speaking, writing techniques and meeting management.

relating to the ethnographic survey. It allows us to think about the role (or the absence) of educational tools and media (Mœglin 2005) in short communication training programs, and to see how they materialize certain conceptions of "useful" bodies of knowledge in "communication".

This research allows us to question the modalities and challenges of projects for mastering communication, the construction of standards and action guides on "effective communication", and the related – logistical and managerial – conceptions of communication. In concrete terms, this is a problem relating to the industrialization of training.

The notion of industrialization is complex, and the goal of the book is not to provide a unique definition, but to identify and analyze its components and its main themes. The collective book directed by Mœglin (2016) distinguishes three interdependent markers of the industrialization of training: technologization, rationalization and ideologization. Technologization differs from technicization in that the devices "add the dimension of the uses they prescribe and the practices they model to the material dimension of the tools and media which is intrinsic to them" (Mœglin 2016, p. 55). "In fact, a framing or formatting effect (in the sense of shaping information) is present in technologization, which obviously does not prevent this framing from remaining relatively open, depending on the richness of the "product uses" prescribed by these devices" (Mœglin 2016, p. 57). We can differentiate two levels of technologization: the promotion and access to training offers (via search engines on their website and the implementation of "interactive" catalogs), and the training offers themselves. Over the past 15 years, there has been a development in e-learning and blended learning training programs, and the implementation of virtual classes. It is nonetheless necessary to draw a distinction between additive educational technologization and substitutive technologization (Mœglin 2016, p. 22). As I will point out in the book, in professional communication training, it is mostly the blended learning offers that are multiplying, that is, forms of additive technologization (even if distance learning offers have developed, especially since the Covid 19 pandemic).

The second marker is rationalization. The notion of rationalization is used in the sense that Weber (1959) stated in *The Vocation Lectures*, a book which contains two lectures given in 1919, one called "Science as a Vocation" and the other, "Politics as a Vocation". For Combès

The last argument which confirms rationalization, and which goes in the direction of industrialization, concerns the penetration of a managerial logic into the educational environment. Knowledge in its generality gradually becomes the object of production regulated on the basis of the performative model of instrumental action (specialization and sectorization of training programs, differentiation in the structuring of content depending on targeted audiences, implementation of standardization mechanisms and new forms of knowledge production) (Combès 1993, p. 42).

This question will be central in the last part of the book, where the extension of the managerial regime will be discussed. For Tremblay, "rationalization, here understood in the Weberian and Habermasian sense, as a constant pursuit of efficacy, yield, productivity, adjustment of means to an end" (Tremblay 1998, p. 45). In this respect, Gadrey (1994), in his work on the characterization of contemporary transformations or the "modernization" of service activities and organizations, distinguishes the professional rationalization of services from industrial rationalization. For this author, the training sector, like other service sectors, is subject to an efficiency logic, the adjustment of means to an end, inspired in a cost/efficacy economic calculation. But, according to him, cognitive and organizational obstacles oppose industrial rationalization (which aims for the massive and standardized production of goods, and is based on a highly Taylorized organization of work).

The professional rationalization strategy aims [...] to make the typification of cases more precise and more systematic, by formalizing the corresponding methods and breaking them into "routines", in order to foster the efficacy of professional working procedures (both in the sense of profit time and quality of response). But it does not associate a range of cases with a range of mechanically prescribed operating instructions [...]. In terms of performance assessment, it privileges the evaluation of the effects or impact of services on users, rather than the measurement of direct productivity gains (Gadrey 1994, p. 186).

As I will show throughout the case studies chosen, even if we observe certain standardization trends in training offers, the rationalization at work concerns, above all, professional rationalization.

Finally, the third marker, ideologization, draws on the work of Habermas (1973), itself inspired by Herbert Marcuse's theories on the ideology of capitalism. For Mœglin, this notion of ideologization is key to understanding what leads actors towards technologization and rationalization. "The notion of ideologization here designates the process through which [...] actors rationalize the rationality of their strategies" (Mœglin 2016, p. 60). Examining ideologization processes clarifies the meaning that actors give to their actions, and the justifications they provide for them. "In other words, they justify the voluntarism of their modernizing strategies and convince themselves of the legitimacy of the priority they give to the optimization of means in relation to ends, to the detriment of any other consideration" (Mœglin 2016, p. 60).

This desire to optimize means to an end is at the core of the question of efficacy which guides this book. This is why it is around this marker – ideologization – that the question will be explored. The term ideologization, rather than ideology, allows us to emphasize processes rather than states considered stabilized. Now, if ideologization is understood as a process for developing the social representations which steer activity and making them visible, it is possible to envision the primacy of the search for efficacy as a form of ideologization.

> Efforts to improve and rationalize are at the origin of the industrialization process, which can be defined as a way of encouraging technical and organizational choices to lower the costs per product unit, with a view to generating revenues and profits. Let us remember that, regardless of their connotations, the notions of performance and efficacy are central in economics: "these are the key terms which summarize all economic problems" (De Bandt 1991) (Delamotte 1993, p. 68).

We may perceive to what extent raising the issue of the efficacy imperative leads to industrialization-related questions.

If we look at its etymological aspects, the term *efficacy* comes from the Latin *efficax*, which means acting, producing the expected effect. Furthermore, it is essential to differentiate efficacy from performance. While efficacy implies the correct use of means and properly fulfilling the function for which the action, thing, individual or organization was intended, performance involves the idea of something outstanding, and, in the field of sport, designates a remarkable achievement (Erenberg 1994). Performance is a result that is considered superior to previous results. Following the footsteps of Bernard Stiegler as to the etymology of the term "performance", Aubert notes that "initially, it refers to a process of perfection in the making" (Aubert 2006, p. 340). Efficacy does not seem related to the question of perfection, but rather to optimization. It falls under the idea of *praxis* and is close to Aristotle's definition of "cleverness", as presented in the *Nicomachean Ethics*: "There is a faculty which is called cleverness; and this is such as to be able to do the things that tend towards the mark we have set before ourselves, and to hit it" (Aristotle 2014, p. 174).

In his *Traité de l'efficacité*, the philosopher and sinologist Jullien (1996) proposed to understand efficacy from the angle of strategy, politics and philosophy, through the history of the European and Chinese cultural traditions, in order to identify two different modes of thinking. According to him, efficacy can be approached via two logics: the European modeling or the Chinese process. On the one hand, it is thought of as the culmination of a planned action, and on the other, as the maturation of a transformation process based on adaptation to situations and circumstances[8]. For Jullien, European thought, heir to Greek philosophy, is based on the means-ends framework; efficacy is thought of as the achievement of a goal (*telos*), modeled and erected into an ideal (*eidos*), which we can only attempt to achieve through force of will. On the contrary, he states, Chinese thought is based on the conditions–consequences model, and efficacy, or rather efficiency, is thought of as a process, rather than as a result: "in short, instead of imposing one's plan on the world, relying on the situation's potential" (Jullien 1996, p. 37).

In that sense, strength and weakness are not intrinsic qualities of a particular person, but depend on the situation. For Jullien, who analyzes this difference between European and Chinese thought through the lens of the texts on the art of war, the Chinese general "does not ask his men to be naturally courageous, as if this were an intrinsic virtue, but, by confronting them with the perilous situation he throws them into, he forces them to behave courageously" (Jullien 1996, p. 41). In its European sense, efficacy implies a desire to master, predict and control in order to "bring means and goals into exact conformity, without doing too much or not enough" (Jullien 1996, p. 67). As Boltanski and Thévenot also point out, "efficacy is part of a

---

8. According to this author, the question of adaptation to situations, come what may, is one of the specificities of Chinese thought (which he develops in another book, *La propension des choses*).

regular connection between cause and effect. The proper *functioning* of beings extends the present into the *future*, opening the possibility of foresight" (Boltanski and Thévenot 1991, p. 254).

Efficacy would fall within the scope of instrumental or purposeful rationality, which, according to Weber, "arranges the objectives and means the best suited to the goals pursued", in order to "achieve the goals it has given itself with optimal efficacy" (Weber 1959, p. 29). Weber opposes instrumental rationality to axiological rationality. As for Dewey, this dichotomy deserves to be discussed further, in order to explore "the immanent normativity of action" (Dewey 2011, p. 46). According to Dewey, who embraces an empiricist approach, values can be observed, they are not abstract ideas. Can efficacy be thought of as a value in Dewey's sense, and how, in this case, can we examine the conditions of its formation? As I will show throughout this book, this may well be crux of the problem: by shifting the focus from ends (thereby ethical questions) to means, does the efficacy imperative not risk hindering us from fairly questioning the ends themselves? In other words, if efficacy is established as a self-sufficient value, how can we ask the question: *Why is this so?*

In order to analyze what this efficacy imperative produces on the mediation of BOK in communication, the first chapter will analyze how communication is structured into products and sub-products, something which raises the question of the boundaries with other fields of training, such as marketing, management and personal development. By considering the question of professionalization in communication or through communication, the second chapter will bring to light the procedures and standards for "communicating properly". By delving into the forms of selection, hierarchization and pedagogic modalities of the mediation of BOK in communication, Chapter 3 will show the way in which communication training programs rely upon heteronomous knowledge in the human and social sciences, inspired by an instrumental approach to communication driven by the quest for certainty. Finally, by showing how communication is particularly at odds with evaluation, the last chapter will call into question the preponderance of managerial models for reflecting on communication.

# 1
# The Promises of Communication Training Programs

Through the analysis of the organizations' rhetoric and their educational offers in communication, the first chapter of this book will focus on the ideologization processes at the heart of the efficacy imperative. More specifically, we will examine how the efficacy principle governs the ways in which educational offers in communication are structured, divided, presented and legitimized.

## 1.1. Diversity of structures, diversity of authoritative discourses

> Since the implementation of the Lisbon strategy in 2000, followed by the Europe 2020 strategy adopted in 2010, ongoing staff training is considered a major issue in knowledge-based economy within the European Union. It must contribute to economic growth, greater competitiveness accompanied by a quantitative and qualitative improvement in employment and stronger social cohesion[1].

According to the 2020 Céreq survey (Center for Studies and Research on Qualifications), European firms are increasingly resorting to training: in 2020, 73% of firms in the 28 members of the European Union (EU) organized training programs for at least one member of their staff; they barely amounted to 60% in 2005. In 2020, the highest share of training

---

1. Céreq Bref, No. 392, June 2020, p. 1.

companies were settled in Latvia and Norway (99%), and the lowest in Greece (22%). France is at the top of the range (79% of training companies). According to INSEE[2]'s 2022 Training-Employment report, the professional training market in France is dominated by private organizations, which represent approximately 80% of the total turnover (estimated at 15.5 billion euros in 2022). The professional training market in France is a fringe oligopoly: not only is it a highly fragmented market, but it is also a market where the largest turnover is recorded by a small number of actors. France is described as a "monotrainer" country, with professional training programs mainly coming down to short training internships (one to five days), most of which do not lead to any diplomas or certifications

> Thus, we face the following paradox: while France comes at the top of EU countries for company expenditure on ongoing staff training and the training rate initiated by firms, it falls at the bottom of the list for the training rate initiated by individuals and leading to a recognized diploma. As a monotrainer, France is caught up not only in a network of practices, but also of actors and institutions, which does little to encourage personal and autonomous initiatives (Fournier 2016, p. 83).

According to the Céreq European survey on professional training conducted in 2020:

> Despite the health crisis, three quarters of firms with 10 or more employees trained at least one member of their staff. In contrast, training modalities changed: more firms resorted to self-training, on-the-job training and remote learning, and less to courses or internships. While part of these developments resulted from an adaptation to the sanitary situation, others could be more structural. Despite such transformations, the share of staff trained by means of courses or internships (47%) remained close to its former levels[3].

While French firms are quite strongly and regularly involved in staff training through the organization of internships, the recourse to other types of training (conferences, seminars, job rotation, on-the-job training) is less

---

2. See: https://www.insee.fr/fr/statistiques/6657644?sommaire=6657784.
3. Céreq Bref, No. 438–439, May 2023, p. 1.

significant than in other European countries, although training has been on the increase since 2020.

Professional training takes greatly varied forms. In 2016, the Adult Education Survey[4], conducted by Eurostat in 28 EU countries, distinguished six types of training, divided into three categories: formal, informal and nonformal:

**Formal**
1. Courses and internships followed inside or outside the firm.

**Informal**
2. On-the-job training
3. Training by job rotation
4. Training in a learning circle or project
5. Conferences or seminars

**Nonformal**
6. Self-training

The professional training system in France favors the development of executives from the largest companies and a specific type of format: the internship, and more specifically, internships offered by private training organizations.

> Contrary to the usage in educational environments, where an internship is considered as a period of ongoing training in a firm, here the term internship designates the periods during which an employee is absent from the workplace to a follow training program within a group (De Lescure 2017, p. 4).

Philippe Carré, professor at the "Apprenticeship and training" laboratory at Paris X University, explains that the canonical internship model still governs an overwhelming majority of the actions currently seen in adult training. According to him, this educational form is inherited from a historically dated school model whose origins can be traced back to "the transmissive conception" of the high school class and the Ferry laws at the end of the 19th century, or even to the Christian schools of J.B. de La Salle a century earlier (Carré 2016).

---

4. See: http://ec.europa.eu/eurostat/web/microdata/adult-education-survey.

Among the professional training structures, Precepta Consult, a research and consulting firm belonging to the Xerfi Group, differentiates[5]:

1. "Multi–multi" proposals, standing for multispecialist and multimodal. These organizations are defined by multithematic training offers and by the plurality of intervention modes (internal and external training, e-learning/remote learning). According to the study's authors, "the strategic priority is to reach a critical national, or even international, size to capture the customers of major accounts". We may also notice that it is these same organizations which are expanding at a global scale. For example, the two multi–multi organizations that we studied are present in 50 and 7 countries, respectively. In 2022, our largest organization reached a consolidated turnover of 233 million euros, equivalent to 14% growth.

2. "Yield" or multispecialist trainers, such as Orsys, Global Knowledge or Comundi, carry out over 75% of their activity in inter-company training. For the study's authors, "yield trainers" are the most exposed to the consequences of the economic crisis.

3. The "certifiers" mostly bring together *grandes écoles*. For the study's authors, their positioning is built upon "excellence" and on more extensive training courses (often leading to certification or diplomas), without neglecting the existence of a varied short training offer, intra- or inter-company.

4. "Training consultants", such as Krauthammer, Mercuri, IFG Langues or StratX, specialize in intra-company missions, through a remarkable degree of integration of production (salaried trainers), and a high level of expertise in their area of specialty.

5. "E-trainers", such as Crossknowledge, Auralog, Télélangue, iProgress, Smart Canal or Hyper Office, are e-learning training companies: their business model is different from that of traditional training organizations, notably by the importance of the initial investment and the logic of the economies of scale which governs them.

According to the editors of the 2017 study by the Fédération française de la formation professionnelle (which became Les Acteurs de la Compétence in 2019):

---

5. Precepta Consult (2015). Les organismes de formation privés. Stratégies et mutations à l'horizon 2015, 2–4 [Online]. Available at: https://www.centre-inffo.fr/uhfp/2014/IMG/pdf/9SAE01-2.pdf [Accessed February 2018].

The division of training into modules, in other words, into homogeneous blocks of knowledge and skills, in which training organizations have been engaged for several years, partly explains why training is becoming shorter and shorter. On the other hand, interns are increasingly shifting towards service and personal development specialties, to the detriment of general disciplines, for which longer training is required. Nevertheless, the number of training hours varies significantly, depending on the audiences and the status of the training providers. In 2013, it amounted to 36 hours for employees, whereas it nearly tripled (109 hours) for job seekers and individuals[6].

This reduction in internship training time corresponds to a modularization growing trend, breaking down training into small, increasingly targeted blocks of skills. This development is part of a loyalty strategy on the part of training organizations. An offers manager explains this strategy of breaking down knowledge into small modules, something which should make it possible to "enhance customer loyalty":

INTERVIEW.– "Web project manager, for example, or E-commerce manager or Web marketing manager, these are the most comprehensive training courses, providing an overall image of a function, throughout a period of approximately 10 days. Between 8 and 10 days. And then, we have more specific internships, on "how to create a Facebook page", for example (professional of course), or natural referencing, or advertising on social networks. This involves breaking down the missions of the communications manager and translating them into precise goals. This is what makes us see customers again. These function as incremental training programs, they are enriched. Customers come for priority training, and then they need additional training on a more specific point. For short training sessions, one has to define precise and reachable goals".

The discourse of this offers manager, whose role is, among other things, to build "products" that best meet the demands of companies and to promote them, clearly shows that modularization is seen as strategic: following a division of skills logic – which deserves to be called into question – it must make it possible to retain "customers". As we will see in the third chapter, this implies a certain conception of knowledge, considered as autonomous

---

6. FFP, Fédération de la Formation Professionnelle (2017). Faire décoller l'investissement dans les compétences. Diagnostics et propositions, October, 32.

building blocks, and the sidelining of more complex and transversal bodies of knowledge, something which fails to fit into this logic of division into operational, tightly targeted goals.

The longest internships (over eight days on average) can be certifying (and in particular, internships which take the title of a profession such as "Communication Manager" or "Community Manager"), but the vast majority of internships offered for employees are brief, non-certifying internships (one to three days). There are two main types of internships, which correspond to two types of relationships between firms and training organizations: intra-company and inter-company internships. The director of a structure specializing in the training of managers and executives in communication (and former marketing director of a magazine publishing conglomerate), offers a rather interesting analogy with the press sector, to differentiate these two types of offers:

INTERVIEW.– "I always draw this analogy with the world of the press where I come from: it's like subscriptions and single-issue sales. When you subscribe, it is much less profitable for a publisher, but you have foresight because of your subscribers: the readers are registered and then they have already paid in advance for X months and services. So, you give them a discount. But single issue sales, if you publish monthly, you don't know how many copies you are going to sell each month […]. In terms of cost per unit, intra-company is obviously less interesting, but in terms of volume, it is far more engaging. And then you establish a relationship. For intra-company training, the customer should be able to choose from sufficiently interesting themes, enticing the sufficient number of employees so that they can be grouped in a course, and this cannot be the case for all employee training needs".

Even if the analogy made by this director is enlightening to ponder the difference between the intra- and inter-company strategies, the inter-company does not entirely fall under the "editorial model", nor does the intra-company fall under the "club model", as conceptualized by cultural industries theorists. For Mœglin, the club model is based on "the principle of subscriber payment, in exchange for access to a fixed set of programs (unlike the flow model), but without, however, encouraging the appropriation of these programs individually (as in the editorial model)" (Mœglin 2010). All things considered, even if intra-company offers greater foresight than inter-company, it does not necessarily amount to a subscription. Even if the implementation of intra-company training programs can enable training organizations to forge closer links with the firms, the "customer" loyalty issue is transversal, regardless of the type of offer.

Following economies of scale logic, large structures deploy a wide range of inter-company internships, whereas the smaller structures often concentrate on intra-company training programs. According to an offers manager:

INTERVIEW.– "The inter-company is a difficult market because you need a base. The entry ticket is high even for the inter-company. You have to reach a lot of firms, you need a lot of space, and logistics behind it too. The offer must be in line with expectations, and this is not easy. This is the reason why there are not so many actors who propose inter-company training in France".

According to the FFP[7], 38% of the organizations adhering to the federation offer "Marketing and Communication" training offers, placed in the third position behind "Management" (57%) and "specific occupations" (53%), and ahead of human resources management (29%), IT (28%), finance and management (26%) and languages (25%). Note that it is difficult to know whether under the "Marketing and Communication" category, the FFP includes communication as a transversal skill (and in particular, public speaking offers). In my opinion, the "specific occupations" category (which comes in the second position), is actually a false category since it brings together extremely heterogeneous types of offers.

The educational structures that offer communication training are very different from one another and operate in a highly competitive market. Thus, visibility and credibility stakes are high, the goal being to establish their authority in the market. Research by Oger (2013) on discursive authority provides important heuristic support, because among other things, it makes it possible to differentiate authority from legitimacy (which is a more sociological concept, superbly developed by Bourdieu). Furthermore, it shows that authority does not reside outside of discourse, it is challenged within it. "Storage of force in signs", "symbolic capital" made of "accumulated credit", authority cannot exist without authorization: it is relational. For Monte and Oger, "authority should rather be considered as the claim to an increase in credibility, fueled by the social status of the speaker

---

7. FFP (2014). Comprendre (enfin!) la formation professionnelle : un enjeu économique, social et sociétal. Report, October, 15.

and/or their institutional position, but which also includes a discursive dimension, as well as a contextual dimension, both closely intertwined" (Monte and Oger 2015, p. 6).

The analysis of authority as understood by Oger invites me to invest in the field of discourse analysis. For Foucault, "discourse is not simply that which translates struggles or systems of domination but is the thing for which and by which there is struggle, discourse is the power which is to be seized" (Foucault 1971, p. 12). This is why "what we are concerned with here is not to neutralize discourse, to make it the sign of something else, and to pierce through its density in order to reach what remains silently anterior to it, but on the contrary to maintain it in its consistency, to make it emerge in its own complexity" (Foucault 1969, p. 47).

Even if our aim is not to analyze all the forms of mediatization of professional training organizations, prospectuses seem to be a suitable support to analyze the discursive use of authority, as well as the editorialization and the valorization of offers:

> Working on one's authority is an investment adapted to such an enterprise, in the sense that authority designates both the concealment of power tools and the performance of such power. It is the promise of a capture without its implementation, a result announced without having to manifest an effort. Authority implies recognition, credit, and obedience to an entity recognized as legitimate. The notion of authority excludes the use of violence, constraint and even persuasion. However, despite the myth of natural authority, authority is neither a force nor an argument, but a construction (Marti 2015, p. 15).

Like Marti, my remarks will not focus on "the efficacy of this power", but on the analysis of "the adoption of authoritative postures to legitimize and give credibility to a discourse and an existence in public life" (Marti 2015, p. 15).

The adoption of authoritative postures in professional communication training involves multiple strategies which correspond, in part, to the great diversity of structures offering this type of training. There are large generalist structures, associative networks, private structures specializing in communication, public *grandes écoles*, private schools, professional journals which offer training in partnership with specialized structures and a plethora of independent trainers who have their own little structure.

I conducted an analysis of self-presentation discourses (Amossy 2010) in the 2018–2019 prospectuses of eight professional training structures (three multi-specialist, three specialist and two *grandes écoles*). This analysis was later updated by an exploration of the 2023–2024 prospectuses of these same organizations, in order to identify evolving elements.

I chose these organizations following several criteria:

– considering the actors who occupy the largest place in the professional training market and have an international presence (the multi-specialists);

– considering the main actors mentioned as specialists in communication training (not only in the interviews conducted, but also recommended by training brokers, or "rewarded" in rankings such as *Décideurs*[8]), (the specialists);

– considering two *grandes écoles* to determine whether university status had an impact on self-presentation discourses and the content of the training offers.

For this study, I did not include consulting firms which offer training services, because these – only a few in number in the field of communication – are mainly intra-company and are not listed in the prospectuses. Nor did I consider any universities (apart from the *grandes écoles*), because they still have a few short training offers and almost no communication internship offers. Finally, I did not choose any associative networks, because, in addition to the fact that they propose a limited number of offers, they are often integrated into the offers of other organizations by means of partnerships.

This distribution of the corpus of prospectuses makes it possible to distinguish three logics in the construction of authoritative discourses: the logic of training specialists, that of communication specialists and finally, the prestige logic of the *grandes écoles*. These logics are not exclusive and can be combined; they are a way of identifying the main argumentative

---

8. The magazine *Les Décideurs* operates according to a survey conducted by managers, who rank training organizations by theme or occupation: http://www.magazine-decideurs.com.

strategies implemented with a view to establishing authority in the professional training market in communication.

The "multi–multi"[9] organization logic, as the Precepta firm describes it – training specialists who offer varied products – brings to the fore their position on the professional training market, the plethoric dimension of their offer, their "quality approach", their expertise in educational engineering and in particular, the deployment of their digital offer. Let us take some examples from the prospectuses to illustrate these different lines of argument.

Activity figures are systematically presented in the first pages of the prospectuses of large training organizations. In a certain way, they constitute proof of the organization's expertise in training, whether in terms of experience, territorial coverage, number of facilitators, number of trainees or scope of training areas.

In one of the first pages of its 2023 prospectus, entitled "Our key figures", the multi–multi B organization presents the following information: over 50 years of experience, seven locations worldwide, 150,000 persons trained every year, 1,500 expert speakers.

It is interesting to note that it is the large organizations that most often resort to branding and come up with slogans. These slogans are in English for the largest structures with an international presence, and in French for the medium ones.

| Multi–multi A | "Beyond knowledge" |
| --- | --- |
| Multi–multi B | "Learning is changing" |
| Multi–multi C | "The art of training" |
| Specialist A | "L'expert médias et communication" |
| Specialist B | "L'excellence à la française" |

**Table 1.1.** *Slogans from large training organizations*

---

9. Centre Inffo (2015). Les organismes de formation privés. Stratégies et mutations à l'horizon 2015. Une étude de la collection PRECEPTA Consult [Online]. Avaliable at: www.centre-inffo.fr/.

The multi–multi slogans focus on questions of learning. According to them, knowledge serves a higher purpose: their slogans, "beyond knowledge" and "learning is changing", illustrate their claim to turn bodies of knowledge into tools at the service of professional success. Educational expertise is therefore at the heart of their claims. As for the slogans of specialists, these emphasize "excellence" and specific expertise in the field of media and communication.

Expertise in educational engineering and in the deployment of the digital offer is another type of recurring argument among large training organizations. I will return to the discourses which present the "digitalization" of training as an educational panacea later in the book. For example, the 2023 prospectus of the multi–multi B organization lists "the 8 reasons why we systematically integrate digital into our thinking":

"1/ To support the transformations of firms;

2/ To train more, at a lower cost;

3/ To make learning more effective;

4/ To improve user experience;

5/ To transcend the simple face-to-face internship;

6/ To promote Social Learning;

7/ To enrich the trainer's posture;

8/ To improve employer brands."

Further in the book, I will develop this question of the idealized and ideological representations of digital technology in training. For the moment, let us note that different challenges emerge: economic challenges relating to performance and the economies of scale (training more at lower cost), and above all, ideological issues which present digital technology as an educational panacea. *Strategies Formations*, which works in partnership with specialists, also speaks of "augmented face-to-face" to describe its "blended" offer. "To transcend", "to improve", "to enrich"… all of these terms clearly show to what extent these discourses participate in what Robert (2017) calls an "*impensé numérique*" (an "unimaginable digital").

Finally, another way for large training organizations to build their authority is to make the collections of works they have produced visible. The most representative example is the "*La boîte à outils de…*", a collection published by Dunod. Most of the time, these works are given to trainees who follow the corresponding training, and are then presented as a "plus", a "bonus" in the prospectus notices. For example, this is evidenced in the description sheet dedicated to "effective speaking" from the multi–multi A organization. Among the "pluses" listed, they indicate that the book *Les cinq clés de la prise de parole en public*, published by Dunod, will be offered to participants.

These publications enable these organizations to present themselves both as actors in the production of knowledge and as those who know how to respond to the social demand for "practical knowledge". In the third chapter, I will examine the claims of these writings more closely, when I address the order of "scholarly" discourses in professional training.

The argumentative logic relating to specific expertise in communication is based on other arguments. Communication specialists insist on their "expertise" specific to the field. For example, the line of products of one of the specialists is called "The Communication Expert". The introduction to the 2018 prospectus from *grande école* B concludes with these words: "(we) are therefore pleased to offer you an expanded range of increasingly expert training courses". In the introduction to their 2018 prospectus, one of the specialists highlights their ranking in *Décideurs Magazine*:

> Beautiful birthday gift for our 25th birthday: *Décideurs Magazine* has just put us back on top of the podium in the Communication category of its annual Guide to the Best Training Organizations in France, with the mention "Indispensable".

Note that expertise can either apply to communication occupations, or to communication as a transversal skill.

A third discursive strategy, which we mainly identify among the *grandes écoles*, is to build their authority upon the institution's prestige, which also enables them to propose longer and more expensive internships. The 2023 prospectus from *grande école* A devotes several pages to the institution's presentation: "since its creation almost 150 years ago, (the institution) has continued to reinvent itself". It is therefore necessary to reflect the institution's prestige on its professional training offers, while showing that these tackle different challenges, as the director of professional training stresses in his introduction: "our goal is to reconcile the institution's intellectual innovation with the concrete needs of firms and public actors, and their perspectives for change". This structure is also the only one which offers alumni dedicated to professional training: the Executive Community.

*Grande école* B, whose 2018 prospectus is much shorter, places less emphasis on the institution's image, which is not presented in its prospectus. On the other hand, it uses authority quotes (Ducrot 1984), the only ones which anchor references within the framework of the human and social sciences. The prospectus is punctuated with quotes by Flaubert and Clémenceau, as well as Barthes and Eco. The quote that introduces the "Digital Communication" line of products: "The universe is a safe of which humanity seeks the combination" is drawn from *Mythologies* by Roland Barthes. The quote that introduces the "Innovative Communication" line of products: "A dream is a scripture, and many scriptures are nothing but dreams" comes from *The Name of the Rose* by Umberto Eco. The link with university research is emphasized in the case of the two *grandes écoles*, as they can present their training as being at a higher level of analysis than the offer proposed by other organizations. For example, the introduction to one of the 2018 prospectuses states:

> The digital is a global phenomenon that we approach in a panoramic way, through the prism of the social sciences. Our goal is not to provide preconceived solutions, but to help executives acquire the height and perspective that will allow them to (re)think their practices, their strategy, their environment to make the digital a lever for transformation.

Despite not being named as such, the industrial dimension is praised as an asset enriching the quality of offers proposed by large organizations, whereas on the contrary, it is criticized by others as being a sign of standardization of the offers, and therefore, unsuitable for executives and managers. This is also why those responsible for training at the *grandes écoles* believe that multi–multi structures are not direct competitors for them:

INTERVIEW.– "Because they do very industrial things/They are never pioneers, for me they are followers/We do not have the same audiences/We follow different processes. They are great industrial war machines of professional training, their entire economy is based on inter-company training".

For her part, the manager of the "Corporate Communications" line of products from the multi–multi A organization explains that the *grandes écoles* are not direct competitors, because they target audiences who already have initial training in communication:

INTERVIEW.– "Compared to the *grandes écoles*, in the communication occupations, we are generalists, we are operational, we are not academics. I do not expect to compete with the *grandes écoles*. Some of my customers come from firms that have appointed them as Communications Manager or Head of Communications, but who have not studied communications and who need an overview of the tools. They did not receive that in their initial training. For those who have specialized training in the field, there is no need for them to come to me. We will see what an audit is, a communications plan, it is an overview of the tools".

Even if the structures can be differentiated according to these three logics, they also operate following transversal logics: they emphasize the trust placed in them by their customers, the expertise of their facilitators, the capacity of the structure to offer "tailor-made" solutions, as well as training certification and evaluation.

For Oger (2013), authority is a relational concept, supported by an issue of trust: we delegate authority, we grant authority. Showcasing "trust" is a necessary part of prospectuses: organizations list the main firms they work for. In a certain way, these lists of corporate logos, often displaying messages such as "they confide in us", allegedly guarantee that the statements are endorsed by the customers (the firms). Besides, the testimonies of trainees in the form of quotes are expected to reflect their satisfaction. The change in enunciation, shifting from the structure's "we" to the trainee's "I" stresses the fact that authority is not self-declared, but is conferred. We therefore come upon what Perelman calls "argumentation through fruits" (Tindale 2009).

The expertise of facilitators is also systematically emphasized in the training prospectuses. This is reflected by one of the specialists, who announces in its first pages: "Our facilitators and actors place their expertise and talent at the service of educational messages. With at least 10 years of professional experience and interpersonal skills validated by a 5-member jury, they benefit from permanent skills updating". Finally, the promotion of a "tailor-made" offer is part of the servuction logic and is there to show the capacity of the structure to be as close as possible to the needs of its customers.

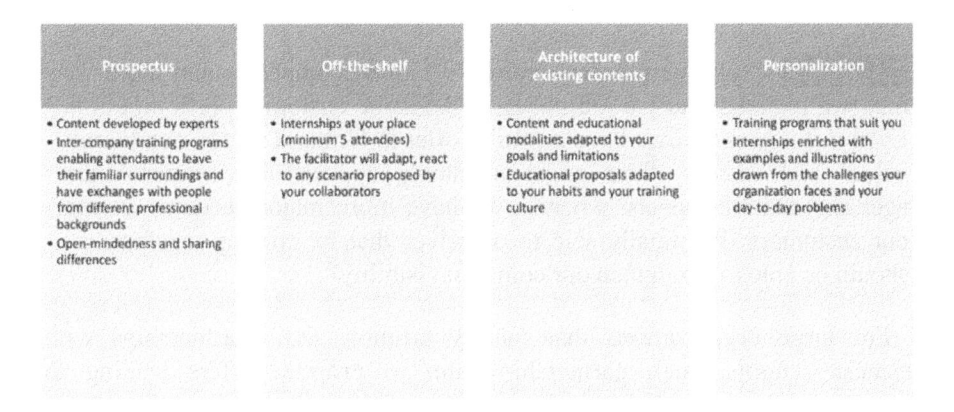

**Figure 1.1.** *Example of a tailor-made offer (inspired by the organization's prospectus)*

The discourse is often deeply engaged, and the argument focuses on the concept of personalized service. In this case, the term "tailor-made" encompasses both genuinely co-constructed offers and adaptations or customizations of standards (also presented in the aforementioned example as "the architecture of existing contents"). This recycling capacity is made possible thanks to the increasing modularity of "brick-based" training offers, thereby making room for multiple rearrangements.

Diploma courses and certified internships are especially showcased, even though they only represent a small part of the offers presented (between 2 and 9% of the communications offers analyzed). Finally – and this is a growing trend in the field of training – organizations are exposing the partnerships they have established. Actually, small structures are increasingly intervening on behalf of larger ones, or small- or medium-sized structures are proposing joint offers. The partnership is then presented as the implementation of complementarity, with each partner benefiting from increased credibility through the partnership.

Far from merely having the goal of complementing expertise, partnerships enable small- and medium-sized organizations to establish more diversified prospectuses of offers. An oligopoly-fringe model, the training market invites fringe actors to join forces in order to avoid disappearing altogether. Among other things, partnerships serve to pool "customer portfolios". This is what the former head of offers at the *grande école* B explains:

INTERVIEW.– "Our partner was really the closest competitor and when we met, we realized that we did not have the same customer portfolio at all. Even if it is true that we have a similar offer in terms of prices, conditions, values and themes, their proposal mainly appeals to communication agencies and freelancers, whereas we have more major accounts among our customers. We finally said to ourselves that by coming together, we should be able to strengthen our common visibility".

For large organizations that mainly promote their partnerships with business schools, such partnerships aim to propose offers leading to diplomas and to highlight the links they could not offer on their own, between initial training and professional training. The introduction to the 2018 prospectus from multi–multi B insists on the partnership the organization has recently established with Brest Business School:

INTERVIEW.– "Our alliance with Weidong, as well as the arrival of the Brest Business School into the Group opened up a new path full of promise for international connections. This unique configuration proposes reboosted blended learning, educational approaches adapted to multispecialization, standardized and tailor-made certification programs, synergies between initial and ongoing training or even interactive and dynamic digital learning platforms". At the end of this introduction, the president of Brest Business School stated: "The complementarity of our two structures creates value. BBS has mastery of certificate and diploma programs, as well as experience in marketing and distribution, not to mention expertise in digital tools".

The case of an association between multi–multi C and a communications specialist is quite interesting to study, because it involves the optimization of the logics identified. As it is a large training structure and at the same time, has resorted to a branding logic and the association with specialists, it highlights their specific expertise in the field of communication. In its prospectus, we find all the forms of argumentation developed by large organizations (number of trainees, experts, training courses, distance training offers), arguments evoked by specialists in communication ("indispensable"), as well as cross-cutting arguments relating to trust ("so loyal") and certifications. The 2023 prospectus also presents "the 9 good reasons" to choose that organization:

– "the most comprehensive offer on the market" (specialist logic);

– "an orientation service that listens to you" (transversal logic, relating to trust);

– "professionals who facilitate learning, and not professional trainers" (specialist logic);

– "designers who are experts in content and pedagogy" (large organization logic);

– "an innovative pedagogy based on practice and the digitalization of the learning experience" (large organization logic);

– "a quality approach (98.2% customer satisfaction)" (large generalist logical);

– "a Corporate Social Responsibility approach" (argument which has not been identified as salient among other structures);

– "an active community" (transversal logic, proposing additional services apart from training such as blogs, breakfasts, forums, etc.);

– "our references" (transversal logic of trust)".

Thus, organizational strategies (such as the establishment of partnerships, branding) coupled with discursive strategies all contribute to "the adoption of authoritative postures to legitimize and give credibility to a discourse and an existence" (Marti 2015, p. 15) in the highly fragmented and competitive market of professional training, because it is in the sense that "speakers are recognized as allegedly holding certain knowledge, a skill, a position, an experience, a know-how so that at first glance, their discourse can be qualified as authoritative, even if its authority is fragile and contested" (Monte and Oger 2015, p. 9).

## 1.2. Segmentation of communication fields

According to the 2017 study by *Acteurs de la Compétence* (FFP until 2019), training in service-oriented specialties is still the most followed, with 60% of interns and 58% of trainee hours[10]. These training courses cover the multivalent specialties of exchanges, management, communication, and sanitary and social specialties. Regarding access to training for "information and communication" professionals, according to a 2016 Céreq study, "information-communication" comes in the 3rd position, just behind "financial and insurance activities" and "public administration", with a 52% access rate to training[11].

Please note that it is difficult to appropriate and comment on the figures above, due to the fact that "communication" can be classified under very different lines of training products. Training in "communication occupations" coexists and sometimes even merges with offers in marketing, management or "digital transformation". As for training in communication seen as a transversal skill (public speaking, "assertiveness", written expression), this can either be included under the "communication" products, or the "personal development" or "professional efficacy" products. It is precisely these fluctuations, these porous boundaries between communication and other fields of professional training that I will study, based on my research analyzing offers within the prospectuses:

> The productivity of a training organization lies in its ability to modify (management) the training activity in the direction of optimization and adaptation to the needs of potential customers (development). The profitability criteria are quite simple: to adjust training durations to goals, to increase the trainer/trainee ratio, but above all, to maintain the attractiveness of the training courses themselves and awaken customer interest (Santelmann 2004, p. 23).

It is precisely this question on the construction of the attractiveness of offers that I will explore through the analysis of prospectuses. From the outset, this shows that we are in a model of diversified production and a product lining policy, with options adapted to a finely segmented target

---

10. FFP, Fédération de la Formation Professionnelle (2017). Faire décoller l'investissement dans les compétences. Diagnostics et propositions, October, 4.
11. Céreq (2016). Employer tax declaration, No. 2483.

(Fichez 1993, p. 111). Although this is a trend in professional training, it is considerably stronger in the context of communication occupations:

> In parallel with this expansion of activity, the number of training courses linked to communication, in all its forms, has multiplied, thereby segmenting the field of communication into occupations (by their name). Even if they differ from institution to institution, these training courses reflect a professionalization dynamic of the information and communication sector, all sectors combined (Brulois et al. 2016, p. 5).

The scriptural economy of a training organization prospectus comes down to the notices listing:

> The list implies discontinuities and non-continuities. It presupposes a certain material arrangement, a certain spatial layout; it can be read in different directions, laterally and vertically, from top to bottom as well as from left to right, or vice versa; it has a well-marked beginning and end, a limit, an edge, just like a piece of fabric. The most important thing is that it facilitates the organization of articles by their number, their initial or by categories. And these limits, both external and internal, make the categories more visible and at the same time more abstract (Goody 1977, p. 149).

I would add that this list organized into sections also gives the impression of a clear division between the fields, even though they are closely intertwined.

A prospectus cannot be read in extenso, it is consulted, and this consultation is done following the summary which formats the classifications within the list. This summary highlights the categorization and classification operations of training offers into products and sub-products. However, it seems relevant to take a closer look at these operations and examine the consistency criteria according to which the offers relating to communication are named and classified. To do this, I analyzed the 2017–2018 and 2023–2024 prospectuses from eight organizations, and I retained the products and sub-products relating to communication as a transversal skill and those offering training for communicators (by examining the "public" box in the prospectus). According to this analysis, the constructions of products and sub-products depend on the positions of organizations – for example, the *grande école* B mainly develops training for communicators, whereas one of the specialists exclusively develops communication training for all executives. But it also reveals fairly mobile, even indistinct, boundaries between communication and marketing, and between communication and personal development (or "professional efficacy").

Offers relating to communication occupations are often included under broader products such as "marketing and communication", or "marketing and corporate communication". Communication would then be a sub-product of this category, but in power relations, after all, it is marketing that takes the upper hand. As a matter of fact, the texts presenting the products mainly use terms associated with the practice of marketing.

The text from the 2023 prospectus by the multi–multi B organization which introduces the "Marketing-Corporate Communication" product clearly shows the influence of marketing on communication:

> "At present, no purchasing decision is made without prior consultation of customer reviews, ratings and social recommendations which influence us more than branding itself. The rapid development of numerous social networks such as Facebook Twitter, LinkedIn, Instagram, Pinterest and instant messaging services such as Snapchat or Whatsapp have transformed the brand-consumer relationship. Consumer actors have taken power! To regain trust, brands must be interesting rather than self-serving. From being transactional and one-off, marketing is becoming relational. The current trend is to invest less in traditional, product-focused advertising and more in customer-focused branded content. A brand is interesting because it brings expertise and knowledge to its customers. Not only is its content ludic and entertaining, but also useful and practical. So rethink your marketing strategy in 2018: no more distributing the same content along several supports and different media... Dare to develop your new, original and renewed content over time and thus become your own media!"

**Box 1.1.** *"Marketing – Corporate Communication"*
*(2023 multi–multi B organization prospectus)*

Although it introduces the "Marketing – Corporate Communication" product, this text speaks of rethinking marketing, and not communication. Communication can appear as a marketing instrument, as a declension of the strategy (designed by marketing) into communication "tools". Even when the "Communication" and "Marketing" products are distinct, shifts between these two professional fields are still quite frequent. For example, in 2018, the "Communication" product from *grande école* A, included an offer entitled "Strategy brand and the customers: learning from luxury customers", whereas it could have been proposed under the "Marketing" product. It is also interesting to point out that for another organization, the "Media and advertising" sub-product is found in the "Communication" line of products, instead of the "Marketing" one. Several 2023–2024 offers are also aimed indiscriminately at marketing professionals. In the "Communication" line of products of multi–multi organizations, this is evidenced by the following training programs: "Responsible marketing and communication", "Evaluating the effectiveness of your marketing and communication actions" or "Evaluating marketing and communication actions: choosing and monitoring your performance indicators".

The products entitled "Digital Transformation" or "Digital Marketing and Communication" are those for which the lack of differentiation (or rather, the relative placing of communication under the control of marketing) becomes the strongest. In concrete terms, the importance given to the digital in training offers in communication has significantly evolved. Throughout the period studied (2019–2024), this is evidenced by the inflation in the number of generic training courses (+ 14.5%) such as "Finding success in digital communication", "Evaluating digital communication", "Digital strategic communication and planning", or the number of training offers relating to social networks (+ 17%), such as: "Optimizing the performance of social media strategies", "Managing the e-reputation of a firm", "Social networks: understanding and mastering Facebook, Twitter, LinkedIn and Viadeo". Finally, over the last two years – and we will return to this – training courses dedicated to the use of Artificial Intelligence (AI) in communication have emerged. Take, for example, "Artificial Intelligence at the service of communication occupations", "Producing content thanks to Artificial Intelligence tools", "3 hours flat to raise awareness on Artificial Intelligence". The text at the beginning of the presentation of the three hour flat offer is as follows:

> Artificial Intelligence (AI) and its applications, such as conversational robots (ChatGPT), is a splendid source of innovation and creativity. This training will allow you to discover the principles of Artificial Intelligence and to implement use cases in your professional environment.

It is interesting to see that technology itself is perceived as a source of creativity. At the same time, this "creativity" is directly associated with the promise of efficacy, as evidenced by one of the goals of the training offer "Artificial Intelligence at the service of communication occupations": "to devise effective prompts to generate text and images".

Thus, the growing importance of questions relating to the "digital" seems to have reinforced a form of primacy of marketing over communication. According to the product manager of the multi–multi A organization:

INTERVIEW.– "The digital has astoundingly addressed marketing themes. Then, this raises the question of the future of communication and of communication services in firms which are increasingly shaken up by the digital. And we can clearly see that the Web and social networks tend to reshuffle and redistribute the cards. This is not obvious. Distinctions are not so neat between customer relations, marketing and communication. In business services, it's not that clear either. I think that now there is real porosity between these different services, plus the IT management. Nowadays, it is not uncommon to see organizations where marketing and IT management merge. There is a real change. So how do we continue to differentiate Corporate communication from the rest? What is it that remains specific to Communication, Customer Relations and Marketing? The boundaries are truly uncertain".

In their study of the links between marketing and communication in the Information and Communication departments of the University Institutes of Technology (IUT), the two researchers in organizational communication, de La Broise and Morillon, highlight what they call their "dangerous liaisons":

Search marketing, e-advertising, direct e-marketing, e-participation… Should we see in this lexicon a radical transformation of the communication function? Indeed, new professional figures incorporating English expressions (community manager, digital planner, social media expert) today carry the technological promises of digital communication. However, it is still difficult to discern among these emerging occupations their explicit connection to a particular function or to a homogeneous professional group (de La Broise and Morillon 2014, p. 166).

In organizations, the adjustment (or entanglement) of two related functions makes it difficult to discern between what (both internally and externally) falls under the scope of communication or marketing, whether in firms or in public service organizations. While not unfounded, this confusion is undoubtedly explained by the expansion of management [...]. Few are the organizations or institutions which currently seem to resist managerial rationality (de La Broise and Morillon 2014, p. 176).

The question of the extension of "managerial rationality" will be key to the rest of the discussion, where I address the relationships between modelization, mastery and the quest for certainty, and describe the quantitative shift at work in the injunction to evaluate communication.

With communication being considered as a "transversal" skill, back in 2018, the offers were included under the "personal development" or "personal effectiveness" products. Between 2018 and 2023, new product categories appeared to bring these offers together. In particular, let us mention the "Professional efficacy" products, which replaced the "Personal efficacy" offer at two multi–multi organizations, and the "Human engineering and soft skills" offer, which appeared in the listings of *grande école* A.

Just like time or stress, communication has to be "managed", or even "optimized", to render any type of professional more effective in any type of situation. Later, I will show that neurolinguistic programming (NLP) is often used in public speaking training, and to a larger extent, we find numerous modelizations used in neuroscience. I will also address the question of professional efficacy being heavily imbued with behaviorist conceptions, which stem from certain social psychology trends reflecting instrumental conceptions of communication.

While during the first years at the information and communication university departments, training in journalism often involves the same initial training as communication (the "information and communication" degrees), the relationships between the "Journalism" and "Communication" products in professional training seem better demarcated than those between communication and the aforementioned areas. Although three of the organizations studied (one specialist and two *grandes écoles*) offer products relating to journalism, their offers contain almost no communication terms. Even if they contain the term "media", media training offers are clearly identified under the "Oral communication" or "Professional efficacy" products, because they are not aimed at journalists, but at those having to intervene in the media.

Finally, communication also has links with graphic design. In that sense, large organizations offer products relating to "Graphic Communication" which mainly include software training offers, such as desktop publishing (DTP). In global terms, all of the offers clearly show the extent to which communication is associated with the mastery of instruments (not only of software or "social networks"), but also management techniques (such as "design thinking" or "creative thinking"). For Grignon, who works on communication expertise within agencies:

> Communication occupations continue to diversify and recompose themselves, in a context characterized by a spectacular technicization of activities. In the professional spheres of public relations, such as in those of marketing and advertising, expertise engages increasingly equipped practices, connected by heterogeneous devices. In particular, Internet tracking software (monitoring tools, analytics, maps, etc.) has gradually established itself as an essential aid for communicators. Although they generally seem to be perceived as simple measuring instruments, these media accompany the redefinition of professions and contribute to the progressive institutionalization of bodies of knowledge, reading skills and know-how (Grignon 2016, p. 24).

The *grande école* B, which targets communication professionals, segments its communication offers more finely. It proposes a segmentation comprising the "fundamentals", intended for all communication professionals on communication challenges ("strategic communication", "innovative communication"), as well as different activity sectors, such as the "Territorial Communication" product (in partnership with Cap'Com), a type of offer which is not sufficiently well represented among other organizations.

The listing testifies to this role of writing which "exteriorizes, crystallizes and accentuates the discontinuity, by conferring a spatial and visual dimension which allows it to be subjected to possible rearrangements" (Goody 1977, p. 186). The construction of lines of products into lists appears both as a differentiating trait ("public expression" in one of the structures, "managerial communication" in another, "territorial communication" in yet another), and as a homogenization of classifications, something which deserves to be called into question, due to the notoriously porous boundaries between marketing and communication, or between communication and personal development.

Organizations also differ, quite relatively, on the basis of the length and prices of the training offered. Even if we can observe some remarkable differences, there is also a sort of standardization of prices, but especially of training temporalities. As we will see in the chapter devoted to temporality, training organizations that used to propose longer offers tend to reduce the duration of their training and align themselves with the shorter temporalities of larger organizations.

The indexing of the training offers (488 in 2019, 519 in 2023) proposed by the eight selected training organizations enables us to see both homogenization and differentiation elements.

Regarding the differentiation elements, we observe – and this corroborates the analysis of the institutional rhetoric – that large organizations offer more "mixed" ("blended") training programs, and 100% remote learning. Two of the multi–multi organizations studied differ on this point. Since 2020 (the year corresponding to the lockdown), multi–multi B has been offering two options for all its internships: one in person, the other as a "virtual class", carried out in a synchronous time (the same duration as the in-person training courses) and different from e-learning modules, which represented 14 out of 96 training offers, in 2023. In fact, e-learning modules are largely carried out on our own, asynchronously with one or more video conferences with a trainer (alone for the "coaching" modality, or in small groups). Also note that even if organization B proposes all of its communication offers both in person and in a virtual classroom, this does not mean that all the internships actually take place in a virtual classroom. For this, it is necessary to grant a minimum number of students enrolled for a session (the threshold generally being eight interns). In 2023, the multi–multi A organization proposed 87 training offers in communication occupations and in communication as a transversal skill. Out of these 87 offers, only eight were 100% remote. On the other hand, 72% of the proposals indicated that they offered "remote activities" in addition to the in-person internship. As we will see later, these "remote activities" are sometimes reduced to the (optional) consultation of online teaching aids before the internship. Synchronous training (in person or in a virtual classroom) therefore remains the main modality – this being notably significant in training offers in communication as a transversal skill (where the interpersonal dimension is particularly emphasized).

Differentiation also takes place in relation to the economy of variety. Specialists B and C, who present themselves as experts in communication occupations, are fully part of a great diversification of offers (respectively 60 and 88 training offers in communication occupations). As for the prices, even if we can notice that the offers from *grandes écoles* and specialized structures for communication training are more expensive than those from other organizations, a communication training program costs a median price of 1,483 euros, and a training program for communication occupations 1,812 euros. It is also interesting to point out that while the organization Precepta classifies universities and *grandes écoles* under the "certifiers" category, the analysis of their communication offers actually reveals that they do not offer more certifications than other organizations. Even if in their institutional rhetoric organizations emphasize their capacity to certify training, certification remains truly marginal in the offers studied.

Whether it is considered as a transversal skill for everyone or as an area of expertise for communicators, communication is listed under different product titles, and most importantly, maintains close or even ambivalent relationships with several other training areas. This makes it possible to begin to bring out the instrumental conception of communication that structures professional training (whether to sell oral or written communication "techniques", or to promise mastery of communication tools at the service of a marketing strategy). The analysis of the titles of the training courses will allow me to delve deeper into this question and unveil the close links which are established between the instrumental conception of communication and the efficacy imperative.

**1.3. Mediation and the performative ideal: the promises of guaranteed learning**

How does a transitive conception of mediation join an ideal of learning performativity? After examining how this conception of mediation is deployed in professional training, I will analyze what I call a "mediagenic" conception of mediation.

In this book, mediation will be understood in the sense proposed by Jeanneret, as a "productive and creative activity which intervenes in the course of communication, by bringing in a new dimension" (Jeanneret 2014, p. 13). The concept of mediation is so important in Jeanneret's reflection on triviality because it is mediations that produce the social circulation of objects and their transformation at the whim of practices. In a broader sense, for the author, this way of understanding mediation involves a certain way of apprehending culture. This posture is properly summed up in the introductory remark to *Penser la trivialité*:

> Everything is transformed, nothing is transmitted from one man to another, from one group to another, without being elaborated, without metamorphosing and without generating something new. If we take stock of this phenomenon, we are led to adopt a certain view of culture and to have certain requirements for its analysis (Jeanneret 2008, p. 13).

So, under what conditions can this type of analysis be deployed?

Davallon explains how the analysis of mediations enables us to grasp the complexity of communication phenomena:

> The first finding is that the notion of mediation appears every time there is a need to describe an action involving the transformation of a situation or communicational device, rather than a simple interaction between already constituted elements, and even less, a circulation of an element from one pole to another. I will argue that there is recourse to mediation when there is a defect or inadequacy in the usual conceptions of communication: communication as a transfer of information and communication as an interaction between two social subjects. With this recourse, the action's origin shifts from the sender actant or interactants to a third party: there is communication through the operation of a third party. The essential question therefore points to the nature of this third party (Davallon 2004, p. 51).

Thinking about mediation means taking into account the fact that communication processes are not linear but discontinuous. These discontinuities are not considered as simple accidents along the way; taking them into account enables the shift from a recurrence-inventorying posture to a dynamic understanding transformations.

This book will specifically focus on knowledge mediation. Hence, the adoption of this conception of mediation invites us to think about what we mean by "bodies of knowledge". As I pointed out in the introduction, bodies of knowledge will not be considered as fixed categories or as contents which could be decontextualized from the communication situations to which they are applied in this book. According to Maury and Kovacs, coordinators of an issue on the anthropology of bodies of knowledge in Information and Communication Sciences for the journal *Études de communication*:

> Far from being a process of contents reproduction, propagation or transmission, the sharing of values and knowledge implies a transformation, a reconfiguration of meanings, diverse and multiple appropriations. Because it is the man, the group, the culture which are at the heart of this process. One of the challenges of Information and Communication Sciences (ICS) is the characterization of the forms of knowledge that emerge and are activated, in human interaction, social practice, the use of techniques and intellectual artifacts (Maury and Kovacs 2014, p. 15).

Based on the book by the Norwegian anthropologist Barth (1969), they insist on the fact that this approach implies not categorizing bodies of knowledge a priori, but understanding them as a relationship modality rather than an inventory modality, and considering the place of the researcher in the observation of knowledge mediation forms (which brings us back to the question of reflexivity).

This joins the perspective, developed by Jacob, in History. In his introduction to *Lieux de savoirs* (Volume 1), he defines bodies of knowledge as "the objects and results of pragmatics which validate and instrumentalize them, disseminate and transmit them" (Jacob 2007, p. 13). In an interview with Müller for the journal *Genèses*, he explains the posture that has governed this vast multi-volume transversal project[12], articulating theoretical perspectives and empirical studies in diverse spaces and temporalities so as to grasp the modalities according to which knowledge constitutes "bodies"

---

12. After *Lieux de savoir. Espaces et communautés*, published in 2007, Jacob directed Volume 2, *Mains de l'intellect*, in 2011, and a third volume should be published in the future.

and a "place" is shared in collectives and circulates across territories. For the historian, bodies of knowledge are defined by their pragmatics:

> For a group set in space and time, these are statements, concepts, ways of doing things that have a particular efficacy and authority, thereby giving meaning to the visible or the invisible world, organizing the perception of time and space, acting on the living or the inert (Müller 2009, p. 118).

For Jacob, what turns these statements into bodies of knowledge is not a particular intrinsic characteristic:

> […] it is a consensus on their efficacy and their authority within a more or less extensive group of actors, from the specialized community to an entire society. This consensus is a cultural variable, which can be based on regimes of truth with a more localized or universal scope. The text *Lieux de savoir* is characterized by an approach which can generally be described as "constructivist", since bodies of knowledge are envisioned as the object and the result of operations, processes and negotiations (Jacob in Müller (2009, p. 118)).

Apprehending mediation as an operator of transformations also leads to understanding bodies of knowledge in a certain way, not as a fixed standard but involving a plurality of statutes, of preparation and circulation modalities.

But this mode of understanding mediation is not the only one. Mediation is a "nomadic" concept (Darbellay 2012) which takes on different meanings and involves different challenges, depending on disciplines and research postures. It is, for example, used in theology to convey that the believer can only communicate with God through intermediaries (priests, angels, prophets, etc.). *Mediare* means being in the middle. Mediation has also been theorized by the sociologists of innovation. Calan and Latour (Latour 1990) primarily consider it as a chain or network of action logics: the chain produces tradition and the network, innovation. In educational sciences, many researchers set the reflection on mediation within the framework of "the Winnicottian hypothesis of transitional space. The activity implemented by an educator, the time and space dedicated to making contact, to the relationship" (Audebrand and Matuszak 2008). Depending on the theoretical framework, emphasis is placed on the actors of mediation, semiotic forms, spatio-temporal landmarks, etc. But another difference is structuring and concerns the intention behind the use of the concept of mediation: to understand phenomena or to evaluate the "effects" of mediation, so as to better frame them.

This distinction between mediation as a concept and mediation as a category for evaluating the efficacy of systems is not only at work in research on education and training, but as Le Marec shows, is also significant in research on cultural institutions. It seems to be a structuring factor when we are working on knowledge mediation. In his article, Le Marec (2006, pp. 9–18) explains that studies on popularization and media functioning are crossed by two antagonistic communication models: the former from the perspective of improving practices, and the latter, preconizing the critical analysis of practices to understand the complexity of social phenomena. This optimization perspective often encompasses an instrumental and linear conception of communication.

"Learn, Apply, Perform" is a slogan promoted by the multi–multi A organization, and clearly embodies a transitive conception of mediation and an underlying performativity ideal. The promise of efficacy through training is made possible by the adoption of a certain conception of mediation, here presented as a guarantor of learning success. The three stages (learn, apply, perform) are deployed in a *continuum*, making it possible to transform the knowledge provided during training into operators of professional efficacy. On a similar note, in the CSP prospectus, we can read the following statement: "Given the fact that success cannot be improvised, our methods are systematic"; the guarantee of success is therefore correlated with the method's mechanics. In its prospectus, this company presents its training engineering method under the label "4 REAL".

| REAL | EFFICIENT |
|---|---|
| An effective training, accessible, with proved simplicity. | Eased transposition for real impact in professional scenarios. |

**4 REAL**
REAL – EFFICIENT – ADAPTED – LEARNING

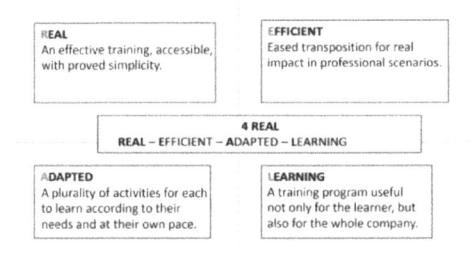

| ADAPTED | LEARNING |
|---|---|
| A plurality of activities for each to learn according to their needs and at their own pace. | A training program useful not only for the learner, but also for the whole company. |

**Figure 1.2.** *"4 REAL" training engineering method (figure inspired by the prospectus of the multi–multi A organization) For a color version of this figure, see www.iste.co.uk/seurrat/mediation.zip*

The terms used for describing this method, which is a trademark registered by this organization, perfectly illustrate the transitive conception of mediation associated with a performative ideal, with a view to guaranteeing the success of training. *"Real"* is part of the promise to adjust training to public expectations, *"Efficient"* crystallizes the idea of the transfer which enables performance, *"Adapted"* emphasizes personalization, while *"Learning"* highlights the spread of mediation "effects" throughout the whole firm. The figures there are presented as proof of the method's validity. Now, as we will see in Chapter 5, the evaluation of formative "effects" is precisely a point which poses particular difficulty, as there is a shift from the evaluation of "results" to the evaluation of satisfaction. In order to make training attractive, educational mediation is presented recurrently under the "pluses" or "pedagogy" sections of the 488 training prospectuses studied as "active", "participative", "interactive". Furthermore, training is often referred to as "action-training". Incorporating the term "action" seems to convey the idea of "classic" training as something more passive, action being the best way to attain the expected results.

The implementation of the rhetoric of the guaranteed efficacy of knowledge mediation in training seems to be linked to a certain conception of mediation which I describe as "mediagenic". I borrow the notion of mediageny from Marion, not as a descriptive category of media phenomena, but as a way that could be described as mediological, of thinking about the perfect adequacy between a promise, its implications and its realization:

> Mediageny is [...] the evaluation of an "amplitude": the reaction manifesting the more or less successful fusion of a narrative with its mediatization, and this in the context – itself also interactive – of the expectation horizons of a given kind. Thus, evaluating the mediageny of a story means attempting to observe and grasp the dynamics of interfertilization (Marion 1997, p. 83).

In this notion of mediageny, there seems to be an underlying conception of the efficacy of media devices which assumes that some (media) forms are more appropriate than others to deploy certain narratives. In another article, Marion (2003) takes the example of the controversy described as especially mediagenic in the written press and which would find a place for "mediagenic redeployment" on the Internet. In my view, this notion of mediageny is interesting not for evaluating the extent of success, but for qualifying a mediological conception of mediation which suggests that such and such form of mediation is especially conducive to guaranteeing operativeness.

In the first part of *Penser la trivialité*, Jeanneret proposes to examine three particularly telling conceptions of the circulation of ideas: their propagation and links with Tarde's social philosophy; their transmission, the guiding principle of Debray's mediological enterprise; and their reproduction, anchored in a semiotics pegged with linguistics. Jeanneret explains that the question of transmission is key to Debray's approach, because he sees it as a specifically important place for the deployment of power. For Debray, the question of the means and techniques is central in understanding transmission phenomena. Unlike the elementary philosophy of Tarde, which neglects forms and envisages a propagation of disembodied ideas, the mediological approach places the *medium* at the heart of its concerns. Jeanneret differentiates mediology as a theory from the series of mediographies exposed in the *Cahiers de médiologie*: "for me there is a mediology, which is a philosophy of the forms of transmission, and a mediography, which is an editorial enterprise bringing together a number of concrete analyses relating to different objects which can structure this transmission" (Jeanneret 2008, p. 37). Even if he insists on the importance of taking into account concrete forms of communication – an importance that the mediological project has particularly emphasized – Jeanneret shows that the conception of transmission expressed by this theory nonetheless raises numerous questions. For the author, what matters most is the elasticity of the notion of transmission itself. As such, the history of the term "transmission" is closely linked to the engineering of technical devices.

This primacy of the technical dimension explains the fact that men have often used the metaphor of the vector to think about communication: this can be summarized by the "telegraph model".

> The bias towards a radically materialist point of view on culture results in an effort to deliberately reduce the world of speculation to that of operational devices. […] In mediology we observe a constant shift from the formulation of messages to the transmission of objects, then from the transmission of objects to the transport of people: in short, from "mass media" to "means of communication" (Jeanneret 2008, p. 39).

I thus propose a shift from mediageny as a category for analyzing phenomena to mediageny as a mode of qualifying the mediological conceptions of mediation. It is then appropriate to further examine which forms of mediation in professional training crystallize these transitive and performative conceptions of knowledge mediation. In other words, how are these promises actualized through the implications of communication?

For Jeanneret,

> the promise and the implication respond to one another. The promise comes down to making a definition of the act of communication and its aim public; the implication creates an object-discourse device which embodies such a claim and most importantly, summons the subjects of communication in a posture, a situation, a context of expression (Jeanneret 2014, p. 66).

The mediagenic conception advances whenever the implication of communication guarantees the success of the promise. In this context, training engineering is presented as the keystone of guaranteed success.

In the field of training, Fichez considers that articulating the question of mediation with that of industrialization makes it possible to understand "the way in which educational situations are affected by industrial trends" (Fichez 1998, p. 192). This, of course, raises the question of the use of tools and media in training, and to a larger extent, the place of training engineering in training structures. On this point, configurations are particularly varied. We can distinguish three types of relationships between industrialization and mediation in training organizations: educational engineering supported by the structures; educational engineering co-constructed between the structure and the facilitators; and finally, educational engineering, which could be described as artisanal and left to the responsibility of the facilitator.

On the basis of what they call "facilitation guides", large organizations, as well as some of the specialists, produce the "educational procedures" which prescribe the contents and mediation methods that facilitators will then have to follow. The production of these "facilitation guides" is structured around certain conceptions of mediation. An offers manager explains that their company owns its educational contents and that producing the "procedures" using common methods helps to promote a "quality process". According to them:

INTERVIEW.– "Above all, it is a quality process that sets us apart from many competitors. It is a quality assurance for customers, for whom our firm constitutes a reference. They undoubtedly know that if they send a trainee at two different periods, the contents delivered will be identical, and there will be an identical quality level. We have very high quality standards, something which keeps customers coming back".

This question of "quality" is particularly interesting to explore in order to understand the complex links between industrialization and mediation. Indeed, for the organizations that rationalize training development processes the most, this contributes to making products comparable following the same quality standard. This evidences the link between standardization and industrialization, where the organization of production aims to limit the differences between the standard and the different products as much as possible. However, it is not possible to compare this with the production of standardized and homogeneous products typical of the Taylorist model (Mœglin 1998, pp. 8–9). As I have been able to observe, large training structures are based on an economy of variety (Coriat and Weinstein 1995). The idea is to reconcile the compliance project with a "quality" standard and product variety. Hence, this involves thinking of recurring forms of mediation disconnected from specific training contents. A training manager of facilitators in a multi–multi structure explains their goals:

INTERVIEW.– "Training other facilitators is crucial because we have an increasing number of external customers. Different facilitators have to share the same practices so that the customer can identify that it is a specific form of training (Name of the structure), with the quality that accompanies it".

For each training program, a "facilitation guide" is developed and presented by the manager as a minutely detailed scenario, timed with all the educational tools, theory, examples, cases, exercises, etc. The trainer is expected to follow this framework to "facilitate" the training. Even if this strongly frames the trainer's practice, they do not necessarily become an automaton. As a trainer from one of the specialized structures points out:

INTERVIEW.– "The training is extremely well structured in advance by the educational procedure. You will do this exercise, go through this step, debrief at this time, etc. Afterwards, it is up to the trainer to own the discussions surrounding the exercise. Although there is a discourse, a framework, everyone makes it their own. And then, as we are all human beings, everyone deviates from it more or less in their own way".

The design of the facilitation guides is strongly oriented by the goal of "seducing" the training audience: this involves varying the teaching methods as much as possible, punctuating the training times in order to elicit and maintain the interest of the trained audiences. This illustrates the link with the question of anticipating public expectations at work in effective rhetoric. For example, one of the multi–multi A organizations has formalized the start-up stage of training, considered a key stage, which they call "taking off". For a training manager of facilitators:

INTERVIEW.– "The take-off is based on the principle that the first minute must involve learning. When we finish the presentation round, it is over. We start action straight away, with an exercise. And at the same time, the exercise's pedagogy includes the goal of trainees getting to know themselves, understanding their training objectives, etc. We can no longer afford to go around the table with the collection of expectations. Our training courses are becoming increasingly shorter and our customer wants learning to take place from the beginning. [...] Our time to train is therefore shorter and shorter, we must be more and more effective. In the evaluations, we no longer want to read verbatim statements such as "we spent the whole morning introducing ourselves", no more of that! We need very precise, highly structured educational goals. So, we created the take-off, and the same happens during the closing session, that is our way of saying goodbye".

In this quote, the link between the forms of mediation rationalization, the shortening of training times and the imperative for educational efficacy is really striking. On another note, for training structures which do not offer pre-constructed training frameworks, this contributes to offering more "low-end" training. For example, for the former head of short training programs at the *grande école* B, multi–multi organizations are not their direct competitors:

INTERVIEW.– "Since they propose very industrial things, things end up being pretty much like a communications pie. To begin with, they are never pioneers or supporters of research, to me they are followers [...]. I know that they propose inter-company communication, but we are not aiming for the same targets".

This position is consistent with the criticisms formulated against the industrialization of training analyzed in the book *Industrialiser la formation, anthologie commentée*. The chapter on the time of criticism[13] (Mœglin 2016) highlights the fact that quite quickly, industrialist thinking in education will come up against its detractors. But these critiques are far from homogeneous and also fit into quite different ideologies. Two extracts (Innis, Piveteau) are analyzed therein. The chapter illuminates major types of critics: the traditionalists and the revolutionaries. The commentary on the text by Innis (Tremblay and Paquelin 2016) – Canadian economist and historian from the beginning of the 20th century and pioneer in the development of communication studies – clearly highlights the different arguments his criticism is based upon: the mechanization and standardization of educational practices and contents would result in a race to the bottom in favor of commercial logics. For its part, the commentary on the text by Piveteau (Mœglin and Petit 2016) explains how this author adapted Innis' criticisms to the French context. As the authors of the anthology point out, its criticism, based on an ideal of democratization of knowledge, is nonetheless based on a certain amalgamation between organizational industrialization and the industrialization of learning. That chapter clearly shows that, even if these critical discourses must be contextualized, the values and forms of argumentation engaged are still at work in contemporary discourses.

In no way is the industrialization of mediation self-evident, as reflected by the plurality of methods of educational engineering. For example, the managers from *grande école* A stress the fact that there is no "rule", that training courses can be developed by the facilitators themselves (who share their opinion on the framework), or co-constructed with the intervenors. As I pointed out earlier, since it is often customary to invite both a facilitator and "experts" to the offers from *grande école* A, the product managers are responsible for ensuring consistency and the articulation of the different intervenors' discourses. *Grande école* A is thus situated between the fairly industrial mediation model by large structures and the more artisanal model, whereas *grande école* B is not engaged in the construction of training

---

13. Chapter whose extracts are commented on by Gaëtan Tremblay, Didier Paquelin, Pierre Mœglin and Laurent Petit.

procedures for inter-company internships. It is different, however, for "tailor-made" offers, for which the structure responds to calls for tender and co-produces educational content and methods with the facilitators to address an order.

This shows that the industrialization of mediation has a variable geometry, depending on the structures and the types of offers (inter- or intra-company). Another aspect for thinking about the relationships between industrialization and mediation concerns the use of tools and media in professional training. Fichez (2000) draws a distinction between the notion of industrialization "in" training (namely the use of tools borrowed from the communication industries for educational purposes) and the industrialization "of" training, which encompasses a more radical transformation process in the way training operates. In this context, the use of digital technologies crystallizes questions about the industrialization *in* and *of* training, letting us see how a conception of media as an instrument for optimizing mediation is at work.

## 1.4. Instrumented mediation: the digital seen as an educational panacea

In the discourse on professional training, the "digital" is presented as a means which holds, in itself, the power to amplify the scope of mediation, personalize it, produce motivation and guarantee performative efficacy. The "digital" is presented as the optimal "instrument" for achieving promises, and the most effective "means" for multiplying formative "effects".

First of all, let us emphasize that it is the term "digital" and not the term "*numérique*" that is used in professional training discourses:

> The French language stands out as being, it seems, the only one to use the Latin root *numerus* ("number"), whereas other languages, even Latin (Spanish, Italian or Portuguese), use, like German, English, Dutch and most European languages, another Latin root, *digitus* ("finger" – it is with the fingers that we count numbers) (Moatti 2012, p. 134).

Originally, the adjective *numérique* is drawn from the technical vocabulary. It designates a mode of automated signal processing. For the researcher, to use the term "*numérique*" as a noun is an abuse of language:

*Le numérique* in its noun form, almost personified, invades everything. The concept is so invasive that it leads us to forget what it relates to (photographic image, musical recording, information processing, etc.): everything converges in *le numérique* (digital technology). The adjective *numérique* abolishes the noun it is supposed to qualify: a shortcut symbol of a hurried world which forgets the noun form, even represses it, to more quickly designate the digital fact (*le fait du numérique*), regardless of the medium (Moatti 2012, p. 135).

Thus, "the portmanteau term *numérique* ends up being used *ad nauseam* to convey the immaterial, to the detriment of the immense underlying material and software base" (Moatti 2012, p. 136). Without going into detail about the controversies over the use of these terms, I will say, based on the reflections of Robert, that "the digital" and its variations such as "digitalization" further reinforce the naturalization phenomena pointed out by Moatti. By highlighting the idea of use in the term *le doigt* ("the finger"), the "digital" makes us forget about the material dimension of digital media, which contributes to establishing "*l'impensé numérique*" (the "unimaginable digital") (Robert 2014).

There are many advocates of the "digitalization" of training, and in this sector we find a certain number of consulting/supporting offers for the "digitalization" of training organizations. What motivates this type of structure is not only to offer consulting services to the training organization, but also to bring together the actors of training, and establish expertise in the field. The *Acteurs de la Compétence* (FFP until 2019) are also highly involved in this subject. They set up a project as part of the *Programme d'investissements d'avenir* (PIA), entitled "*La formation digitale au service de l'employabilité et de la compétitivité*". This project, with a budget of 2.55 million euros and deployed since January 2018, aims to "support the digitalization of companies in the sector in order to measure the digital maturity of training companies and to offer support in the transformation of their practices[14]".

All these actors insist on the fact that "digitalization" does not imply the end of face-to-face practices, but rather an enhancement of face-to-face/digital complementarity. According to the *Acteurs de la Compétence* (FFP until 2019):

---

14. See: https://lesacteursdelacompetence.fr/.

The market is actually moving towards a complementary integration of digital solutions, also offered by new entrants in the sector, with the educational expertise from professional training actors. Training thus becomes "multi-modal" and is based on "blended learning", which combines face-to-face and the digital. This makes it possible to adapt the training courses to each profile, their expectations, needs and constraints. The offer of blended learning tailor-made devices is a key to developing effective training[15].

The quote above clearly crystallizes the ideal of educational efficacy supported by the growing use of digital devices in professional training. Although blended learning is presented as a mixture, almost as a "perfect method", the modalities of such a mixture do not seem to be self-evident. Hoping to distance themselves from this fashionable term, some researchers prefer to use the term "hybrid", "because it refers to the creation of a new entity whose major characteristics are the presence-distance articulation and the integration of technologies to support the teaching-learning process" (Charlier et al. 2006, p. 482). In this clever cocktail, which is supposed to guarantee the success of blended learning or "hybrid training", the challenge is to show the complementarity between the "assets" of face-to-face and remote training.

In blended learning, digital technologies (*technologies numériques*) are presented more as additive technologies than as substitutive technologies. Nevertheless, this articulation is not the only trend in professional training witnessing more and more actors specializing in "100% digital" training and landing on the professional training market, such as Google, who have not historically been active in the training sector. Grignon (2016, pp. 123–139) examines the way in which Google frames the ordinary practices of communication professionals. Through the sociosemiotic study of the "Academies" which accompany some of its software (Analytics, AdWords, YouTube, etc.), the author shows how the firm cultivates its control over the knowledge, skills and values which circulate in highly varying socio-organizational contexts and contribute to the progressive reconfiguration of the expert/lay landscape in the world of communication. The example of the Google Academy discussed by Grignon clearly shows

---

15. See: https://lesacteursdelacompetence.fr/.

the way in which technologization and industrialization are accompanied by ideologization processes.

This question of ideologization is also explored by Bullich (2018) in his article on "the platformization of training", where he analyzes "the economy of promises" (Joly 2015) of online training platforms – mainly Massive Open Online Courses, MOOCs – such as Skillshare, Udemy and Open Classrooms. For the researcher, the main promises of these platforms are customization and personalization, empowerment and inclusion in a community. As I pointed out earlier, the training organizations studied for this research project offer more "mixed" training than completely remote asynchronous training, such as the platforms studied by Bullich. In this way, they attempt to show the interest in the connection between activities carried out in groups (mainly in person but in the case of multi–multi B also in a "virtual class") and online activities, performed individually in an asynchronous manner. This enables them to continue to legitimize their historical activity, in this case training internships, by showing how their "effects" are "amplified" through supplementary digital devices. Despite these differences, we find important links between the economy of promises analyzed by Bullich in these platforms and the promotion discourses of the offers listed in the prospectuses of five out of the eight organizations studied. If this statement is valid for only five out of the eight organizations studied, it is because the deployment of "mixed" offers requires significant investment that the smaller structures studied cannot currently make. Despite this, during my interviews with the director and the educational director of one of the specialized structures, both stressed the fact that they want to develop this type of offer, and in 2018, they launched an initiative (*Convention industrielle de formation par la recherche, CIFRE*) with a doctoral student who has worked on this subject. On the other hand, the low use of online training modules can also be presented as a choice. For those responsible for the "Communication" product of the Executive Education department in *grande école* A:

> INTERVIEW.– "We are thinking about developing a bit of remote work, but we will continue to work mainly in person. Students who choose training at *grande école* A still have this expectation. There is mutual enrichment and the network, as well as the ability to meet directly and exchange ideas with our experts".

This interview was conducted back in 2019. Since then, in 2021, *grande école* A has set up an offer promoting "interactive conferences" followed by "workshops", but its training offers are still mainly face-to-face internships.

On the other hand, the five training structures which offer complete remote learning or "mixed" training offers develop a whole rhetoric praising the interests of this type of system:

> Undoubtedly, the promise that is most often evoked by these platforms is that of personalization. This is aimed at both students and facilitators. First of all, this promise comes in the form of a use that is publicized as immediate, continuous, ubiquitous and at will. "Learners" are thus summoned to work on the platforms considered and to exploit the learning possibilities of "ATAWAD" methods ("Any Time, Any Where, Any Device") (Bullich 2018, p. 18).

The personalization they promise is also accompanied by an abundant offer: the prospectuses are regularly supplemented to ensure that there are enough products to suit to everyone's aspirations. We find this same rhetoric in the prospectuses of large training organizations.

As previously mentioned, the multi–multi B structure is the one that develops this type of offer the most. It even has a product called "NExT". In the prospectus, such offers are presented as a real blended experience or 100% digital, with personalized coaching throughout the whole course. Thanks to the flexibility of these courses, NExT is the right answer to help optimize training management and improve learning efficacy. Personalization is therefore presented as a guarantee of success. The ubiquitous dimension is also particularly highlighted: the online and offline modes are adapted to smartphones and tablets, have a ludic character, with short sequences accessible anytime and anywhere. Learning and training become a pleasurable experience thanks to Pocket Impulse's gamification and mnemonic activities. The flexibility promised by such devices allegedly promotes learner motivation, motivation being necessary for empowerment, understood as "increasing-capacitation", that is, a "rise in each person's capacity to act" (Bullich 2018, p. 21). For the multi–multi B organization, its offer "encourages stronger engagement on the part of learners and constitutes the ideal educational complement to strengthen the performance of multimodal systems".

The platforms analyzed by Bullich exclusively offer online training, whereas the training organizations that I studied insist on the complementarity of the "assets" of each modality (so as not to disqualify their historical activity as providers of face-to-face training). Digital offers are therefore presented as "augmented face-to-face", supposedly "optimizing face-to-face time". In its prospectus, the multi–multi A organization explains that "digital classrooms favor greater efficacy, thanks to the alternation of teaching methods". They argue that the "digital" enables us to "work on virtual situations and to transpose learning with complete peace of mind: before, during and after training". In its 2023 prospectus, the multi–multi B organization presented a diagram which clearly embodied the transitive ideal of "transposition" crystallized around the use of digital technologies in training.

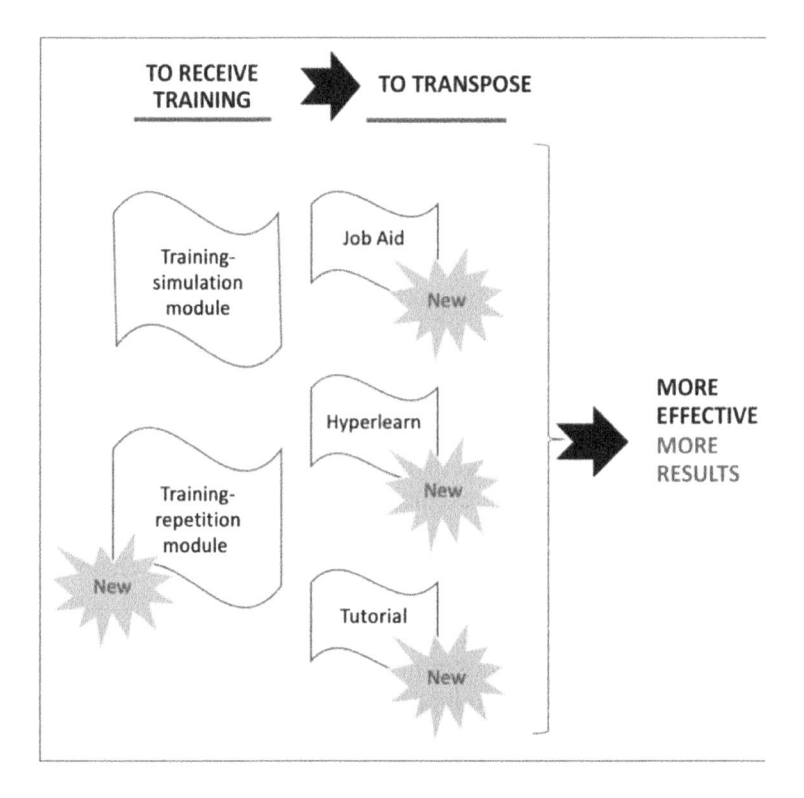

**Figure 1.3.** *Transposition diagram (figure inspired by the prospectus from the multi–multi B organization). For a color version of this figure, see www.iste.co.uk/seurrat/mediation.zip*

Thanks to the example above, we can see to what extent technologization reinforces ideologization around the efficacy imperative. First of all, this is visually embodied by means of a three-phase structure (training, transposition, results) connected by directional arrows, in a linear and almost mechanical conception of mediation. The repetition of gestures and the simulation permitted by digital devices is supposed to enable, de facto, the "transposition" of acquired knowledge into the professional world and its use at the service of efficacy and performance.

It is interesting to note that what organizations call "blended learning" designates extremely different practices. When we look at the training prospectuses of the five largest organizations, 56% of the training offers were labeled as "blended" (or with the mention "+ remote activities") in 2019, and 71% in 2023. Sometimes, the "blended" modality is reduced to making online documentation accessible for download before the internship, or a video extolling the merits of the training that will follow. Without minimizing the influence of these media transformations in the field of professional training, I would say that this mediological conception over determines the role of the technical device in knowledge mediation:

> The terms "extend", "reinforce" or "multiply", to describe the contribution of mediatization to mediation, are misleading if they give credence to the idea of a simple amplification of the second by the first. Mediatization is not the transposition of mediation. Their respective ways of processing knowledge, of constructing bodies of knowledge, of addressing the learner differ completely (Mœglin 2005, p. 78).

My aim is not to deal with the full extent of the problems relating to the development, mobilization and promotion of digital devices in professional training, whose variety and plurality are faithfully represented in the publications of the journal *Distance et médiations des savoirs* (DMS). My purpose is to explore how the emphasis of training organizations in blended learning is part of a mediagenic conception of mediation, where digital technology is considered as an instrument for optimizing training "effects". The growing use of online modules is leading to an increasingly strong modularization of "brick" content. This modularization, which has made segmented training times shrink (like the "3 hours flat" and "speed learning" offered by large organizations), is also leading to an increasingly robust division of fields of knowledge and, as I will see later, to a primacy of schematic knowledge more suited to mediation in short temporalities.

Mœglin analyzes this shift from the service logic to the "self-service" logic. According to him, this actually leads to a shift in the center of gravity of the educational process:

> [...] this substitutes the priority traditionally given to the development of educational contents and methods with a completely different priority. And what is this priority? To facilitate the access for "users" (according to the appellation in vogue) to sets of educational resources simply made available to them. And this, at the cost of modularizing resources, their disposition and combination in educational environments where users are invited to pick up what sparks their interest, according to a unique and personalized training path (Mœglin 1998, p. 107).

For the researcher, this position leads to a reversal, to a form of "unaccountability upstream in favor of downstream, making the pupil or student assume responsibility for the success (or failure) of a system where the learner is the main (if not sole) actor, in the name of official guidelines "placing the learner at the center of training"" (Mœglin 1998, p. 108).

To be able to distance ourselves from the "economy of promises" underlying the discourses promoting digital training offers, we must take a closer look at such devices in order to see how these pretensions are embodied in communication engagements. I will not conduct this analysis here, as training for communicators (and even more, public speaking training) is still poorly invested in by digital devices. Why? As I will show in the section devoted to "paradigm shifts", this could be due to the fact that training in communication (as a transversal skill and as an occupation) is imbued with an interpersonal conception of communication; organizations seem to consider that communication training is less suitable for "digitalization" than other areas of training, such as accounting or executive secretariat. A product manager interviewed in 2018 expressed the following: "We had an e-learning training program in oral communication and it did not reach such a large audience, except for a few trainees who were unable to attend. In oral communication, they tend to seek face-to-face communication".

Observation of the training prospectuses shows three salient points regarding the relationship between educational offers in communication and digital devices: the specialized training organizations and the two *grandes écoles* studied do not currently offer remote training modules (even if one of their projects is to develop supplementary online modules). Since 2020, large organizations have offered some "100% remote" communication training programs, but most of all, offers presented as "blended". Remote training offers offered by large organizations only correspond to 1/8th offers. They further reinforce the logic of content fragmentation and the reduction of training length. The two emblematic remote products from our two multi–multi organizations are respectively entitled "Speed learning 3 hours" and "3 hours flat". These offers often relate to the instrumental mastery of such and such digital medium and in particular socio-digital networks, as evidenced by the titles of these offers:"3 hours flat to promote your image remotely"/"3 hours to develop your visibility on LinkedIn"/ "Social networks: understanding and mastering Facebook, Twitter, LinkedIn"/"Corporate social network: the keys to successful deployment"/ "3 hours to decode nonverbal communication"/"3 hours to manage your emails efficiently"/"Turn your emails into an asset".

It is interesting to note that this "dematerialization" of media, according to the term used by the actors to describe these digital documents, is not unanimous among facilitators. Actually, some facilitators think that interns – who for the most part do not print digital documentation and consult it shortly before training – will use it much less, unless it is distributed and used during training. This is why two facilitators brought printed documents during two of the training programs attended, one of them emphasizing that some of the documents were *spare*, and the other, that the material had been printed at the instructor's expense.

The fact that training in communication strategies and public speaking does not involve a remote learning modality does not necessarily mean that a reflection on the tools and media of professional communication training and their links with an instrumented design mediation is not relevant. As Mœglin (2005, p. 86) does when he refers to the stick used by Socrates in his demonstration of the Meno to analyze its usability, it is appropriate to pay attention to the plurality of tools and media which simultaneously configure the forms of mediation and contribute to the construction of mediation conceptions.

In public speaking training, a certain technical device seems essential: the camera. Even if some facilitators use PowerPoint and others do not, or some distribute documentation and others very little, all of them use the camera as a mode of deciphering and "revealing" the functioning of the public speaking. For the educational director of one of the specialized communication structures:

INTERVIEW.– "There is a very important element in this know-how, in this transfer of know-how, which is the camera [...]. The video-recording will allow us to ensure that we are as objective as possible. Because if there is no video-recording, there will only remain my memory, which is infinitely subjective [...]. The video-recording cannot simply be blamed for being biased or a lie. If something is recorded, this means it has been produced. We don't know where it came from and I don't want to get into the origins of why, but just concentrate on the effects. The interest of the video-recording, is that it also makes it possible to slow time down, which is a problematic factor in communication".

This statement is marked by an immanentist conception of meaning, a conception based on the idea of the transparency of semiotic phenomena: images speak for themselves, their discourse being univocal and universal. Watching a video-recording is supposed to produce a revelation or at least "trigger" the encouragement of the communication practices of interns to evolve in the right direction. As the speaker becomes its own audience, they must understand the "effects" of discourse so as to better control them. Most of the time, the intern will end the program with a stock of videos on a USB stick. Video-recording is at the core of public speaking training, which devotes a great deal of time to viewing and commenting on recordings of oral performances (which means that each oral performance is "watched" twice: once live and once recorded).

In the public speaking training followed in one of the multi–multi organizations – a training module which, as I have pointed out, is the most expensive of the public speaking training programs offered by the structure – the individual meetings between interns and the team of facilitators are there to optimize the time spent with each person commenting on their own video, without interns spending too long reviewing each other's performances. This is similar to "media coaching" methods, as analyzed, for example, by Le Bouëdec in her current thesis. She proceeds with an organizational analysis of media training and media coaching. Based on three years' experience as part of *CIFRE* in a communications consulting agency which specializes in media speaking, she analyzes "the bond that unites a communications agency with its customer organizations in the search for 'effective' communication" (Le Bouëdec 2016, p. 27).

The search for "educational efficacy" at the service of "professional efficacy" governs knowledge mediation choices. In this view, other small tools, which may seem trivial, are also interesting to show the way in which they present themselves as instruments for optimizing public speaking, or the activity of communication professionals: post-its and index cards. These small tools play a prominent role in training programs, as they constitute a "set which is both heterogeneous and interdependent of other devices which happen to be available in a given context and generally guide social activity" (Jeanneret 2014, p. 13).

As I have pointed out, few printed materials are distributed during the training observed, but one type of format is still the favorite: the index card. This, as I have already emphasized when I analyzed training prospectuses, is a "unit of information", "a summary of information" (Gardey 2008, p. 162). As I have seen in my previous works on training kits (Seurrat 2010; Marti and Seurrat 2018), the index card invites conciseness and content hierarchization. Furthermore, Gardey emphasizes that the index cards published by organizations are "most often preformatted documents which lead to the restriction and standardization of the information provided at each stage of a procedure" (Gardey 2008, p. 162). The index cards distributed in training programs in communication planning materialize the idea of planning and the importance of carefully following the procedure's steps.

In public speaking training, the index card used is the Bristol type, which the speaker must use to best prepare for an oral performance. Handed out blank, it is then associated with oral writing instructions. It is presented as the essential tool to best control the course of our discourse. It embodies the concept of a simple and impactful discourse. The facilitator announces the activity that will be carried out with this "Bristol smart card": "we are going to work with Bristol index cards. On each index card, you will write an idea in one sentence and no more, and at the bottom, what supports your idea, a number, for example".

**Introduction**
- 3P
- Goal
- Plan

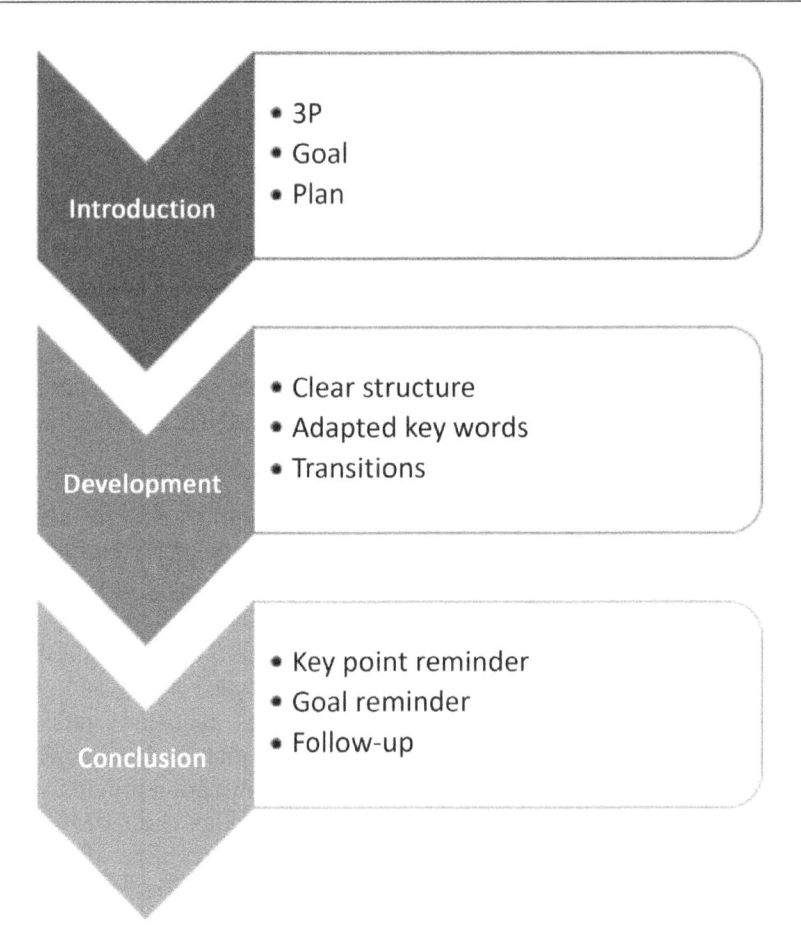

**Development**
- Clear structure
- Adapted key words
- Transitions

**Conclusion**
- Key point reminder
- Goal reminder
- Follow-up

**Figure 1.4.** *"Bristol smart card" (inspired by a training teaching aids from the multi–multi A organization). For a color version of this figure, see www.iste.co.uk/seurrat/mediation.zip*

Index cards are tools for prefiguring discourse, and also tools for prefiguring the speaker's postures. For example, a facilitator advises us to draw a "smiley" at the top right of each card, so as to never forget to smile. As an intellectual mnemonic technology, and an operator of action, the index card must enable us to control our statements and actions so as to bring them into line with the expectations projected by the audiences.

In public speaking training, post-it notes are often used by interns to formulate their evaluations of the oral performances of other group members. Due to its very short format, the post-it encourages the intern-observer to formulate the evaluation in a few words. In one of the organizations, a post-it writing grid is also provided to participants: for each oral performance, interns are invited to write the first name of the person who has just spoken on a post-it, draw a heart next to what they preferred in the performance and an arrow pointing upwards to denote what can still be improved. It is interesting to note that, in this perspective for assessing interns, the co-learner is not asked to write a "minus" sign (which would denote a lack), but an arrow, representing the possible margin for progress. Each intern then leaves with a collection that can be consulted again at will. In Chapter 5, I will show how, through hermeneutic marking, the framing of communication assessment (of oral communication services and the communication "actions" of professionals) standardizes the apprehension modalities of communication.

Whether digital or not, professional training tools and media are the operators of action which "instrumentalize" training and are supposed to amplify its scope. In this, they participate in a mediagenic conception of mediation which presents them as optimization instruments. These concepts expressed by the training organizations seem to echo the formulation of interns' expectations.

## 1.5. The explicit request for communication "tools" and "techniques"

In short nondegree professional training programs – even if most of the time those who pay are not those who attend the training – the logic of servuction is at work. This requires the offer to adapt to expectations. The formulation of promises is an obligatory and recurring part of training programs, which presents itself as a response to a request. In that sense, the promise always comes second, after the enunciation of expectations. Here, I follow Jeanneret in his characterization of promise stricto sensu, as the "explicit expression of a proposition on communication and what it can bring to audiences" (Jeanneret 2014, p. 14).

The profiles of those trained in "communication occupations" and, even more so, those trained in communication in general are extremely heterogeneous. In the three public speaking training courses observed, the interns' occupations were quite different: customer relations manager, salesperson, network development manager, management controller, distribution manager, developer, salesperson, laboratory manager, marketing manager, director of an accommodation institution for dependent elderly people (EHPAD), general director of services, financial director, head of internal audit mission, etc. Note, however, that almost all of the interns were executives. The higher the hierarchical level, the more opportunities to speak in public, but above all, the higher the expectation to persuade our audience. The companies represented are also quite diverse, despite there being an over-representation of large companies: BMW, Total, Disney, Alcatel, EDF, Danone, Sanofi, etc. The professional profiles of those trained in strategic communication and planning are logically narrower in terms of "communication functions", but we note a fairly large heterogeneity of functions and hierarchical statuses: communications manager, communications assistant, director communications manager, head of corporate social responsibility (CSR), director of Africa communications, product manager, advertising space purchasing manager, HR communications manager, public relations manager, marketing and communications manager. As their title clearly shows, certain functions are at the crossroads of marketing and communication. Large companies are also the most represented: Total, Orange, Citroën, Siemens, Areva, etc.

On the other hand, there are significant differences in the professional experience of trainees, which ranges from one or two years, to over 20 years. This heterogeneity of profiles is common in intra-company training, and is presented by facilitators not as a difficulty for establishing common frameworks, but rather as an asset for training:

OBSERVATION.– "Some of you have initial training in communication, others do not, some already have extensive professional experience, others are at the beginning of their career. You are a heterogeneous audience, this is normal in training and this is what makes it so rich".

A significant proportion of interns are undergoing "professional reconversion", with a past in occupations relating to management assistance, marketing, commerce or journalism. This is also a point often stressed by the product managers from multi–multi organizations: their audiences need "to grasp the basics", because many of them do not have initial training in communication.

Finally, being a participant in these training courses myself, my status as a teacher–researcher and the projection this role elicited deserves to be further explained. My status as a communications researcher has led many trainees and certain facilitators themselves, to see me as an "expert". Despite not being stabilized and changing depending on the contexts between researcher and expert, the distinction seems important to me, as we are discussing training practices. For Delmas:

> The expert can be characterized as a specialist capable of providing a wealth of knowledge, constituted by such person, but often developed by others. It responds to a request […]. The researcher, on the other hand, defines its activity on the basis of a knowledge production project, whose practical impact is not the main concern (Delmas 2011, p. 11).

To this, I may object and say that researchers do not think on their own, but develop bodies of knowledge "in the company" of others who have preceded them, or with whom collaboration takes place. Research can also be applied to social demands (notably within the framework of funded programs), and the relationship with the "practical impact" varies depending on the disciplines and research positions. Still, should we not ponder the distinction between the researcher and the expert? I do not think so, but I believe that everyone must think about this boundary in their practice, but also in their research ethics.

Being assigned this "expert" label produced a certain discomfort in me during group work, because group members could expect me to have "the solution" to the case studies, while certain facilitators could ask me to confirm their statements, especially when they referred to "theory". It is precisely this relationship to certainty – which I will call into question in the third chapter of this book – that seems to be one of the frameworks of the debate between the expert and the research postures in the human and social sciences.

I would like to implement a comprehensive reading of the expectations of trainees in the professional training programs followed. It is neither an evaluative nor a justifying reading, but a reading "which refers to the meaning given to it by the actor in a given situation, that is to the 'good reasons' they have for acting in that way and not otherwise" (Berthelot 2001, p. 242). Formulating trainee expectations at the beginning of the course is a mandatory activity in all the sessions observed. It clearly demonstrates the supply–demand logic, even if the interns have not necessarily chosen the training themselves and are not the ones paying for it. The formulation of expectations as soon as the training begins has, as a corollary, the assessment statement at the end of training and the evaluation questionnaire, which mainly concerns the adequacy between the expectations and the completion of the training program.

Out of the 38 occurrences of explicit formulation of intern expectations at the start of training (an intern can formulate several expectations) jotted down during my observations, 19 mention a need for "tools" or "techniques", that is, over half of them. Furthermore, the need for tools is almost systematically associated with the occurrence of efficacy, performance or improvement (15/19):

OBSERVATION.– "I need tools to improve my performance". "I need tools to be able to transmit information more effectively". "I would like to master short sentences in order to have a more impactful discourse". "I wish to obtain the keys to success". "I need to acquire communication techniques to know how to communicate effectively with a nonspecialist audience". "I need to go through the whole range of communication tools to be more effective in my practice". "I want to strengthen my methodology to be more effective in my duties". "I am looking for keys to better know how to build a communications plan".

The relationship between means and ends which is at the heart of the question of efficacy is also explicitly exposed in certain formulations of expectations: "I need to acquire tools to go faster"/"I need to become more efficient with the same budget".

It is also necessary to differentiate certain expectations specific to public speaking training, and media training expectations raised by programs in strategic communication and planning. The question of self-confidence is a fairly present expectation in the context of public speaking training and media training (8/22):

OBSERVATION.– "I hate speaking in public, I would like to be more comfortable". "I would like to become more comfortable, to be more concise". "I desire to know how to manage my stress better when I speak in public". "I have already made several appearances in the media. I would like to know how to get to the point, gain self-confidence and know how to avoid any tricky questions".

These remarks are consistent with the fact that these training programs are either classified under the "Communication" products, or under the

"Personal Development" and "Personal Efficacy" products. On the other hand, we will see that the use of the notion of "personal efficacy" in certain works in psychology is quite instrumental and strongly associated with the question of self-confidence.

Another expectation often expressed (7/22) regarding public speaking training concerns the ability to persuade:

OBSERVATION.– "I need to elicit adhesion". "I need to become more impactful". "What I expect from this training program is to give me the basis to better convince in meetings".

This expectation joins the performative ideal which can already be detected in ancient rhetoric, the idea that mastery of language can make it possible to anticipate and control the reception of our audience. As for training programs in strategic communication and planning, they raise expectations relating to the strengthening of the intern's legitimacy in relation to peers, as well as and above all, the hierarchy.

OBSERVATION.– "I would like to be able to have my communication plan validated by my superiors". "I need to know how to convince my superiors of the strategic importance of communication". "I hope I can gain credibility with my superiors".

This quest for legitimacy is partly explained by the fact that these are training programs oriented to occupations, and that they mainly address the "communication function". Further, drawing on the work of researchers from the *RESIPROC* network, I will show that the communication function struggles to move away from an instrumental vision.

Finally, among the professionals undergoing reorientation, it is the question of "methodology" that stands out the most:

OBSERVATION.– "I am shifting from marketing to communication, and I want to strengthen my communication methods and tools". "I have a background in accounting. I want to learn to prioritize by having a tighter grip on methodologies". "As I do not have a background in communication, I have methodological gaps". "I have been parachuted into communications and I am waiting to obtain methodology to gain rigor and credibility".

Later, I will show that the definition of what a "method" is raises questions in the context of professional training and in relation to what we can understand by "methodology" in the human and social sciences. For the moment, let me stress that "methods" in training are mainly procedures and lists of mnemonic tasks, which perhaps serve less to apprehend the complexity of situations – to gain understanding – than to claim mastery over the course of things to act upon. It is nonetheless necessary to note two expectations formulated as part of the training program in strategic communication and planning of *grande école* A, and which relate more to distancing than to the mastery of tools or procedures:

OBSERVATION.– "I would like to have a more global vision of the communications function". "I chose this training to gain height". "I would like to have more effective communication and a more structured discourse to be more credible in my occupation".

Thus, communication, presented as a transversal skill, is believed to foster "professional efficacy" in all occupations. The mastery of "communication techniques" becomes a factor to gain in professional efficacy. Communication, seen as a set of skills linked to occupations, becomes the very object of the quest for efficacy. Communication is then either an efficacy factor – a means for achieving it – or an object that must be shaped in view of the efficacy imperative.

The promise of efficacy is highly present in institutional rhetoric, especially among large training organizations. Let us take, for example, the introduction to the 2018 prospectus of one of the multi–multi organizations, signed by its president. It opens like this: "Our mission is to make every moment an opportunity to learn; a rich and stimulating experience with a single goal: efficacy". It ends with: "Inventing solutions that combine innovation, agility and efficacy: that's also what it means, bringing you 'Much more than knowledge', a formula which refers to the slogan 'Beyond knowledge'. Knowledge is therefore at the service of a value: efficacy".

The formulation of training promises by facilitators always follows the statement of trainees' expectations. It is important to emphasize that this formulation only occurs at a second moment, because the statement of the promises is directly presented as an adequate response to expectations. The facilitators also rely a lot on the formulation of expectations, even if this means directly using certain expressions from the trainees to demonstrate that the training will respond to them:

OBSERVATION.– "You are waiting a lot for methodology, which is very good, because that is precisely what we are going to work on during these two days". "During this training program, you will acquire methodologies and learn how to position yourselves". "In addition to the methodology, we will exchange best practices and we will see how we justify the role of communicators at a time when budgets are being cut". "How do you design a communication strategy with high added value? How do you optimize the implementation of communication, learn how to evaluate it and integrate the digital? This is precisely what we will see during this internship". "At the end of the internship, you will be secure".

Facilitators nonetheless insist on the limits of the training program and above all on the fact that its success depends on the involvement of trainees and their ability to use the learning acquired during training in their professional life. In this, efficacy as a promise is differentiated from performance.

OBSERVATION.– "It's not about performing miracles, it's about giving you a larger perspective and efficacy in your speaking addresses. You should emerge from this training program with greater flexibility, gaining perspective and efficacy". "There is no magic wand. The success of the training program depends on your involvement".

The promise of increased efficacy seems particularly linked to the use of adequate means in relation to the temporal constraints of the action:

OBSERVATION.– "We are going to see a whole series of tools and method stages to design better communication plans. So far, you may have done it intuitively, now you will do it in a stronger, more convincing manner and you will gain efficacy. It will take a little longer upstream, but it will save you time afterwards".

The modalities for referring to efficacy are therefore expressed differently: instead an imperative, it becomes a quest to which promises are made. But it seems to me that the quest and the promise contribute to the naturalization of this imperative as self-evident. It appears that the variation of discourse acts relating to efficacy particularly resonates with instrumental conceptions of communication. Seen as a series of (writing or oratory) techniques, or as a series of tools (mainly from management sciences), communication becomes the preferred territory for deploying performative efficacy.

# 2

# Mastery Over Communication: Professionalization and the Injunction to Efficacy

This chapter delves into the relationship between the injunction to professionalism and the need for efficacy. The claims of professional communication training crystallize around a "professionality transfer", allegedly conferring increased professional efficiency. The researcher is then invited to explore the order of discourse in the expertise of communication facilitators, as well as the conceptions of "professionality" that structure the professional training programs studied. Thus, by considering the question of professionalization in communication or through communication, this chapter will bring to light the procedures and standards for "communicating properly". The promises of professional training mainly imply that facilitators will "transfer" their expertise to trainees and that, thanks to training, interns will be able to benefit from a gain in professionality, reflected by the optimization of their professional efficacy. This chapter will look at the forms of legitimization of communication expertise and the links between the injunction to professionalism and the efficiency imperative.

## 2.1. The figures of facilitators and the legitimization of communication expertise

In this competitive professional training market, one of the main challenges for structures is to establish their authority. This is based on different logics that depend not only on the positioning of structures in the market, on their specific "self-presentation" modalities, but also on a recurrent and transversal discursive strategy, emphasizing the expertise of facilitators. All training structures promote the expertise of their facilitators, because the instructor is the figurehead, the main actor in professional training. It is precisely this category of communication expertise that will be the subject of this development. The credibility of the training's promise of efficacy is linked to the legitimizing discourse of the training body, but most importantly, to the training situation itself and the presentation of the facilitators' expertise.

This category of expertise has been invested in a certain number of research works, mainly in sociology (Trépos 1996) and in political sociology (Delmas 2011). It has also been the subject of specific research in information and communication sciences. The work of Bouzon (2002), for example, focuses on the relationships between risk management and expertise, that of Tavernier (2009) concerns the mediatization of expertise, whereas research by Grignon (2015) is dedicated to the construction of communication expertise in consulting agencies. This research project particularly echoes the works by Grignon, as it involves exploring the specific forms of construction of communication expertise, not in agencies but in professional training.

According to Jaillet:

> The expert's keystone is the ethos. It is the quality that makes the expert someone endowed with a presumption of trust. But this presumption must then be transformed into certainty, it must be cultivated, preserved, seized (Jaillet 1998, p. 38).

The expert is the one who must have specialist knowledge, the one summoned to address a request or respond to an order. For Delmas, "crowned as an expert, the professional, specialist practitioner or researcher, is encouraged to take on a new role, subject to determinations which differ from those governing their usual activity" (Delmas 2011, p. 11). This change of universe is reflected on multiple levels: modification of the time horizon, concern to carry out "useful work", fulfillment of "normative performances", taking into account conditions such as social acceptability and the feasibility of prescriptions. "Expertise has a mainly pragmatic dimension; here it will be defined as all the bodies of knowledge mobilized for action" (Delmas 2011, p. 16). In this context, the expert is not only the one who knows, but above all, the one who knows how to do things. This seems to correlate with the promise of efficacy at work behind the question "how to master such or such type of situation?". The facilitator can then be considered as a "professional" (as defined by Jeanneret), an "actor who makes a public statement on communication in order to legitimize and promote a certain way of taking action professionally" (Jeanneret 2014, p. 14).

Smaller structures often present profiles of their training programs on their website. The formula used by one of them "professional facilitators and experts in their field" clearly highlights the dual professionality expected from the facilitator: knowing how to train, having teaching skills and being able to prove their expertise (in particular based on their experience) in the professional field in question; in this case communication. In the short descriptions below the facilitators' ID photographs, the emphasis is more on professional experience in the field of communication than on experience as a facilitator.

As we will see, even though the educational frameworks and contents can be more or less prewritten by the structures themselves, the facilitator is ultimately the one who is expected to deliver the promise. As I have already stressed, drawing on the work of Oger, authority is a relational concept: it is in the relationship that the facilitator builds with his audience that authority can be deployed. This is why, in their introduction to the book *Expertise, Communication and Organizing*, Treem and Leonardi explain that it is necessary to adopt a communicative approach to expertise, because expertise is not an intrinsic property of an individual but "an attribution that emerges in social interaction" (Treem and Leonardi 2016).

This invites the researcher to explore the *order of discourse* communications expertise: "what is the status of the individuals who – alone – have the right, sanctioned by law or tradition, juridically defined or spontaneously accepted, to proffer such a discourse?" (Foucault 1969, p. 51). One of the first arguments is to present themselves as experts, as specialists who have a set of particular skills.

> With an origin in engineering sciences and techniques, the category of expertise designates the possession of specialized knowledge on a specific phenomenon, likely to authorize an opinion which can arbitrate over a political, legal or technical decision, thus shedding light on a problem and identifying resolution practices (Jaillet 1998, p. 17).

For Jaillet, the main skill of an expert is the rhetoric with which its serious character is demonstrated. As relevant as the implementation of this rhetorical approach may be, the question of communication expertise cannot be reduced to it. Indeed, the competence of "experts" in training also lies in their ability to organize and communicate knowledge. But it is true that, in order to make certain bodies of knowledge visible, it is first important to demonstrate that the facilitator is in the right "place" (Flahault 1978). Now, this place is relative to the promotion of the mastery of two areas: pedagogy (and more specifically, andragogy[1]) and communication.

How do facilitators highlight their "communication" expertise, what are the typical paths and profiles that emerge, and what are the methods by which expertise is showcased during training?

From the observation of the eight training programs, several possible configurations with differentiated forms of expertise distribution emerge: training courses with a single facilitator ("Strategic Communication and Planning" from *grande école* B, "Optimizing your oral communication" from *grande école* A and the two training courses in media training); pair training ("Exposing, Argumenting, Persuading" in a specialized structure with an actor/journalist duo); "choral" training ("Public speaking: persuasion techniques" in the multi-multi A organization, with five facilitators from different professions); and finally, the articulation between the facilitator's training and occasional interventions by experts ("Designing and managing a strategic communication plan" in *grande école* A).

In public-speaking training programs, the actor/journalist duo is quite common and is presented as a guarantee of complementarity. This translates a distribution of skills between actors and journalists, thereby claiming to address a "complete" approach to public speaking. In fact, the actor is instructed to transmit skills in terms of body language, voice and stress management, whereas the journalist is assigned to teach trainees how to produce impactful statements, relying on "short sentences" and anticipating the reactions of their audiences. The introduction to a training program made by an actor in the specialized structure evidences this.

OBSERVATION.– "I am a trained actor, we are going to work together on the messenger, tomorrow with Élodie, journalist, you will not work on the content which is specific to you, but on the structuring of your oral

---

1. From the Greek name *andros* ("man" in English), andragogy "designates the methods used in adult training. This notion, distinct from pedagogy (training children), appeared for the first time from the pen of a German grammarian, Alexander Kappen, in 1833. In the 1920s, the idea was taken up in the United States, then was disseminated in certain circles by the work of Malcolm Knowles in the 1970s and 1980s". *Les Grands Dossiers des Sciences Humaines, "De la formation au projet de vie"* 2015, No. 1, glossary p. 24.

presentation". The educational director of this same structure explains: "We will initially use the know-how of journalists, which is, between quotes, 'marketing on information'. This is something we are not taught at university, that is to say, how to do it in so that information is fit for consumption, adapted, attractive".

This expertise distribution between the one who knows how "the messenger" must behave and the one who knows how "the message" must be formulated in order to be impactful is not unrelated to a certain instrumental conception of communication, where the "nonverbal" can be separated from mastery over the verbal. This logic of expertise compartmentalization, which helps to isolate dimensions of communication which may acquire an autonomous form, was even more marked in the public speaking training program that I followed in multi-multi A organization. This training program, which is the most expensive in their prospectus (the other speaking training courses are conducted either with a consultant/actor duo, or with a single facilitator), is presented as choral training, making room for "tailor-made" training. It proposes combining the expertise of two consultants specializing in speaking, an image coach, an actor and a lyric singer. Each facilitator profile is assigned a training goal: *enhancing your image* (image coach); *structuring your message* (consultant); *gaining confidence* (actor); *mastering your voice and diction* (a singer). The orchestration and temporal sequencing are done in connection with the distribution of this expertise: plenaries with the two consultants, workshops and 15-minute meetings with each of the "experts" (actor, image coach and singer) and finally, two major oral sessions (at the beginning and ending of the training) with the entire team.

In the "Designing and managing a communication strategy and plan" training program from *grande école* A, the expertise distribution is done differently: the facilitator, former communications director of *INALCO* (*Institut national des langues et des civilisations orientales*), is present throughout the three days of the training and invites "experts" for occasional presentations (for two hours). Every day, an intervenor, introduced as a specialist in a given subject, makes an expert presentation on said subject: a consultant, former research director at TNS Sofres, a new media manager at Vivendi and an agency director specialized in measuring the efficacy of communication are the three "experts" who took part in this training.

Whatever the configurations, the facilitators and intervenors showcase, at the beginning and then throughout the training, their professional experience as trainers, and also and above all in the exercise of an occupation: journalist, actor, communications director, etc. The account of this professional experience establishes their legitimacy to transmit knowledge and know-how relating to the goals targeted by the training program. The life story, more or less developed, is a necessary step to legitimize an expert's professional position.

OBSERVATION.– "I am a former journalist. I have worked for several television channels, notably for the BBC". "I was director of communications at *INALCO* for 6 years and, before that, director of communications at the University of Poitiers and in town halls". "I have been working in communications since the 20th century" (laughter) "I was a director in a large international company". "I was director of internal communications in several large groups for around thirty years".

It is not surprising that training prospectuses mainly highlight the fact that their facilitators know their "field" in depth. As Douyère and Le Bouëdec point out, the facilitator's professionality is "a secondary professionality, which depends on primary professionality" (Le Bouëdec and Douyère 2016), something which should be stressed. We could even say that the primary professionality is a prerequisite for the second professionality (being a facilitator), but that it is this second professionality that must enable the primary professionality to professionalize trainees.

According to the prospectus from *grande école* A:

> The training programs offered in *Executive Education* are complete, they combine theoretical framing and operational declensions. They are delivered by experts, actors of their time, in full mastery of their skills and with solid experience: professionals from the business world (managers, consultants, lawyers, journalists, etc.), recognized in their sector of activity, French and foreign public service experts (senior civil servants), professors from (school name) and other major schools or universities, researchers from (school name) and our partners: thanks to them, training benefits from the latest advances in research in economics, political science, sociology, history and law (2017–2018 Prospectus, p. 13).

The complementarity publicized combines scientific knowledge with practical experience. Reference to research is presented as cutting edge, making it possible to provide training with the most recent knowledge in a field. Nevertheless, it is interesting to note that, during the training course, this academic highlighted her career much less than the other facilitators from the other training courses observed. She quickly introduced herself as an "academic", without mentioning her status as a professor, her university or even her research (which she talked about later, because I asked her the question). Although she published a certain number of works on tales and their oral transmission, she did not talk about them. Paradoxically – but perhaps this should not be read as a paradox – she placed greater emphasis on her "ancillary" activities in radio broadcasting and the moderation of scientific or professional events (proof of her commitment to the *praxis*).

OBSERVATION.– "I just returned from China where I was at an international forum. I had to summarize the 22 communications in seven minutes! Fortunately, I counted with techniques and I relied on my know-how". "I hosted many official ceremonies, and, for that case, I always take note of who to thank so as not to forget anyone".

In their self-presentation, facilitators rarely mention the training structure where they work and emphasize their own structure more. This happens because most facilitators have their own small training structure, and some of them even hire other facilitators themselves. In fact, training structures are increasingly outsourcing their facilitators because they need numerous trainers to diversify their offer. However, due to the lack of enough training days, they cannot afford to request exclusivity. Most facilitators also mention the fact that they train on behalf of different structures. In one of the training courses observed, a facilitator had even left the logo of a competing structure on some presentation slides. Consequently, the differentiation sought by education structures is ultimately limited. Finally, the consulting activity is presented as a corollary to training, a way for the facilitator to update skills and show that they are still in vogue. Trainers are also called "consultant-facilitators" in certain training structures.

OBSERVATION.– "I also work directly for large companies, for example, I was recently in charge of training 250 communicators from the *RATP* group, I had to contact a few freelancers, but it was me who designed all the training's educational engineering".

Success stories from consulting missions often punctuate the facilitators' oral interventions. For example, during her "plenary", the image coach showed two photographs of women and asked the participants to attribute personality traits to them. After showing the interns that the two women were very different, she announced that they were in fact the same woman:

OBSERVATION.– "This is Agnès, one of my customers. The first photograph is before the makeover. She wanted to be more feminine, to gain self-confidence. The bet paid off, didn't it?".

In all cases, facilitators must show that they are still linked to the primary professional activity, which is also a selection criterion for training organizations.

It is nonetheless necessary to differentiate between two main forms of legitimization of facilitators in the field of communication: facilitators in communication as a transversal skill and facilitators in the communication professions. If we take a closer look at the training programs followed – in this case, public speaking training and training in strategic communication and planning – public speaking facilitators introduce themselves as coming from "other" environments (notably journalism and theater), whereas facilitators in strategic communication and planning present themselves as more experienced peers who could have been the hierarchical managers of trainees. Therefore, this involves differentiated claims to "professionality transfer".

In public speaking training, the emphasis is on the difference between, on the one hand, the interns' occupations (even though most of them do not perform communication functions, they are called "communicators" insofar as they attend the workshop to "optimize" their communication in a professional context) and, on the other hand, journalists and actors. At the same time, there is the interest in knowledge "transfer" and know-how from other action frameworks.

OBSERVATION.– "The big difference between the actor and the communicator is that the communicator must constantly decipher nonverbal cues and adapt to an audience". "You are not expected to play the actor". The actor is immersed in emotion and waits for the audience to approach. The communicator is the opposite, they must go towards the audience and avoid being centered on emotion". "Actors have a certain number of tools which can be useful to managers. Journalists have a number of useful tools as well".

Other more unusual universes are summoned in certain training programs. The specialized structure studied, for example, calls on an airline pilot for training on managerial communication called "Captain Speaking", as well as a negotiator from the French National Gendarmerie Intervention Group (*GIGN*), for a training course called "Elite Negotiation". The director of the structure explains this approach.

INTERVIEW.– "We adopted this principle of looking for executives outside the company for sharing effective tools with managers [...]. We met an Air France airline pilot officer. We did a lot of lab work and we created the Project Pilot training program. Because ultimately, what does civil aviation come down to? It's about getting people from point A to point B safely, managing a crew [...]. For negotiation, in the same way, we sought the best practices in completely different worlds. Who are the best at negotiating? The *GIGN*. We made contact with former *GIGN* negotiators and we built a training program via acculturation. We got to know each other, tried to identify the suitable tools and discarded the nontransferable ones, those too specific for each occupation. And we built a training course called Elite Negotiation".

It is interesting to note that there is a question of efficacy transfer: a practice that is effective in one context is also expected to be effective in another. The operation of selection and qualification of a practice as "effective" or as "best practice" is not discussed, presented as self-evident. This same director points out the following.

INTERVIEW.– "Beyond the somewhat 'wow' effect for executives and company managers of spending a day with a *GIGN* negotiator, there must be real relevance, that is to say, the transfer of know-how. The *GIGN* negotiator works in highly specific situations, with specific requirements, excessive constraints, but the interest is to transfer their skills to other working contexts".

Through this recurring use of the term "transfer", there is a certain, transitive, conception of knowledge mediation which precisely obscures the plurality of mediations at work in an educational situation. The communicational approach invites us, on the contrary, to think of mediation not as a place of passage but as a transformation process. As Jeanneret points out, "the expression 'knowledge mediation' assumes that bodies of knowledge are produced in certain places and 'mediated', that is to say, that a set of actors, operations, productions contribute to their circulation, transformation, making them suitable for reappropriation" (Jeanneret 2004, p. 21). As I will see in Chapter 3, one of the significant mediations in professional training is the mediation which I describe as casuist (Seurrat 2016) and which involves constructing best practices, that is to say, norms based on the generalization of situated experiences.

The facilitator's experience is crucial in training in strategic communication and planning, even more than in public speaking training. Facilitators in specific skills for communication occupations often have "senior" profiles: they have made training a second professional life and present their career paths as a guarantee of credibility and as proof of their ability to grasp trends.

OBSERVATION.– "What I can tell you after over twenty years in supporting change is that even when the changes are painful, when there is honesty and frankness, it gives you credibility". "In over 25 years, I have clearly seen that profiles and expectations have changed". "I have 25 years of experience in communications after studying at Sciences Po and Harvard".

Even though the notices for training offers often have a section dedicated to promoting the training pedagogy (presented as "active", "participative", "innovative", "immersive", "practical", etc.), it is not the pedagogy that fuels the argument on the facilitator's expertise, but rather their prior professional experience. A former monitoring director at *AFPA* (*Association pour la formation professionnelle des adultes*) rightly criticizes the fact that training structures which train employees in companies hire less professional facilitators than professionals who provide training.

INTERVIEW.– "They hire company executives who work with other company executives, so they consider that their experience gives them the skills to train, which is not necessarily the case… Their training potential is drawn from the company and, with this formative potential, they train other executives. But actually they are organizing meetings between more or less qualified experts. This is quite different from a structure like *AFPA*, where we have 4,500 full-time facilitators on permanent or fixed-term contracts".

If the words of this former monitoring director can be so critical of the training programs offered by large organizations, it is also because his structure, *AFPA*, mainly trains job seekers or people undergoing professional reconversion, whereas the private structures analyzed in this research project mainly train company employees. As was shown in Chapter 1, the articulation of these two professional training challenges is not easy. Unlike centers like *AFPA* where most of the facilitators are employees within the structure, professional training organizations mainly rely on independent workers. A manager of the "Digital Transformation" product from a multi-multi organization explains that the outsourcing of facilitators is even more striking in the training offers for communicators.

INTERVIEW.– "We have internal facilitators, but it turns out that, on the communication products, there are few of them, there have been quite few in fact during the history of this product. They are mainly consultants, external facilitators. People who are employed, working in companies, or who have their agency, or who are freelance. We recruit specialist professionals for their skills and their expertise. As regards their educational capacity, we are responsible for training them".

Thus, for the recruitment of facilitators, training practice is less important than experience (expertise) in the field concerned. This is why large training structures, and also smaller ones, set up training schemes for facilitators. This is not the case for the *grandes écoles*, which mainly recruit their facilitators in the intervenors' networks of their institutions, assuming that their experience is sufficient and that they will therefore do not require training as facilitators.

Experience as a facilitator seems less important than a background in the occupation associated with the field of professionalization of the training program. However, over the last 20 years, education and training occupations have undergone heavy professionalization. Laot and de Lescure explain that the term "trainer" appeared in the 1960s and that the creation of *INFA* (*Institut national pour la formation des adultes*) in 1963, and then *AFPA* in 1966 encouraged the emergence of that occupation (Laot and de Lescure 2006).

For Delamotte, professionalization can be considered in three ways (Delamotte 1998, pp. 76–92). A first, somewhat simple, definition argues that profession corresponds to a job, and that professionalization comes down to the emergence and development of job categories. In the field of professional training, with the development of large training organizations and the creation of numerous small structures, we have witnessed an expansion of this profession since the 1980s[2].

A second conception of professionalization, "more open to the complexity of phenomena [...] corresponds to the frequently expressed idea that it is necessary to professionalize".

> To 'professionalize' is then understood as increasing skills and shifting from a sort of amateur or craftsman status to a 'professional' status, with all that this word suggests of skills and seriousness in practice (Delamotte 1998, p. 76).

Therefore, "an activity becomes a profession when specific, constituted and legitimized bodies of knowledge establish the exercise of an occupation" (Delamotte 1998, p. 76). Over the past 15 years, we have observed the creation of Master's degrees specialized in educational engineering and the development of training courses for facilitators. It is also interesting to note that training courses for facilitators often focus on the use of games in training, which contributes, as will be seen in the third chapter, to a mediagenic conception of games as an educational panacea.

Finally, in third place, for Delamotte:

> We can finally approach the concept of profession by considering the collective organization of jobs. We speak of professionalization when an activity, which is primarily a source of income, becomes socially structured (Delamotte 1998, p. 77).

This structuring is remarkable for the creation of networks such as the FFP in 1991, which presents itself as "the platform bringing together all the key actors in human capital"[3]. In *Les professions de l'éducation et de la formation* (Bourdoncle and Demailly 1998), approximately 40 authors analyze the transformations of professions in the three major sectors of education: school education, ongoing training and higher education. Some chapters are dedicated to adult training. As Bourdoncle and Demailly point out in the introduction to the book, even though the training profession

---

2. The 2016 *DARES* surveys identify 140,000 facilitators working in training organizations (source: FFP 2015, p. 11).
3. See: https://lesacteursdelacompetence.fr/.

attempts "to be unified under a sole identity", it "is no less fragmented into numerous and unstable job profiles" (Bourdoncle and Demailly 1998, p. 18).

The research I tackled in communication training clearly shows both the fragmentary nature of this profession and its unstable dimension. This secondary professionality (which depends on a primary professionality) seems all the more unstable in the field of communication occupations, whose rapid transformation is constantly brought to the forefront. Several facilitators, in search of both interventions and legitimacy, also told me their wish to provide courses in the information and communication departments, or even asked me how they could apply for associate lecturer positions.

Even though the backgrounds, statuses and ways of doing things of facilitators are highly diversified, they all deploy the same promise, that of a "mastery" of communication which should make it possible to increase their professional efficacy.

## 2.2. "Mastering" communication to gain professional efficacy

The two main types of training programs (in communication and for communicators) and the two main types of facilitators (the ones coming from a different professional field and the more experienced peers) correspond to two main types of claims relating to the mastery over communication and the efficacy imperative. In both cases, the facilitators are the ones who introduce themselves as being able to transmit such mastery over communication to trainees. But while in the first case, mastery over communication is a means for gaining professional efficacy, in the other case, it is an end in itself for communication professionals. Again, in both cases, the issue of mastery is linked to the uncertainty underlying any communication situation, whether it is a communication situation in a professional context (oral or written) or the implementation of a communication strategy on the part of communicators.

For Boltanski, uncertainty unfolds to varying degrees. According to this author, the strongest degree is called "radical uncertainty" and concerns "the question of knowing what it is going on with what is" (Boltanski 2009, p. 13). Uncertainty gives rise to worry, and this worry is a driving force for seeking ways to ward off what seems beyond our control. For Jeanneret, uncertainty is constitutive of any communication process, social actors being confronted on a daily basis with "the essential – rather than accidental – heterogeneity and discontinuity of communication processes" (Jeanneret 2008, p. 137).

Jeanneret coined the expression "cybernetics of the imperfect" to designate this "conception of communication which excludes the possibility of completely understanding and mastering it, because actors 'navigate without any instruments', as the Greek sailor who pilots a ship" (Jeanneret 2014, p.11). For Jullien, the European conception of efficacy refers to "the good pilot as the one whose ability makes it possible to best exercise mastery, in the face of the uncontrolled movement of the waves" (Jullien 1996, p. 25). The central challenge is therefore to strive towards a "cybernetics of the perfect", even in the face of contingencies. In his doctoral thesis, German (2017) calls into question the way in which the actors in the museum field attempt to keep at bay the "cybernetics of the imperfect" by equipping the project with a "perfect cybernetics of exchange" (Jeanneret 2014, p. 280), a project that seeks to "optimize the transitivity and predictability of communication" (Jeanneret 2014, p. 280). This shows how the desire to predict the behavior of museum audiences leads to "the (fantasized) attainment of impeccable knowledge of possible expectations, something which could be used in the elaboration of programs (program: 'thing written in advance', the Latin equivalent of prescription)" (German 2017, p. 139). This is part of an ideal of perfect concordance and of perfect congruence between what has been "prefigured in anticipation of a situation" and "what is really figured as it unfolds" (Jeanneret 2014, p. 180). Such desire to anticipate the reaction of museum audiences (as analyzed by German) fully echoes the desire to anticipate the course of communication exchanges in the public speaking training programs studied.

In communication training programs falling within the "Personal Efficacy", "Professional Efficacy" or "Personal Development" products, communication is presented as a means, as an instrument to be mastered in order to gain professional efficacy. The question comes down to convincing "non-communicators" of the importance of communication in all professional practices, and even more markedly in management functions: communication is at the service of success for every professional. This joins three frameworks of thought which, in a distinct way, all make communication a tool at the service of efficacy: sophistry, Goffmanian sociology and the psychology of personal development.

Sophistry is a school of thought born in the pre-Socratic era of Athens in the times of Pericles:

> [The Sophists are] professional educators, itinerant foreigners who trade in their wisdom, culture and skills, like the hetaeras trade in their charms. But they are also men of power, who know how to persuade judges, turn around an assembly, make an embassy succeed, give laws to a new city, train in democracy, in short, carry out political tasks. This double mastery has its source in the mastery of language, in all its forms, from linguistics (morphology, grammar, synonymics) to rhetoric (the study of tropes, sounds, the appropriateness of discourse and its parts)[4].

In *The Sophist*, Plato develops a rather sharp criticism of those he calls "the masters of deception", because they know how to confuse us by resorting to verbal tricks. For the philosopher, sophists represent otherness and we must learn to protect ourselves against the traps they set (Teisserenc 2012). What is this mastery that Plato feared, and which made him warn us to arm our thinking against the techniques of sophists? It is what we call rhetorical efficacy. In this respect, the link with the search for efficacy through a mastery over communication is particularly strong.

In his article entitled *"Rhétorique et herméneutique"* (*Rhetoric and Hermeneutics* in English), Molinié explains that "efficacy is the sole touchstone of speech acts, regardless of their appearance" (Molinié 2007, p. 433). For the author, this is based on two devices: an affinity system and a unity system. The affinity system is based on the affects–words relationship, whereas the unity system relies on argumentative construction. We find these two aspects in public speaking training, which can generally be divided between, on the one hand, training sequences related to the management of emotions, proxemics and the adoption of attitudes and, on the other hand, sequences linked to the construction of discourse, the use of rhetorical tropes and the search for impactful formulations. Efficacy is played out in this desire to predispose a relationship with a particular audience, which must enable the attainment of the speaker's ends:

> Efficacy cannot make the slightest distinction between the poles of the one who speaks and the one to whom or for whom one

---

4. Encyclopaedia Universalis.

speaks, any more than the relevance of the idea of a truth or of a feigning of affects: there is an ethico-pathetic continuum which is experienced in the total act – production-reception – of discourse as interrelational dynamism (Molinié 2007, p. 438).

As Amossy points out:

> In ancient Greece, self-presentation was first thought of as a practice of influence. Its study is based on the principle that it is impossible to make someone adhere to your views, to make them opt for a way of seeing or doing, without first making yourself credible in their eyes (Amossy 2010, p. 32).

Public-speaking training is there to provide trainees with added credibility. Although all of the structures mention "rhetoric" or "oratory art" in the title or in the content of certain training notices dedicated to public speaking, *grande école* A is the structure where this filiation is emphasized the most, as evidenced by the syllabus of its training offer "staging your speech" (Box 2.1).

---

**1. Getting prepared to intervene**

**Preparing yourself physically**

Why is it appropriate to warm up physically? All of the keys to breathing properly and working on your voice.

**Managing concentration**

Learning to focus on the subject and managing body and speech rhythms (tempo).

**Managing stage fright**

When speaking, presence is important. It is important to turn stage fright into an asset. With one aim: to achieve your goals.

**2. Implementing your speech**

**Using body language**

Face, gaze, hand: so many parts of the body that potentially carry speech and are language allies. How can you use them in front of an audience?

> **Preparing the right type of speech**
>
> Orally, a good speech requires knowing how to exploit suspense and to structure the speech accordingly. Which rhetorical elements should be mastered?
>
> **3. Staging your speech**
>
> **Knowing how to narrate your speech**
>
> To achieve this goal, you have to develop a good mental attitude and remain enthusiastic about the subject. Discovering the keys to achieve this.
>
> **Knowing how to persuade**
>
> It is advisable to have defined the right goals, to wish to persuade and to organize your train of thought to achieve this. Interacting with your audience is an art that needs to be mastered. Managing speaking time is important, as is the ability to know how to conclude.

**Box 2.1.** *"Staging your speech" (inspired by the teaching aids from* grande école A*)*

"What matters is the impact of the 'how' rather than the 'what'". This sentence, which closes the description of the training program, clearly shows that, according to the efficacy logic, the means are more important than the ends. At the heart of Plato's criticism of the sophists is not the immoral but the amoral dimension of this practice. At the beginning of the syllabus description, we can read: "to speak out = to take power". This shows that effective rhetoric serves the quest for power and that communication is designed as an instrument to achieve this end.

"Storytelling"[5], which is a recurring training offer in the prospectuses analyzed, appears as a variant of the dimension of unicity of effective rhetoric. Mastering narrative construction must serve as a lever to persuasion. This is demonstrated by the presentation of the training courses dedicated to storytelling in the prospectuses observed.

---

5. Term popularized after the publication of the book by Salmon, C. (2007). *Storytelling. La machine à fabriquer les images et à formater les esprits*. La Découverte, Paris. It should nonetheless be noted that even though this author seems to emphasize the "novelty" of storytelling, the question of the construction of stories has long been addressed by narrative semiotics and narratology.

For example, specialist C proposes (and this is illustrative of the trend towards the increasingly advanced modularization made possible by distance learning media systems) innovative "mobile learning", which are video tours of approximately one hour at the price of 44.99 euros. One of the videos offered is called "the basics of storytelling" and is presented as follows:

> Storytelling, the term occupies a nice place in the ranking of buzzwords who liven up the conversation threads on social networks, communicator sites and trendy conferences. But what is storytelling? Is it effective? How is it produced? How do we use it?

The training offer alleges knowing how to "use" the tool (rhetoric, storytelling) to increase efficacy.

The "Optimizing oral communication" training, which I attended at *grande école* A, was particularly nourished by references and exercises in rhetoric and narratology. This is related to the fact that the facilitator was an academic specializing in "oral literature", and more specifically in the transmission of tales and legends. Since her introduction to the training program, the facilitator announced this anchoring in rhetorical practice, something which should enable the deployment of professional efficacy.

INTERVIEW.– "How do you share your beliefs without imposing them? In particular, we will work on argumentation and suggestion. This engages the relationship with the rhetorical foundations. Argumentation is the skeleton of discourse. By additionally working on the suggestion, we will access a field for remarkable improvement".

She then invited us to read, in her booklet, the description sheet dedicated to figures of speech or to practice "drawing straws" exercises, which involved finding an impactful ending to short stories (The Stories of Nasr Eddin Hodja). As pointed out by Le Bouëdec and Douyère in their analysis of media training, these training courses aim to "ensure control of the production, as well as of the interpretation of discourse" (Le Bouëdec and Douyère 2016, p. 51).

> The identification of the modalities of discourse circulation in the public space, of the forms and arguments which arouse conviction, or which are perceived as such, have equipped this function, which has turned into expertise. A communicative

"body of knowledge" has thus been constituted, which integrates supposed audience expectations or intermediaries with regard to the speeches delivered. [...] For the authors, "this knowledge on how to 'communicate properly' [...] builds this speech so that is 'well' transmitted and 'better' received, renewing a tradition anchored in ancient sophistry and rhetoric" (Le Bouëdec and Douyère 2016, pp. 44–45).

Its art lies in adaptation (as defined by Jeanneret), that is to say, a "rhetorical strategy adapting a message to an anticipated recipient by betting that its appropriation by the audience and its circulation will be favored" (Jeanneret 2014, p. 10). Rhetoric therefore has a double side: descriptive and normative, it "relates to analysis but also to efficacy, because at the time it enunciates standards, rhetoric establishes uses and values" (Jeanneret 2014, p. 97).

For Soulez, who analyzes the use of rhetoric in Aristotle, it involves far more than the art of adaptation. His hypothesis is that it "can be read as a theory of reception, or rather of the audience, within a theory of discourse production" (Soulez 2004, p. 89):

> We often think that Rhetoric considers the relationship between the speaker and the audience, as an "adaptation" of the speaker to the audience, as if it were, on the one hand, a simple adjustment to the audience, on the other hand, of the transformation of a "message" which preexists the speech one wishes to deliver. In a far more decisive manner, the fundamental principle of Aristotelian Rhetoric the analysis of discourse according to opinion ("endoxa"), as opposed to science or Being. To place opinion at the heart of discourse production is to radically introduce consideration for the audience, meaning that the speaker must strive to produce a speech to respond to a plurality of receptions beforehand. [...] The anticipation of audience interpretation in the form of a "response" in the Gadamerian sense presupposes a discourse efficacy which is not based on the power of words themselves but, one could say, on the projection of the effect that the audience can achieve (Soulez 2004, pp. 90–91).

Rhetoric, as used in professional training, is mainly presented as the art of constructing an impactful speech. Even though the bottom line is to adapt our speech as best as possible to the audience expectations, the latter are not called into question: the challenge lies in transmitting "rhetorical techniques", stages in the construction of speech or tropes. Rhetoric is seen in its instrumental dimension, a dimension that is also developed by Bautier in his book *De la rhétorique à la communication* (Bautier 1994), where he shows to what extent this instrumental vision of rhetoric runs through our contemporary world. It is therefore not specific to the professional training studied, but is one of the markers of the trivialization of instrumental conceptions of communication in our societies.

While the use of rhetoric in training mainly emphasizes the construction of speech in order to increase the speaker's power, another recurring promise of public-speaking training relates to the mastery of nonverbal communication. For this, we find certain mentions quite allusive to "the silent language"[6] and to the work of the so-called Palo Alto school with the fairly recurrent use of Watzlawick's formula, which has become almost proverbial: "we cannot not communicate"[7]. Although it is never quoted, it is also possible to perceive a connection with Goffman's work. Erving Goffman's first book, *The Presentation of Self* (first volume of *The Staging of Daily Life*), is fully part of the so-called interactionist movement and explores the ways in which individuals establish interpersonal relationships. Amossy explains that Goffman stands apart from the rhetorical tradition, but that he also addresses the question of ethos, which he calls "the presentation of self" in his reflection:

> According to him, the way we present ourselves to others in daily interactions constitutes a practice on which depends not only the efficacy of our action in society, but also social life as such [...]. Far from focusing on oratory practice, he studies the entirety of social behavior in a given context as it is translated by clothing, gestures, facial expressions and everything relating to the staging of our own person apart from language (Amossy 2010, p. 48).

In *The Presentation of Self*, Goffman develops the theatric metaphor: the social world is a theater where the challenge lies in preserving the individual's face. Therefore, "the individual will have to act so that he intentionally or unintentionally expresses himself, and the others will in turn have to be

---

6. *The Silent Language* is a book by Edward T. Hall first published in 1959.
7. "We cannot not communicate" is one of the five great axioms of communication defined by Watzlawick et al. (2011).

impressed in some way by him" (Goffman 1959, p. 17). As in the theater, there is a stage, a backstage, actors and an audience. The actor's challenge is to be as credible as possible in the character played, so that the audience can believe in what they see and hear. According to Goffman, it is then behind the scenes that we can perceive "the true face" of the actor, a face which, in "staged" social interactions, is adorned with a "façade". It is possible to see that the effective interaction in Goffman is the one where the actor manages to maintain the face. This concept where strategy dominates human communication is particularly suitable for the postures adopted in professional communication training. This could account for the almost systematic presence of actors in public speaking training. The actor's expertise lies in the ability to teach us how to "maintain the face" and to manage impressions.

The "Women acting" training program proposed by one of the specialized structures is a good example of the link between public speaking training and Goffmanian sociology. The training program's presentation is as follows.

> The expression "female leadership" is now used in many professional training programs. Their promise is to help women develop managerial skills and leadership strength. Rather than considering that there is an exclusively feminine type of leadership (as opposed to another, masculine one), the intention is to help women who access responsibilities within the firm. This support helps them to develop soft skills as well as hard skills.
>
> In addition, it contributes to overcoming many cultural and behavioral biases and to highlighting the best version of themselves. This makes them able to shine and to make others shine!
>
> "Women acting" training, entirely tailor-made, is deployed by female experts for female leaders. The purpose of this program is to enlighten and equip participants to manage tasks at the highest level of responsibility within the company, in an environment that remains predominantly male.

**Box 2.2.** *Presentation of the "Women acting" training in the organization's prospectus*

In its presentation text, the insistence on the question of posture, on learning to be and maintain a position as a leader, clearly shows the extent to which the challenge is to control "one's image" in order to control "one's perceived image". For this, the expectations of leading women on stage are broken down into different components – vocal expression, gestures, clothing, make-up – and the actor, a stage professional, must enable them to optimize these "tools" for strategic purposes.

In the psychology of personal development, we also find this personal efficacy goal. Personal efficacy is also developed as a concept by certain psychological researchers. This work, which is quite normative, aims to identify the components of personal efficacy and, thereby, to provide elements for achieving it. Bandura, professor emeritus at Stanford University and Canadian psychologist, developed a theory he calls "social cognitive theory" and proposes the concept of self-efficacy. Self-efficacy concerns the beliefs that an individual has in their own capabilities for action, regardless of their objective abilities. For the author, self-efficacy beliefs constitute the key factor in human action. If a person feels that they cannot produce satisfactory results in an area, then they will not try to bring them about. In order to act effectively, the person must develop a feeling of personal efficacy (Carré 2004, pp. 9–50).

Several researchers in psychology and educational sciences claim to be part of this "positive psychology". This is the case of Lecomte who, in "*Les applications du sentiment d'efficacité personnelle*" (Lecomte 2004, pp. 59–90), proposes to identify the characteristics of "effective teachers" and "effective schools":

> Effective functioning requires both skills and efficacy beliefs for them to be properly used. Different persons with identical abilities, or the same person in different circumstances, may perform poorly, adequately, or outstandingly, depending on variations in their self-efficacy beliefs. The initial skills level influences the performance obtained, but its impact is strongly mediated by self-efficacy beliefs (Lecomte 2004, p. 61).

The researcher then deduces the elements which, in his opinion, characterize the "effective school":

> In high-achieving schools, principals are not only administrators, but also educational leaders who seek methods to improve teaching, whereas in low-achieving schools, principals function primarily as discipline administrators and stewards. The competent school leadership of a principal builds a sense of educational efficacy in teachers (Lecomte 2004, p. 69).

There is, here, a transitive, even epidemiological, conception of efficacy: the leader's efficacy produces, in turn, efficacy in the subordinates.

Although the direct reference to the work of Bandura is not present in the training programs I followed, the goal of reinforcing the feeling of the ability to act is central. The fact that communication is listed under the "Personal Efficacy" products is non-negligible. More than understanding the complexity of communication phenomena, the question is to be convinced of an individual's power to act through and upon communication.

## 2.3. Reinforcing the professionalism of communicators

In training programs designed for communication professionals, the facilitator's expertise must be used to reinforce the professionalism of communicators. This development concerns the relationships between the injunction to professionalism (Boussard et al. 2010) and the efficacy imperative. What makes up the professionality of communicators and what can serve as a standard for evaluating their professionalism?

As Dadoy explains, the term professionality comes from the Italian *professionalità*, a noun defined as "the professional character of an economic activity" (Dadoy 1986, p. 69). The suffixity indicates "the quality of". Professionality is what allows us to qualify an actor as a professional:

> The Italian concept of professionality, which continues to be, more than ever, at the heart of the debate between the actors of the national system of industrial relations, still retains a dose of mystery, probably due to the fact of not having exhausted all its potential. This polyhedral concept, which allows for the reading of various dimensions and the consideration of various parameters, is recent enough to have not yet found, in most dictionaries, the translation of its multiple meanings, other than the traditional ones which do not fully acknowledge the socio-economic processes that have recently begun and are now irreversible (Weiss 1983, p. 371).

The rhetoric on the qualities required for the exercise of such or such communication occupation as described in the prospectuses and, even more, the discourse of facilitators during the training course on strategic communication and planning that I observed are interesting material for analyzing the social representations of the professionality of communicators.

In the prospectus of specialist C, the section devoted to the "Communication Expert" product is punctuated with inserts signed by working professionals, who enumerate the qualities and skills required for the "correct" exercise of such or such communication occupation. For example, on page 41, just before the instructions for the "Communications Assistant" certification training, there is an insert dedicated to this function:

> The Communications Assistant is often a multitasker, playing out different roles, under pressure, he or she must cope with numerous requests from superiors and the communications team. Rigor and method are the key words for this position. Thanks to your intervention, there is not a grain of sand in the cogs. We count on you. So, valorize your skills! Organization, sense of anticipation, writing, communication, you are the real right arm of the comms' manager!

First, the communication function is valorized. This is a particularly transversal point in the professional training of communicators and emphasizes what is at stake in the quest for legitimacy in these occupations. Secondly, there is a focus on the representations of the professionality of the communications assistant: versatility and ability to organize and anticipate, in other words, mastery over the "cogs" of communication. We can clearly see the extent to which a text like this is imbued with both normative conceptions of the occupation and, de facto, instrumental and logistical conceptions of communication.

In a similar way, just before the notice dedicated to the "Communications Manager" certification training, we can read the following insert:

> Being a Communications Manager is a real occupation! Demanding, serious and exciting, engaging advanced skills. This is why it is essential to be well trained to acquire all the methods in order to design a relevant strategy, manage an effective communication plan and make the most of the digital sphere.

Insisting on the specificities of the professionality of communicators means arguing in favor of the need for training for these audiences. The facilitator of the training in communications plan dedicated a large part of the introduction to the presentation of "the communication function". According to him:

OBSERVATION.– "The communication function is a supporting function for all media: HR, marketing, quality, management". "It is one of the most transversal functions, which is also why it fulfils a complex and strategic function". "Being comfortable and knowing how to listen is essential. It is true that a communications manager must be able to communicate with the surface technician as much as with the hierarchy".

For the facilitator, the communicator must exert three roles: as a strategist, as a methodologist and as a manufacturer.

The strategist is associated with the management team. The methodologist suggests ways to implement the strategy. The manufacturer develops the tools. The three roles are therefore complementary.

The facilitator then listed the challenges inherent in this function:

OBSERVATION.– "Reducing the gaps between the perceived image and the image transmitted". "Reinforcing the coherence of different communication forms". "Adjusting messages to the targets' concerns". "Implementing rigorous piloting methods". "Producing and piloting indicators". "Becoming a privileged management tool".

The above-mentioned remarks show that it is important to promote these functions, to show their indispensable nature, and that this is achieved by highlighting the "strategic" dimension of communication. The most frequently highlighted qualities are relational in nature, associated with listening and organizational skills. The skills enumerated also relate to the mastery of tools, methods (mainly procedures), which must make it possible to certify the quality and rigor of work: the means to guarantee the efficacy of the action. Last but not least, we find statements relating to mastery over communication: "getting the most out of it" and "reducing the gaps" are all goals that mark the desire to reduce the uncertainty specific to any communication process. Training programs are thus presented as enabling the acquisition of these skills, skills that can only then be deployed in practice, in the implementation of the training acquired in the daily exercise of the occupation.

This echoes the words of Gilbert de Tressac for whom:

> The notion of skill is an intermediate notion which allows us to think about the relationships between work and the bodies of knowledge held by the individual; actually, what influences the success and performance levels of individuals is not limited to the knowledge they possess, even though the knowledge accumulated through training and experience constitutes an essential condition for success (de Tressac 1996, p. 224).

For the author, we sometimes tend to place the notions of qualification and skills in competition:

> The opposition between the two notions is not played out between themselves, but within each of them, where two conceptions of qualification-skill confront one another: the first favors the instrumental dimension of qualification or skill, its functional value. The second one favors the political dimension, the social and conflictual aspect: in this second conception, there is a desire to link potential and social relationships, the qualities possessed and their hierarchization, the explicitation of skills and the use of such explicitation (de Tressac 1996, p. 233).

These two conceptions can coexist, all the same. In the professional training of communicators, we find not only the statement of the functional, instrumental value of skills, but also – and often based on the questions and remarks of trainees – the discussion regarding the definition and recognition of these skills through social relationships and more specifically, the hierarchical relationships experienced within the firm. This leads to questioning the notion of professionalism.

For its part, professionalism refers to the question of the recognition of professionality and the standards associated with it. The work from the RESIPROC network, linked to certain work in the sociology of work and in educational sciences specializing in adult training, makes it possible to question the constitutive dimensions of the professionalism of communicators, in terms of historical developments, paradoxes or even norms.

For Domenget, professionalization lies between the demand for professionality and professionalism requirements. For the author, "the question involves not so much being interested in professionalization, in the sense of the process of recognition of a professional group, but of analyzing a broader phenomenon, the rise in professionalism standards, whose nature has changed" (Domenget 2016, p. 28). For Wittorski, author of an HDR (qualification to direct research (French diploma)) accreditation to supervise research on the relationships between training, work and professionalization (Wittorski 2005), professionalization is not an unequivocal reality, but an issue that raises both modes of definition and of evaluation differentiated depending on the actors and debates, or even the tensions, within organizations. For the author, professionalization concerns "the continuous evolution of an individual's professional skills associated with increased efficacy" (Wittorski 2009, p. 781). We therefore see the close link between professionalization and the efficacy imperative that I wish to invest more precisely in the context of communication professions.

Evetts, sociologist at the University of Nottingham, proposes a distinction between what she calls professionalism "from within" and professionalism "from above" (Evetts 2003, pp. 759–776). This distinction seems particularly interesting in the context of communication occupations, and, among other things, illuminates the tensions that run through them. For the author, it's a question of two disjointed but articulated processes. Professionalism "from within" is endogenous and initiated by the workers themselves who attempt to create control over their activities and in particular over the elaboration of the goals assigned to their activities. Professionalism "from above", on the contrary, relates to hierarchical constraints, to the management the organization's standards and to the framing of their activity by persons outside the profession.

For Boussard et al., the coordinators of the book on *the injunction to professionalism*:

> Being a professional means not only judging oneself as such, but also being recognized as such by external actors participating in the work activity as peers, hierarchical superiors, subordinates, customers, outsourcers, etc. (Boussard et al. 2010, p. 12).

As a result, this qualification as a "professional" becomes a multiple-scale challenge:

Being qualified as a professional is not only the target of the demands and coordinated strategies from workers who try to valorize their activity, have their knowledge recognized, establish control over the access to their specialty, increase their legitimacy, etc. It is not only the product of an internal definition controlled by the workers concerned; it is dialogical, because it supposes being recognized by the other actors with whom these workers interact when carrying out their activities. Moreover, it is dual since it also results (and this, increasingly), from an injunction transmitted by these actors, whose aim is to mobilize workers, improve their performance, reinforce the sense of responsibility and increase their efficacy (Boussard et al. 2010, p. 17).

The professional no longer refers only to the figure of the qualified and expert worker, autonomous, driven by values of commitment and responsibility and involved in an expressive and creative activity; it also designates a set of imperatives imposed from the outside on workers, subject to new definitions of their missions and confronted with efficacy standards governing their activity (Boussard et al. 2010, p. 13).

This requirement for efficacy linked to the extension of the managerial model in organizations[8] raises specific questions when we consider communication occupations, the training associated with them and more broadly, the communication conceptions and standards that these trends valorize. The collective book entitled *Les acteurs de la communication des entreprises et organisations, pratiques et perspectives*, directed by Lépine et al. (2014), questions the growing predominance of models and practices drawn from communications marketing, as evidenced by the authors' introduction:

Briefly stated, the opening question for this book is the following: in a context of predominance of managerial models, are communicators in a crisis of meaning in their practices in relation to the representations they have of their profession, or, amidst of logic of tension, are they trying to build an observable specificity in their practice? The hypothesis is that the crisis in the profession is part of a societal crisis, involving the sense of

---

8. This question will be the subject of Chapter 4.

work and the firm, implying a profound mutation in the communication function (Lépine et al. 2014, p. 6).

Professionals in the communication occupations particularly struggle with this "professionalism from above" and should particularly develop postures, methods and arguments to maintain their specificity, to justify their actions and to show their capacity to respond to these imperatives:

> Whatever the sector of activity, but more acutely in the commercial sphere, the professionalization of the communication function is largely conditioned by its capacity to defend a specific contribution, specialized skills as well as methodologies and tools which are unique to it and therefore justify adapted training and differentiated practice (Lépine et al. 2014, p. 141).

Lépine works more specifically on the question of the evaluation of communication, which will be treated in further depth in Chapter 5:

> As a management function, communication acquires credibility through the implementation of dashboards. Likewise, the actors of this function are led to negotiate their place and the recognition of their professionalism by adopting reporting management standards which make the validity of their actions understandable to leaders (Lépine 2014, p. 160).

These questions are also raised in the book *Professions et professionnels de la communication* (Gadea and Olivesi 2016), who explain that the transformations in communication professions are linked to the use of digital technology and the fact that new professions, related to marketing, IT, management, etc., are demanding tasks that traditionally fall within its scope The doctoral research carried out by Grignon focuses on the equipment associated with the communicators' expertise and on the standards accompanying it.

> Monitoring software, analytics, maps, etc. are essential tools for communicators. While they may be perceived as simple measurement tools, they accompany the redefinition of professions and contribute to the institutionalization of knowledge, reading skills and know-how (Grignon 2015, p. 24).

Training internships for communicators thus present themselves as places for reinforcing this professionalism in tension, as adjuvants to the imperatives which govern the professionality of communicators. From an etymological point of view, the internship initially designates the "stay that a new canon must complete for a minimum time at a place in their church to be able to enjoy the honors and income of such prebend" (Guénée 2017, p. 7). It is interesting to highlight this idea of the benefit that the internship brings in terms of legitimacy to exercise a function.

Recurring remarks from interns in the strategic communication and planning training programs observed clearly highlight the tensions expressed by communicators and the difficulty for managing this quest for the recognition of their professionalism.

OBSERVATION.– "For our function to be recognized, we must always prove that it is useful". "We are always asked for more with lower budgets". "More and more, we are asked for technical, graphical skills, etc. Initially, we had to be a conductor and now we are asked to be highly technical". "At Orange, it is marketing that has the power".

Therefore, there is a certain hiatus between the insistence made during training on the strategic dimension of communication and, on the contrary, the testimonies of different interns who declare not having any control over the definition of their organization's strategy.

Martin-Juchat conducted a study to observe the perimeter of actions assigned to communication through agencies selling strategic consulting services. To do this, she analyzed the rhetoric from communication agencies, surveys from occupation observatories and had interviews with agency managers. Through this study, the goal was:

> [To] observe how, since the 1990s, the identification and distribution of the different missions assigned to communication within companies have evolved, marked by several closely interrelated processes previously observed: instrumentalization, technicization, greening, commodification and marketization (Martin-Juchat 2014, p. 57).

Also relying on previous research conducted with Lépine in 2009 (on communication directors) and in 2012 (on the representations of the occupation by communicators), the researcher detected that the so-called "strategic" communication function is often relegated "to the simple choice of techniques matching the goals established by others" (Martin-Juchat 2014, p. 55). However, according to Martin-Juchat:

> The instrumentalization of the function is not unrelated to an intentionality of the profession which has found in the tools a means of justifying its activities and building its legitimacy, in a context where the return on investment (ROI) logic is imposing itself (Martin-Juchat 2014, p. 69).

When the interns of the training courses observed deplore the fact that their function is not sufficiently recognized in their organization, the facilitators do not contradict them, but all insist on the possibility of gaining legitimacy thanks to training. According to them, the mastery of tools and methods – which are, as we will see, mainly drawn from the management sciences – will allow them to obtain this much sought-after legitimacy:

OBSERVATION.– "This morning, we will see how to optimize the communications plan. This is essential not only for your own credibility, but in a broader sense, for the credibility of the communications function". "This type of tool takes time to formalize, to format for the company, but afterwards, when you use it, your hierarchy will look at you differently".

The quest for authority in the eyes of our own hierarchy is also subject to "techniques", to formalisms proposed during professional training. For example, during one of the communications plan training sessions, the facilitator proposed different "tools" to reinforce the credibility and legitimacy of communicators concerning their hierarchy.

OBSERVATION.– "I will give you another little tool that is useful for problem solving. It is a super simple tool, understood by everyone and super effective for making decisions in meetings and making your approach understandable by the hierarchy.
Observation    Goals
Cause          Solutions
Do you know the communications triangle? Through this little communication triangle tool, you can dialogue with your management and legitimize your approach".

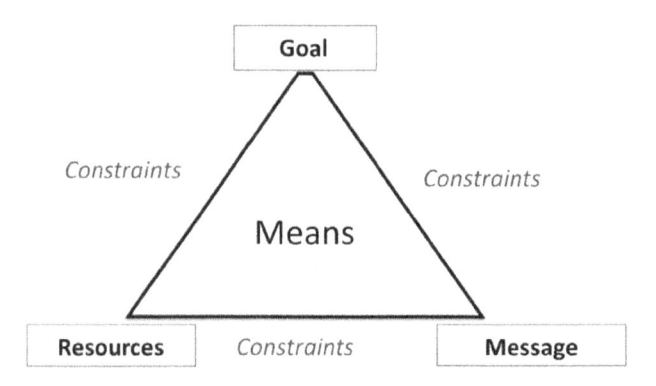

```
              ┌──────┐
              │ Goal │
              └──────┘
               /    \
   Constraints/      \Constraints
            /  Means  \
           /           \
          /             \
   ┌─────────┐         ┌─────────┐
   │Resources│Constraints│ Message │
   └─────────┘         └─────────┘
```

**Figure 2.1.** *Communications triangle tool (inspired by the teaching aids from* grande école B*). For a color version of this figure, see www.iste.co.uk/seurrat/mediation.zip*

This diagram, whose origin is not mentioned, embodies an instrumental conception of communication which goes against any semiological or semiotic reflection on the relationships between signifier, signified and referent. The forms of communication are thought of as a means, independent from the "messages", and the action presented under an agonistic light: knowing how to overcome constraints to achieve our personal goals. The "good" professional is therefore the one who is judged as effective in fulfilling the responsibilities of their role. The professionality required for (or vindicated by) communicators is strongly influenced by managerial standards. Communication training programs promise interns that they will learn how to position themselves within the recognition space of their profession.

For Boltanski and Thévenot, the "valorized subjects" of the "industrial city" are the professionals perceived as "functional, operational beings" who must show "their ability to integrate into the *cogs* or *gears* of an organization" (Boltanski and Thévenot 1991, p. 255) to ensure predictability and reliability. We can therefore argue like Delamotte that "the professionality", which draws attention over the know-how, is fictitiously neutral. "Professionalization actually corresponds to a new model of commitment to work in relation to two partly contradictory obligations: autonomy and conformity" (Delamotte 1998, p. 78). It seems to me that professional training is precisely a privileged place of research to observe this articulation between autonomy and conformity. Fictitiously neutral, the professionality of communicators, as well as communication perceived as a means for gaining additional professionalism, are imbued with binary and dichotomous conceptions of communication that I will examine in the following sections.

## 2.4. The argument of the paradigm shift and communication conceptions

How can we propose to master communication (either interpersonal communication or strategic communication) in such short training periods, between one and three days? This was one of the first questions that I pondered at the beginning of this research project and which was linked to a major point of differentiation between the initial or ongoing training courses I teach and the short training courses observed: the temporal dimension. It seems that one of the major arguments for claiming to have "effects" on trainees in short-term courses – whether in speaking training or strategic communication and planning – is the presence of "a paradigm shift" and that it is by integrating change that the trainee will be able to see professional practice optimized. All of the training programs observed, either communication training courses or programs for communicators, invite trainees "to change their paradigm". This change should make it possible to better understand "the reality" of modern communication, while such awareness is supposed to produce training effects on trainees, and this within a short time frame. In addition, these "paradigm shifts" are far from devoid of normative conceptions of communication. Here, I will examine the two main types: the opposition between information and communication, and the "digital revolution".

The notion of paradigm was developed by Kuhn (1962) in *The Structure of Scientific Revolutions* and is now commonly used to designate a way of seeing or a method to be followed. For this historian and philosopher of science, a paradigm corresponds to principles and methods shared by a scientific community at a given period of time. It is a "universally recognized scientific achievement which, for a time, provides model problems and solutions for a community of researchers" (Kuhn 1996, p. 10). Although the paradigm is an authoritative model, it is only temporary, since it will later be replaced by another one. It can therefore be thought of in its normative dimension.

> Close historical investigation of a given specialty at a given time discloses a set of recurrent and quasi-standard illustrations

of various theories in their conceptual, observational, and instrumental applications. These are the community's paradigms, revealed in textbooks, lectures, and laboratory exercises. By studying them and by practicing with them, the members of the corresponding community learn their trade (Kuhn 1996, p. 43).

By extension, the notion of paradigm is used in training, not to explicitly refer to disciplinary knowledge, but to qualify a way of thinking, a way of understanding communication. In this, the paradigm makes part of a polyphonic authority:

The paradigm shift is at the basis of what Oswald Ducrot called *polyphonic authority*: inherent in the argumentative functioning of language, it is based on the fact that a (P2) proposition draws its legitimacy from a prior proposition (P1), whose assertion, simply shown by the speaker, has thereby acquired a force of truth which provides an argument for P2 (Oger and Monte 2015, p. 8).

In the same way, the "paradigms" presented in training courses are starting points which are not open to discussion but are presented as truths that will come to support the prescriptions made in training.

The first "paradigm shift" mentioned both in public speaking training and in strategic communication and planning refers to the transition from the information society to the communication society. Underlying this idea, there are fairly reductive conceptions of information and communication which present them as opposed.

The facilitator from *grande école* B began her training on strategic communication and planning by asking participants what they thought were the differences between information and communication. Their responses were as follows.

OBSERVATION.– "To inform is a downward posture". "In communication, there is exchange". "Information is the content, while communication is the link".

The facilitator concluded with the following.

OBSERVATION.– "You are right, information is one-sided, communication is relational". "The role of the communicator is to understand, to make people understand, but also to make themselves understood". "The communicator is the facilitator, the go between".

We confirm the extent to which these polarized discourses construct opposing, and therefore, reductive representations of information and communication. Information is presented in a dysphoric logic, as a downward message-diffusion model, whereas communication is understood in a euphoric logic, as being both the source and modality of the richness of exchanges deemed symmetrical. In the same way, a facilitator hosting the communications plan training explained the following.

OBSERVATION.– "Sender and receiver are replaced by the encounter, we are no longer fulfilling an information role, but a mediation role. [...] Here is the paradigm shift: the paradigm is the basic system of thought. For example, when we thought that the Earth was flat, our system was self-centered, the Earth was the center of the universe. That was the paradigm. If we think that the only actors are formal actors, we will make big mistakes in terms of communication. This implies a change in mentality: shifting from information to communication. We are now talking about stakeholders instead of targets. The target is too static, we no longer manage content but interactions".

An intern reacted to this: "we are too focused on following the same models, even if everything has changed".

In public speaking training, facilitators also insist on the fact that it is necessary to shift from an information logic to a communication logic. One of the facilitators from the specialized structure explained the following.

OBSERVATION.– "My job as an actor is really to turn their brains around, in the literal sense of the word. That is to say, we will no longer be interested in what they have to say, but in what the other will receive. In fact, we completely change our point of view".

It is interesting to note that it is not only the "new paradigm" which crystallizes simplified and instrumental visions of communication. The argument is actually based on the assumption that there is an "old paradigm" which may have been relevant for a time. This previous paradigm, part of a mechanistic conception of communication, is just as normative and schematic as the one that comes to chase it away. The "paradigm change" then becomes an injunction to adapt it to the "contemporary world". The change is presented as absolutely radical: we are expected to reverse our point of view, our priorities, and transform our practices in order to finally apprehend the "reality" of communication.

This primacy of communication over information is consistent with certain academic publications such as the renowned book by Bougnoux entitled *La communication contre l'information*. In this book, the author insists on the primacy of the relationship, on its anteriority in relation to information: "the enigma of the relationship infinitely precedes our knowledge contents and what happens is that it exceeds the measure (in the overflows of love, religion or identity passions)" (Bougnoux 1995, p. 10). In this point, the author is in line with works from the "Palo Alto school" (which he uses extensively in his previous book, *La communication par la bande* (Bougnoux 1991)). *La communication contre l'information* is part of a systemic conception of information: "the informational or semiotic relationship in general inserts a third term or an intermediate space between the transmitter and receiver, which we will call *différance* (Derrida), the interpretant (Peirce), or more generally, computing" (Bougnoux 1995, p. 21). Here, it is possible to see connections between this approach and the "paradigm change" proposed in professional communication training. Note, however, that Bougnoux develops a critical approach to the "excesses" of media communication whereas, in training, communication is represented – from a euphoric perspective – as being a positive approach in itself.

The most explicit filiation, one which abandons the "paradigm change" of polyphonic authority to embrace the authoritative quote, is the reference to Wolton's works. While few academic authors are cited in professional training, she was quoted in four of the training courses I followed.

OBSERVATION.– "Here is the quote from Wolton, who is one of the great communication gurus: "it is not enough to inform, to communicate". "As Wolton, a major researcher at CNRS, said, communication is more important than information". "The term *communication* has been overused, we associate it too much with communication technologies, whereas communication is being with others". "Wolton, a CNRS researcher on communication, offers a beautiful definition: communication is the art of living together". "I recommend two easy-to-read, inexpensive little books:

*Le procès de la communication* by Philippe Wellhoff which has just been released, and the little book by Wolton, *Informer n'est pas communiquer"*.

In her essay *Informer n'est pas communiquer* Wolton (2009) sets out to explain why communication is the great challenge of the 21st century. For this, she argues that communication is more important than information: "the more easily we can communicate, the more we want to see each other physically. So much the better. We are social beings, not information beings" (Wolton 2009, p. 17). "Thinking about the transition from information to communication means detechnizing communication, putting technology in its place" (Wolton 2009, p. 78). The conception presented in this essay (without generalizing this to all of Wolton's writings) is part of a more global project which seems more political than scientific, promoting the principles of "cohabitation". For the author, "we must manage the lack of communication through negotiation so as to reach cohabitation" (Wolton 2009, p. 21).

This conception is far from unanimous within the sciences of information and communication where instead of opposing information and communication, the challenge is often to conceptualize their links and to think of them jointly in view of understanding symbolic and social processes. As Boure points out in his introduction to the book *Les origines des sciences de l'information et de la communication*, the specificity of France is that it brings together "what is generally separated abroad: information and communication" (Boure 2002, p. 10).

The second "paradigm change" presented in the context of the training in strategic communication and planning that I observed (and in the presentation speeches of numerous training offers from the "Marketing and Communication" and especially the "Digital Transformation" products), concerns "the digital revolution". For example, at the start of her training on strategic communication and planning, the facilitator announced: "the paradigm shift is the new deal in communication, and the new deal involves the Internet. There is before and after the Internet".

She then drew on the board, the "communication diagrams" before and after the Internet:

IN THE PAST

*Firm*

⇓

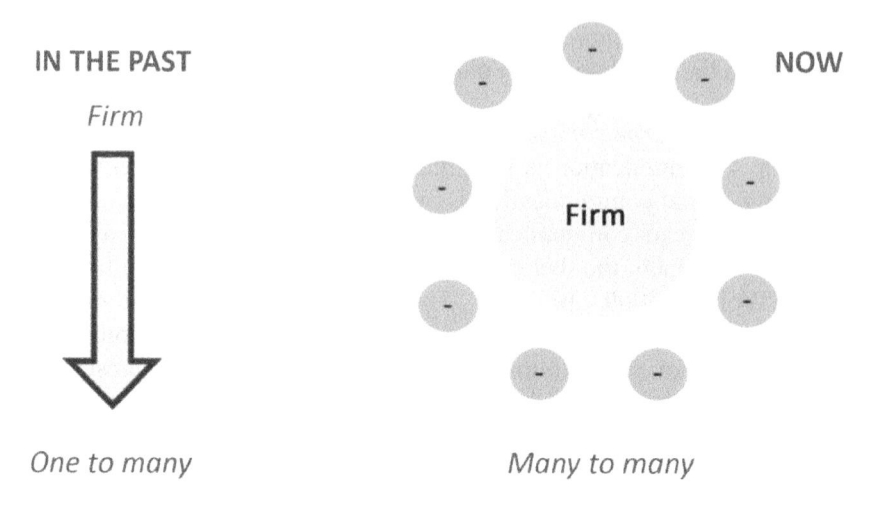

*One to many*

NOW

**Firm**

*Many to many*

**Figure 2.2.** *"Communication diagrams" before and after the Internet (inspired by the teaching aids from* grande école B*). For a color version of this figure, see www.iste.co.uk/seurrat/mediation.zip*

She then asked the participants: "how much information about the firm do you think is not produced by the company?". The participants suggested percentages between 30% and 70%, to which the facilitator responded the following.

OBSERVATION.– "80%! Yes, 80%! The company is deprived of its communication. It lost its control and its mastery". "But in this cacophony, we will have to listen to the firm. How can you make your communication audible and credible?". "There are still companies that are immersed in this single transmitter/receiver diagram. As a consultant and facilitator, I see this in a lot of companies. The question is: how to become a conductor, produce content that can be exchanged by the different actors?". "The comms' bunker is over, the role of the communicator is to explain to others that the situation has changed. To do this, you have to change your mindset". "80% of messages cost nothing on the digital sphere but are difficult to master. So it's in our interest to go on the Web and try to create a good buzz".

The facilitator did not explain how and in what context these percentages were developed. The intention was not to have them discussed, but to create a "trigger", the premises for argumentation. The rest of the argument, focusing on the "digital revolution", emphasized the mastery of social networks and the imperative to create a "buzz". For this, "influencers" were often mentioned, as they are the one who should know how to identify and to draw attention so that they act in favor of the firm's strategy: "Influencers, you have to know how to identify them, convince them and use them well!"

Before starting "the communications plan methodology", a facilitator concluded:

> What changes does the digital bring in, and how does this impact the communications plan? We have shifted from a single logic to a 360° logic, we changed from the multimedia to cross media. We are completely reversing the way in which we see things. We no longer communicate about something, but with someone.

This concept of rupture, revolution, is not new when it comes to approaching computerized media. As Jeanneret explains in *Existe-il (vraiment) des technologies de l'information et de la communication?*, it does not help to "cultivate discernment". The researcher then invites us "to avoid getting caught up in the abstraction effect of those who ask us to consider the object as an essence, something 'in itself'" (Jeanneret 2017, p. 71).

In the above-mentioned discourses, computerized devices such as "social networks" are thought of as facilitators or even multipliers of exchange. Their use and configuration are self-evident. For Robert, "that which is self-evident is placed in a position as not to be questioned, and/or for which questioning is not/no longer legitimate, what does not need to be justified, in other words, what exceeds political justification tests" (Robert 2018, p. 36). *L'impensé numérique* is characterized by a naturalization of the digital and therefore does not allow political questions to be asked: "the unimaginable digital offers a naturalized and simplistic representation of ICTs behind which the shift in political prerogative can unfold with complete impunity, since it is neither spotted nor called into question" (Robert 2018, p. 7). For the author, this unimaginable produces an obscuration of the political logics at work in the digital economy.

Furthermore, at the heart of this idea of "paradigm change" associated with the advent of the Internet and especially the "Web 2.0" is this idea that firms, brands, should be in permanent "conversation" with the audience.

This "conversational model" is derived from the "Cluetrain Manifesto" or "manifesto of the obvious" which is a text published in 1999 on the Internet and then in 2000 in the form of a book by Levine et al. (2000). This book, which had great success in marketing and communication consulting agencies, develops the idea that with the Internet, "markets become conversations between companies and potential consumers" (Levine et al. 2000, p. 14). This conception of the "conversational model" is analyzed by Patrin-Leclère:

> Like the eponymous armchair invented in the 17th century to facilitate confidences (two places seated head to tail), the "conversation" appears here as a conditioning, a device characterized by the intention of promoting communication between the possible participants. The term designates both an imagination and a possible practice without necessarily being proven, to the extent that the device pre-exists and survives the use that could be made of it (Patrin-Leclère 2011, p. 4).

This conversational model obscures the technical and symbolic mediations specific to computerized devices and naturalizes the practices associated with them in order to highlight a utopian conception based on the symmetry of exchange.

In his doctoral thesis, German analyzes the way in which this "conversational model" is notoriously present in the communication strategies of museums:

> The relational "paradigm" is based on the encounter and mutual reinforcement between the (communicational and professional) pretensions of mediated and mediating industries, and the deployment of their favorite devices (which exercise de facto pretensions) to address the uncertainties experienced by the media industries regarding the production and promotion of the cultural objects they develop (German 2017, p. 274).

This relational conception is notorious in the rhetoric of networks described as "social":

> At a time when battles are raging over how to qualify what is presented as the epiphany of true society (*social media*) and

how we got into the habit of using the term *social* to designate databases, YouTube, Facebook, Twitter, Pinterest have created a shortcut between the industry of passages and the financialization of data. Why? Because they are documentary panoplies designed around small written forms, which draw all their force from the semiotic transmutation of all our statements (Jeanneret in Patrin-Leclère and Seurrat 2015, p. 42).

Whether in the paradigm shift from "information to communication" or "the digital revolution", we come across a primacy of the relational component, but above all, of the unthought of politics (*un impensé du politique*) and, more specifically, the political and economic dimensions mediations of communication.

It is because these conceptions of communication are instrumental that they are particularly suitable for short professional training periods. According to Miège, theories that aim to provide a general explanation of communication all present fairly similar limitations and deficiencies: reductionism, abstraction, the primacy given to a paradigm, and the confusion, voluntary or unconscious, of the instances under consideration. For the author, "this is even more acute when interpersonal or linguistic communication is supposed to 'represent' the whole of communication in society" (Miège 2004, p. 185). In short training programs, these explanatory models of "communication" are chiefly mediagenic, because they easily adapt to the promise of providing the keys for understanding communication within a short time frame. In that sense, they act as a starting point for prescribing standards of action that update them. The paradigm shifts presented in the introduction to professional training therefore appear as "anticipatory stories", which establish the general framework where such recommendations will be deployed.

# 3

# Procedures and Standards for "Communicating Properly"

Two main types of knowledge are engaged in professional training, at the heart of the facilitators' claims to expertise: "tools" and "techniques", which correspond to procedural knowledge, and experiential knowledge. To feed the professionalism of trainees and increase their efficacy, the promise to "communicate properly" is deployed through the presentation and implementation of communication "tools" and "techniques", as well as the formulation of "best practices". Mediated in a short time frame, knowledge is presented as a "turnkey" and embedded in a transitive conception of mediation. This invites me to apprehend the construction of procedures and standards through the mediation of practical knowledge and to call into question the place left to creativity and reflexivity in this quest for control and mastery over communication processes.

## 3.1. Toolboxes and communicational claims

What are the communicational claims of training programs in communication? Jeanneret defines the "communicational claim" as the "mode of intervention in communication processes which in a deliberate or insensitive manner hierarchizes elements, determines crucial conditions and legitimizes a certain competence to intervene" (Jeanneret 2014, p. 14). The communicational claims of professional training programs involve a "how-to" approach that must grant a communicational "power to do", allegedly conferring social power. Before delving into the forms of mediation of practical knowledge in the following chapter, I will tackle a reflection on the communicational claims of training programs. Prior to going into detail on the production of professional training "tools", this chapter will analyze the discourses that explicate the claim to the mastery over communication "tools" and "techniques" for increasing communication efficacy.

For professional training in communication considered as a transversal skill, the gain in "professional efficacy" must result from the mastery of "communication techniques". In professional training for communication occupations, the development of professionalism in communicators is correlated with the mastery of tools that, as we will see later, are mainly borrowed from the management sciences. Here, I will not focus on the foundations of such or such "tool", but, more generally, on the claims deployed in the discourses presenting these communication "tools" and "techniques".

At the heart of the rhetoric on communication "tools" and "techniques" is the promise of mastery over communication, which correlates to highly instrumental conceptions of communication. This is evidenced by some of the facilitators' introductory remarks:

OBSERVATION.– "Communication is a discipline, like learning how to drive or to play tennis. Everyone has a capacity for progress". "Technique is not what formats, but what sets you free". "For example, you all master grammar and, at the same time, you all express yourselves differently. It is necessary to accept this discipline and little by little it will become something natural. What is interesting for us today is to become more efficient orally, and to achieve this, one must work on the message perceived". "The key to the efficacy of a communications plan is knowing how to properly identify the targets".

In my thesis, defended in 2009 and entitled *Les médias en kits pour promouvoir "la diversité"* (Seurrat 2009), I analyzed documentary objects called "kits", which had been designed to train media professionals and audiences in "the fight against discrimination" and "to promote diversity" in media. I aimed to study how these projects intended to act on the symbolic in order to influence the social sphere. I showed that the "kit" was marked by a logistical vision of communication and its social efficacy. Through the compilation of media fragments, those objects are presented as digests, as media metonymies. Kits are designed as an aid that should enable the user to grasp media, both figuratively and literally. A support for discourse, the kit is an object conceived to be used. In order to approach these "intellectual technologies"[1] (kits), I had identified three logics[2]: a pragmatic logic for elaborating practical knowledge, a hermeneutic logic for contextualizing the interpretation of media and a normative logic instituting values ("the promotion of 'diversity'").

Stricto sensu, in the professional training programs observed, there are no kits (in the form of specific documentary combinations), although constant references are made to "toolboxes". The "toolbox" may sometimes designate "a specific method" or refer to what has been acquired during the training as a whole. Even though admitting that the use of a "toolbox" works as a metaphorical modality, the three logics I identified in my thesis still seem relevant to address the claims of professional training in communication.

The Centre national des ressources textuelles et lexicales (CNRTL)[3] from the Centre national de la recherche scientifique (CNRS) informs us of the etymology of the term "kit":

> *Kit* is a term derived from the Middle English form *kit(te)* and designates a container. Borrowed from Middle Dutch (whose meaning is "container for a liquid"), the term acquired the more general signification as a "container", and from there, a "box for transporting a product, equipment contained in a box, equipment for a soldier, a box with tools". In the 20th century, "equipment enabling somebody to self-build an object sold in separate parts" (1955)[4].

The history of the term is marked by a progressive synecdoche: from a container – a receptacle – the term "kit" ended up designating the entire contents of a box. The *Trésor de la langue française informatisé (TLFi)* takes up other uses of the term "kit": "a lot of articles constituting the soldier's equipment (1785), then the necessary traveling items (1833) or an assortment of tools (1833)"[5]. The kit is defined as an object that contains a plurality of elements, an assortment and an equipment set. These different

---

1. Taking up Mallarmé's expression "intellectual technologies", which the poet uses to qualify the operation of classifying sciences, Jack Goody describes as intellectual technologies objects which make such classification possible, the ordering of bodies of knowledge (Goody 1977).
2. I explain these three logics in further detail in Seurrat (2010).
3. Available at: www.cnrtl.fr.
4. Available at: www.cnrtl.fr/etymologie/kit.fr.
5. Available at: http://atilf.atilf.fr/tlf.htm.

elements must reunite what is necessary and indispensable. The use of the term "kit" can also denote that it is the bare minimum, as in the case of a "survival kit". The idea of utility is also constitutive of the term.

As a specific "method", "the toolbox" is presented as a synthetic summary of the stages of a procedure, something we should bear in mind. This is evidenced by the "survival kit" used in the transition from the written to the spoken form proposed in the public speaking training from the structure specializing in communication. This "kit" is an index card describing the procedure to be followed, very much like a cooking recipe, in order to prepare an oral presentation.

---

**Conclusion**

Start by writing the ending, what you want to demonstrate, the end result, and support it with three undeveloped arguments, only mention them.

**Development**

Develop and articulate the three arguments by giving precise facts and figures. Thus, your messages will have an impact.

**Introduction**

Reuse your conclusion by adding a catch-phrase and one or two elements from each of the three arguments.

Put everything back in order and there you have a structure which will enable you to maintain coherence, flexibility and security.

---

**Box 3.1.** *"Survival kit" index card (inspired by the teaching aids from the specialized organization)*

"The CDI method", proposed in "The Media Acting Guide" from this structure specializing in communication training, is presented as a "survival kit", as the essential kit to become prepared for "proper communication", even when the professional only has little time. The claim is visually expressed: the index card pinned on the wall with the three words "conclusion, development, introduction" points to the steps not to be missed, the "checklist" to remember. At the bottom of the index card, there was an insert in the shape of a suitcase[6], conveying the idea of baggage (the knowledge acquired that the intern will be able to take home once training is completed). This showcasing crystallizes the means–end relationship underlying the efficacy logic: it all boils down to guaranteeing a certain efficacy, even when the means are limited.

Multi-multi organizations are those which most frequently use formulations to designate the equipment required for mastering communication situations. For example, during the training course on public speaking, we saw "the communicator's magic lantern" or "the Swiss army knife of public speaking". Like the toolbox, the Swiss army knife is presented as a compendium of essential tools for practice. The "Swiss army knife of speaking" comes in the form of a table that the professional must complete to prepare for a public speaking presentation. The goal is to vary communication methods as much as possible in order to reach the largest audience.

| Pictures (visual, auditory, kinesthetic, olfactory, gustatory) | |
|---|---|
| | Emotions |
| Anecdotes | Repetitions |
| Narrative | Reformulations |
| Quote | Transitions |
| Comparison | |
| Metaphor | Slogans |
| Figures | |
| Examples | |

**Table 3.1.** *"Swiss army knife of public speaking" presented during the "public speaking" training from multi-multi organization A*

For the facilitator:

OBSERVATION.– "It's an extraordinarily useful tool. It falls within the scope of manipulation techniques. In short, I'm not telling you to manipulate your audience, manipulation depends on the intention, but if you use the Swiss army knife, you will gain in efficacy".

---

6. Due to copyright reasons, these visuals could not be reproduced in the book.

This grid for constructing a speech is part of a pragmatic claim, proposes a certain way of apprehending discourse and finally, constructs a normative model of what a "good speech" should look like. The three logics identified in my thesis (pragmatic, hermeneutic and normative) are also operative for apprehending common types of formalism in professional training.

Used for referring to the entire training, the expression "toolbox" emphasizes the exhaustive aspect of the training program: the trainee has everything needed to use later in professional practice. This is evidenced by the conclusions of two facilitators teaching training programs in strategic communication and planning.

OBSERVATION.– "You now have a fairly complete toolbox, it's up to you to make the best use of it and above all, to put it into practice on a daily basis! Test it little by little, all in life is made up of communication situations!". "After all, we end the course with a full toolbox. I want you to know how to use it and for you to want to use it. Then, improvement in communication is something that happens over time, it lasts a lifetime!"

The publications from multi-multi A organization entitled *"La boîte à outils de…"* articulate the material dimension of the toolbox as a documentary arrangement with the claim that they constitute a thorough equipment set for such or such type of professional. The structure presents the collection on its website in these terms:

> DUNOD, publisher of knowledge texts for over 200 years in the fields of business, engineering and personal development, with a background of over 3,500 titles and our firm, leader in professional training in the same fields since 1926, have naturally come together through a partnership for promoting the books of our authors/facilitators.

Under the "Communication" line of products, we find *La boîte à outils du responsable de communication* (Jézéquel and Gérard 2016). Sold in bookstores, it is also given to trainees as part of the "Communications Manager" certification training courses. On the Dunod website, it is presented in the following terms:

> How to conceive a communications plan? What methods should one choose to steer and evaluate actions? How to optimize communication through images, writing and the Web? What

tools should be used to encourage effective press relations, boost public relations, communicate in times of crisis or develop internal communication? How to work with agencies? Discover 60 essential tools for practicing business communication on a daily basis. This 3rd edition contains updated examples and a new social media tool.

The book reunites a series of index cards numbered at the top right by "tool" number. These index cards are all structured in the same way, in four stages: the presentation (often using a diagram) of the "tool", an argument entitled "why use it?", "methodological" advice on "how to use it" and finally, a section entitled "how to be more efficient", explaining how to optimize the strategy for maximum efficacy.

Let us take the example of tool #13, entitled "The new influencers". To begin with, this is introduced by a bubble diagram with silhouettes connected by multiple arrows. The diagram represents a certain conception of communication, viral and organic, on the Internet. The text then explains the importance of knowing how to master this "tool", namely "influencers":

> New influencers have an increasingly strong impact on the community of Internet users who follow them. To build effective relationships with them, it is necessary not only identify them, but also to find the right words (Jézéquel and Gérard 2016, p. 48).

In the "why use it?" section, the authors insist on the need to build "regular and authentic relationships" with "influencers". Then, in the "how to use it" section, they explain the steps to follow and identify "influencers" (in particular, through mapping) and to best adapt the messages for them. Finally, in the "how to be more efficient" section, they provide additional advice on how to optimize the "tool's" use: "respect their freedom of tone" and "strive to build a long-term relationship" (Jézéquel and Gérard 2016, p. 50).

At first glance, the book's promises focus on the "how to" aspect, which must serve to attain mastery over communication for efficacy purposes, putting forward an instrumental conception of communication and, in the case of this index card, of social actors. The book is presented as a compilation of "essential" tools for fulfilling the role of communications manager. This refers to the primary use of the term "manual" as defined by

Alain Choppin[7]. In his book, *Manuels scolaires: histoire et actualité* (Choppin 1992), he explains:

> Etymologically [the manual is] a book that is held by hand or is within reach: it is necessarily easy to handle, with a reduced format and weight. In the 19th century, it used to designate a practical guide, a collection of pieces of advice, recipes or rules (the perfect gardener's manual, the artilleryman's manual), a meaning it has retained in our days [...]. It is hardly used in the educational field, except, judging by certain passages from Flaubert or Verlaine, with a pejorative connotation (when speaking about teaching routines) (Choppin 1992, p. 11).

We are not dealing here with the "manual for the perfect gardener", but with the "manual for the perfect communications manager".

Regardless of whether it qualifies specific "methods" or it refers to training as a whole, the toolbox is always characterized by a structuring element: its intended use. All of the facilitators insist on the fact that the toolbox's potential cannot be deployed without practice, the daily exercise of professionals. In this sense, it is up to the intern to fulfill the promises of mastery delivered by the toolboxes. This is evidenced by the various comments made by facilitators in the training courses observed.

> OBSERVATION.– "The hammer is a tool, you can use it to build something but you can also use it to hit your neighbor". "I am offering you a tool case from where you take what is useful to you". "It is important for you to master these tools, but most importantly, for you to know how they can be of use for you". "Then, it is necessary to put these tools into practice on a daily basis, so as not to miss what you have learned in the training program". "Today we studied a lot of methods, I hope it's quite concrete and above all, that you'll put them to good use. It's not the tool as such that is of interest, but what it will be used for".

---

7. Alain Choppin's book offers a multidimensional history of school manuals: the forms, practices, discourses, educational policies, which have contributed to forging and transforming the forms and representations of school manuals. Through his analysis of the criticisms and defenses of manuals, he raises a certain number of imaginaries regarding these objects which, on certain points, can shed light on the imaginaries the "toolboxes" crystallize.

Thus, it is its use that gives the toolbox all of its meaning as it is during use that its potential is realized. As Souchier points out, "in other words, it is in the action, in the hand of the Companion, that the tool's collective intelligence is revealed. The tool only exists in that it evokes both the use and the actor" (Souchier 2004, p. 43).

The "toolbox" rhetoric thereby functions as a summary of professional training claims: it will provide the equipment and utilities required for mastering communication. Through its rhetoric on communication "tools" and "techniques", professional communication training deploys three logics: (1) a pragmatic logic highlighting "practical knowledge"; (2) a hermeneutic logic we could also reclassify as a "logic of elucidation" of communication problems; but above all (3) a normative logic which establishes values that are not, as was the case of the kits studied in my thesis, relating to "living together" but to efficacy, or rather, a movement seeking to establish efficacy as a value that may suffice in itself.

### 3.2. Prescription and planning to "master" communication

While facilitators insist on the appropriation and freedom of use of the tools offered in training, it is still the prescription that predominates in professional training. As I saw at the beginning of the chapter, the injunction to professionalism is strongly marked by standards, and "the 'professionality' which polarizes attention on know-how is fictitiously neutral" (Delamotte 1998, p. 78). In this development, I will focus on the different enunciation modalities of standards in professional training in order to understand the links between the enunciation of standards, professionalism and the efficacy imperative. To apprehend these relationships, I will rely on reflections relating to the performativity of language and on diverse conceptions of planning.

For Austin (1962), a speech act has three dimensions: the locutionary act, accomplished when we correctly formulate an utterance; the illocutionary act, performed by the speaker on the receiving agent, which expresses the speaker's intention; and the perlocutionary act, which relates to the effects on the addressee targeted by the locutionary and illocutionary acts. Austin paid particular attention to the type of utterance described as performative (in English *to perform* conveys the idea of "doing, accomplishing"). A constative utterance, such as "your phone is ringing", seems to describe a situation, but can also modify the behavior of the receiving agent (who may stand up to pick up their phone). While remaining constative, the utterance therefore has an implicit performative dimension. John Searle (1969) developed Austin's proposals by proposing new classifications, which he includes under the term "speech acts". Kerbrat-Orecchioni took up and explained the general categories of illocutionary acts for Searle. The latter draws a distinction between five main types of speech acts: assertive, directive, commissive, expressive and declarative:

> Assertives aim to engage the speaker's responsibility (to varying degrees) for the existence of a state of affairs, regarding the truth of the proposition expressed, and their adjustment direction goes from words to the world. [...] As for the illocutionary purpose of directives, they constitute attempts on the part of the speaker to make the listener do something; attempts which can be modest ("invite to", "suggest", etc.) or on the contrary "ardent" ("order", "claim", "insist") depending on the degree of intensity of the goal's presentation (Kerbrat-Orecchioni 2001, p. 21).

In professional training programs, the enunciation of standards is mainly done in two stages: an affirmation on communication or on the expectations from the audience (assertive), followed by a prescription (directive).

OBSERVATION.– "The news is what people are interested in, you always have to find a hook with the news". "Your audience expects something concrete, not something abstract. It is necessary to provide figures, examples, tangible things". "This is the overall picture of communication, to communicate properly, to be a good communications manager, you must ask yourself the right questions and be rigorous in your methodologies".

We note, however, that there is a certain attenuation of the directive dimension of the speech act through the recurrent use of impersonal expressions. Instead of "you must", facilitators are more likely to start their recommendations with "it is necessary to…" (*il faut que* …). The impersonal turn constructs a form of enunciative erasure (Rabatel 2004) which makes it possible to present the recommendation as coming from the expectations of the audience or the hierarchy of interns, rather from the facilitator.

OBSERVATION.– "It is necessary not to say too many things, there is a need to prioritize". "It is necessary to always bear the starting point and the arrival point in mind, and not to lose focus". "To be a good communicator, good listening skills and rigor are needed".

However, these classifications are fraught with certain limitations. For example, the same verb can correspond to different illocutionary acts ("I swear that it's true" is an assertive act, whereas "I swear to tell the truth" is a commissive act). But, most importantly, all of the language acts proposed by Searle can be at the service of prescription. For instance, the promise may have incentive value. When a facilitator promises trainees that such or such tool will be effective, it is perhaps less the promise that counts than the goal in itself, which is to have the "tool" used. Consequently, the broader category of the performative in Austin (1962) is more suitable for encompassing the plurality of these modalities. Not only does the training prescription involve discourses, but also varied writing formalisms (diagrams, tables, check lists, etc.). From the Latin *praescriptio*, stemming from *praescribo* and derived from *scribo* ("write") with the prefix *prae-* ("before"), the prescription implies a certain prefiguration, a programming of the action. Now, the forms of prefiguration of the action are numerous and quite varied in training programs. For example, during her intervention as part of the training in strategic communication and planning, a new media manager from Vivendi preconized the most favorable times of the day to intervene in such or such "social network". The recommendation, which concerns the temporal scheduling of actions, is both discursive ("the best times to post") and figurative: the box construction, the use of the clock and the "social networks" logos in the original visual aids (which could not be reproduced here) are all ways of prefiguring and scheduling the action, as are the brief excerpts in each box.

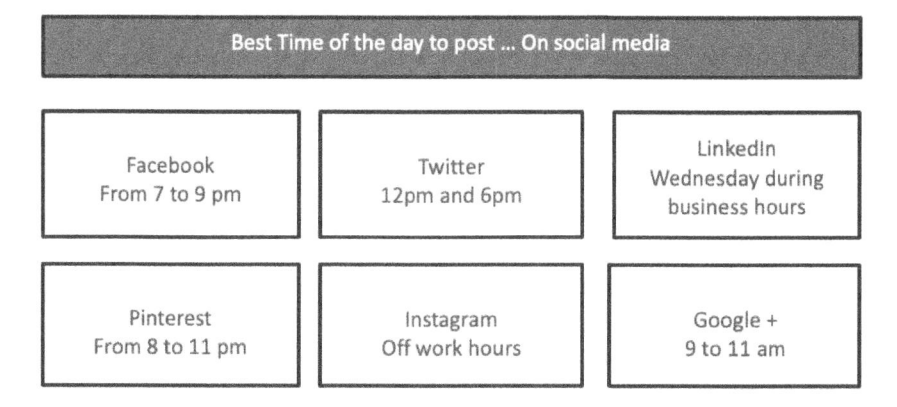

| Best Time of the day to post ... On social media |||
|---|---|---|
| Facebook<br>From 7 to 9 pm | Twitter<br>12pm and 6pm | LinkedIn<br>Wednesday during business hours |
| Pinterest<br>From 8 to 11 pm | Instagram<br>Off work hours | Google +<br>9 to 11 am |

**Figure 3.1.** *Scheduling of actions (diagram inspired by the teaching aids from* grande école *A)*

In this way, the above-mentioned representation is at the same time a list of assertions that must serve as prescriptions. It is interesting to note that Searle's speech act theory (1969) involves a certain conception of communication: it is both analytical and normative. In fact, one of the questions that animates Searle is related to the conditions of success or failure of illocutionary acts. In this we can somehow suspect a search for efficacy. To do this, Searle will develop a reflection on the conditions under which an illocutionary act is or not successful. For Searle, an act is not true or false, but a failure or a success[8]. Searle sees language as a kind of game, with constitutive rules that must be respected to achieve its ends.

The analysis of forms in the enunciation of standards in professional training cannot be limited to the analysis of speech acts, for two reasons: the first reason is that, as we have seen, the prescription can be made in ways that transverse speech acts; the second reason is that it is perhaps in the formalisms taught in professional training that the normative dimension is the strongest. In concrete terms, although this primacy of standards tends to sidestep the debate around values:

> Standards define appropriate behavior, at the level of customary, or required conduct, at the level of morals and laws; they therefore imply the existence of general principles in whose light prescriptions and prohibitions can be legitimized. It is to these principles that we tend to give the name of values in contemporary sociology. While standards are rules of conduct, stipulating the appropriate behavior for a given actor under specific circumstances, values are criteria to judge on what is desirable, defining the general ends to an action[9] (Chazel, *Encyclopaedia Universalis*).

Procedural bodies of knowledge, as understood by Barbier, are statements particularly imbued with standards. The author defines them as "a series of operations likely to lead to a given sort of results" (Barbier 1996, p. 16). In this regard, the "communications plan", which is the subject of specific training (also among the most requested training courses for communication occupations), can be considered as a macro-prescription

---

8. On this question, we find an interesting development in Reboul (1992).
9. Chazel, F. *Norme et valeurs sociales. Encyclopaedia Universalis* [Online]. Available at: https://www.universalis.fr/ [Accessed March 5, 2018].

made from a scheduled sequence of prescribed stages (each containing their own prescriptions). For Bonnet:

> By prescription, we mean more or less formal orders for activity, intervention or behavior, orders whose origin can be hierarchical due to decision-makers, or regulatory or even place in a context of political or technical change, or any other event requiring a response in terms of production of meaning by the actors invited or forced to act (Bonnet 2015, p. 68).

The communications plan can then be thought of as a series of action orders (to diagnose, develop messages, draw a budget, evaluate, etc.), each containing their own prescriptions (to diagnose by establishing barometers, to develop simple and impactful messages, to evaluate with metrics, etc.).

In the three training courses I followed, the facilitators invited the interns to build the summary of a communications plan. The goal was to see whether they found the right items and placed them in the right order. Training programs in strategic communication and planning can be seen as a format associated with an upstream formatting, which is the communications plan. Even though facilitators arrive more or less quickly at the communications plan and develop its different aspects – some focus on the "diagnosis" section, while others insist more on the "evaluation" section – all of them follow the pattern of the communications plan as a framework for part of the training. In this case, the communications plan comprises seven stages: diagnosis, goals, targets, messages, actions, tools, means and evaluation.

– A "strategic planning" tool: the communications plan is the document that is supposed to be at the heart of "the communication function". It formalizes a strategy and lists the stages and means to be deployed to guarantee its success.

In his article entitled "*La cognition située, une nouvelle approche de la rationalité*" (Laville 2000, pp. 1301–1333), Laville proposes an analysis of the forms planned action may take. According to the author, there are several conceptions of the plan that can be articulated with one another: the plan as a program, the plan as a resource, and, within the plan as a resource, the plan as a framework and the plan as communication:

> Classical planning theory dispenses entirely with reactive behavior. It is based on a total reduction of action through

planning and conceives the plan as a program controlling the behavior of agents. Following this conception, the agents proceed in two phases: they construct a plan (construction phase) and then execute it (execution phase). If the environment changes before the complete execution of the plan, the construction of a new plan is undertaken (Laville 2000, p. 1321).

The communications plan is a program that must guide the action of communicators. The facilitators also insist on the fact that it is necessary to respect the order of the stages and not to ignore any of them.

OBSERVATION.– "Being methodic is essential, because in everyday life we don't have time to break everything down, it is necessary to know the stages and place them in the right order". "The communications plan is used to structure your actions and not to forget anything important; it is necessary not to skip any stage; otherwise the entire methodology would be ruined".

When the plan is seen as a resource, it constrains the action without fully determining it. Laville takes the example of a person about to descend a series of rapids in a canoe and who carefully plans the route. However, the plan thus formed will not determine the details of the behavior during the course of action, because the contingencies that will appear remain unpredictable: "the plan serves as an internal framework for the routines the agents are equipped with to be triggered" (Laville 2000, p. 1322). In strategic communication and planning training programs, the question of contingencies is not central in the facilitators' rhetoric, although it becomes a subject for discussion as a result of the questions raised by trainees. These mainly concern the lack of means to implement the initial diagnosis or the final evaluation.

For example, an intern points out to a facilitator that the communications plan used as a recurring pattern at his business slightly differs from the one taught in the training course. The facilitator responds: "yes, of course, we've seen the academic summary that we find in comms' books, but in real life, it's a little different".

Finally, the plan can also be considered as a mode of communication. This is particularly palpable in the situation where the communications plan is presented as the preferred tool for establishing a dialogue with the hierarchy.

OBSERVATION.– "Formalizing your approach is essential for giving credibility to your role". "This type of tool takes time to become formalized, to be formatted for the firm, but afterwards, once you use it, your hierarchy will look at you differently". "The communications plan is used for persuading your hierarchy".

These remarks suggest that the communications plan fulfills less of a "methodological" function for communication professionals than an argumentative function for the hierarchy. It must serve to give credibility to a legitimacy-seeking function. Mastery over the plan thereby intends to reflect the communicator's professionalism, to align the expectations from such a role with those of marketing. The very structure of the "communications plan" is therefore quite normative and evidences a logistical vision of communication. It perfectly corresponds to the consequentialist logic of efficacy, as analyzed by Jullien:

> In the alternative sketched, the first path traced, the "European" pathway to modeling, implies a means-end relationship. An end being conceived ideally, we then look for the means to implement it and turn it into a reality (with all the intrusion that this "entry" into reality may involve – both relatively arbitrary and forced). Or, to present the approach the other way around, by *plan*, in the sense of action plan, we mean any elaborate project comprising an ordered sequence of operations, as means, intended to achieve the intended goal (Jullien 1996, p. 59).

For Jullien, the plan serves as a framework for thinking: "it is through it that we understand action, from it that we expect efficacy [...] We can rework this framework, redefine one of its edges – but it is difficult to go beyond it" (Jullien 1996, p.60).

Planning (in public speaking and as a communication strategy) therefore appears to be a form of professional rationalization, as analyzed by Gadrey (1994). For this author, the permanent rationalization of professional work manifests on two levels: a cognitive type of rationalization and an institutional type of rationalization.

[The cognitive type of rationalization] is based on the typification of cases, the relative formalization of processes (or intellectual methods) for problem solving and the use of a repertoire of "routines" that individuals may have acquired on a personal basis, but which often exist as skills collectively disseminated within and by the organization. For the most part, methods are the combination and coordination of appropriate routines, following the breaking down of one complex intellectual task into smaller components likely to match such routines (Gadrey 1994, p. 172).

As taught in professional training programs, the communications plan represents a good example of this decomposition of intellectual tasks underlying a cognitive type of rationalization.

The institutional (or regulatory) type of rationalization/formalization is a "process enacting the rules to which an entire profession is subject" (Gadrey 1994, p. 174). For Gadrey, these rules demarcate what is certified by the firm and what is not. The institutional type of rationalization will therefore legitimize certain forms of cognitive rationalization by transforming them into official processes. As a communications manager at Orange pointed out, the communications plan is a formalism that cannot be modified. These forms of rationalization are related to the fact that professionals cannot "practice their profession without a minimum 'typification' of the cases they come across, mastery over the appropriate methods and the activation of operating routines" (Gadrey 1994, p. 174). These procedures must thus make it possible "to achieve an economy of means in the management of time and effort" (Gadrey 1994, p. 174), which brings us clearly back to the question of efficacy.

The communications plan properly embodies the concept of "method" used in short professional training programs. The *Dictionnaire historique de la langue française* explains that the term "method" comes from the Low Latin *methodus*, which used to be employed in medicine, geometry and rhetoric. Borrowing from the Greek *methodos*, a combination of *meta* and *hodos* (which means "road, path"), the method refers to a path. In my opinion, this suitably matches the idea of method as we understand it in the human and social sciences. Then, as pointed out by the *Dictionnaire historique de la langue française*, there was a shift from the idea of the path followed, and the term acquired a normative connotation (the path to be followed). The method became synonymous with process, technique and the means in the sense of "the way of doing things":

> The "method" in training therefore refers to applying techniques, the paths to follow in order to acquire professional credibility. Another way to strengthen professionalism is to draw inspiration from "best practices".

The recurring emphasis on "best practices" in professional training therefore contributes to this professional rationalization and the circulation of standards for "communicating properly".

## 3.3. "Best practices" and the circulation of standards

The enunciation of professional standards involves the prescription of procedures and forms of action planning; in professional training. It is also accompanied by the enunciation of "best practices". I draw a distinction between the enunciation of "best practices" as an illustration of the norm and the case study as an educational practice (which I call "casuist mediation" and will be more specifically addressed in the chapter dedicated to mediation practices in professional training). Here, I focus on the enunciation forms of standards, through the listing of "good examples", of "success stories" in professional training. This modality for exposing and illustrating professional standards is highly present in professional communication training programs. The enunciation of "good examples" drawn, among other things, from the professional experience of facilitators gives substance to the standards and shows their actualization in practice. The example is directly associated with a fairly dichotomous judgment: there are good examples to imitate and bad examples to avoid.

What are the conditions of "enunciability" for "best practices"? It seems that:

> They are not simply the signalization, at the level of verbal performances, of what could be deployed in the order of the mind or in the order of things; but they appeared by virtue of a whole set of relations that are peculiar to the discursive level (Foucault 1969, p. 129).

In my Master's degree research paper (Seurrat 2005) and later in several articles (Seurrat 2011), I worked on the development and circulation of "best practices" for "the management of diversity" in various firms. That work explored the way in which experience is turned into generalizable knowledge. How are situated actions established as "best practices"? My question related to the processes of qualification and transformation of actions listed in favor of "diversity". To do this, I studied the institutional, social and semiotic processes that favor the transition from a situated practice to a recommended practice, in other words, the modalities according to which singular actions become exemplary ones. That work made it possible to show that "best practices" have a temporary status, which depends on the authorities and actors entitled to formulate such a judgment. By researching databases on "best practices" from business associations, this work illuminated the role of architexts in making heterogeneous practices coherent and legible. In the context of the professional training programs observed for the present research project, "best practices" were not listed in documentary bases, but enunciated during the training to give substance to the recommendations made by the facilitators.

In French, "*bonne pratique*" is assimilable to the English term "best practices", in which the insistence on efficacy is remarkably clear. Briefly stated, "best practices" are those whose results can be proven. In this way, the series of "best practices" can be understood as:

> These collections of prescriptions […] which prescribe an action, which formulate a program; they lead to an extension of the knowledge available to the specialist and even the amateur; they invite us to 'put to the test' the recipes (to 'test' them, to 'experiment' with them) and to carry out a comparative evaluation of the results (Goody 1977, p. 235).

This ideal of the reproducibility of practices may serve to repel the anxiety caused by the uncertainty of the professional world and perhaps, even more markedly, the universe of communication professionals.

The "good examples" are offered like a florilegium by facilitators to trainees, but the latter are also invited to contribute their own to this "common pot". Training programs, especially inter-company ones, are seen as moments for sharing, for "benchmarking". Benchmarking ("yardstick" or "reference point") is a practice that involves comparing an individual's actions or products to "the competition" in order to position themselves and, above all, be inspired to "get the best out of it" (Gautron 2003, p. 17). In professional training for communication occupations, facilitators insist on the opportunity that the training offers them for exchanging "best practices".

OBSERVATION.– "I invite you to exchange best practices, to share your experiences". "Share your examples of success or failure, put them in the common pot, we will be enriched by the experiences from each and every one".

This echoes the remark from a former facilitator at one of the multi-multi organizations, for whom the exchange between interns can be more important than the training contents delivered by the facilitator:

> In inter-company training, they expect to encourage a debate with other professionals, an exchange of practices, benchmarking. The content of the training course sometimes almost becomes a pretext.

In training programs in strategic communication and planning, the "best practices" put forward by facilitators are often audiovisual advertisements. Their short format and their relative meaningful autonomy (which enables facilitators to spend little time presenting them) seem to function as a good introduction to the series of varied examples, considered as models for action.

The facilitator from *grande école* B, whose talk focused on the importance for brands to construct meaning by communicating "values", played a whole series of advertising films (like an Indian commercial for laundry detergent Ariel attempting to deconstruct sexist stereotypes), to demonstrate the efficacy of "authentic" discourses. He concluded the series of examples with: "You see, the most important is to make sense. How? It is necessary to focus on the firm's purpose and legitimacy".

Unlike case studies which are built upon educational stages and there is a problem to be solved, the successful example is valid in itself and becomes the subject of a few remarks, as evidenced by these comments from of the three training courses on strategic communication and planning.

OBSERVATION.– "See how ingenious this ad is?". "We understand why this video created a buzz!". "It's a good example that can inspire you". "We can clearly see that, when it is suitably conceived, disruption works effectively".

The emphasis is often placed on the "creativity" of advertisements. Even though communications managers can participate in the development of advertising campaigns, they are not, most of the time, the ones who create them. At first glance, we may think that the repetition of what has already been done or said is not compatible with the idea of creativity. The injunction to "creativity" is thereby often accompanied by the production of "best practices" benchmarks. Levoin and Oger, who worked on creativity prizes in education (Levoin and Oger 2012), show that such prizes are part of a "best practices" diffusionist model, supposed to encourage innovation. They show that this circulation of "best practices" materializes through a number of recurring forms, such as rankings and educational guides. For these authors, the visibility of "best practices" is far from specific to the education sector and is more broadly part of socio-political models which they describe in these terms:

> The generalized circulation of entrepreneurial models, the promotion of principles characteristic of a new conception of 'governance' and, in the symbolic order, the promise of social regeneration (Levoin and Oger 2012, p. 121).

For example, an intern from the strategic communication and planning training course dictated in *grande école* B was invited to briefly show the other interns a document for framing needs – internal to her company – detailing who should carry out which task, with what means and within what time frame. She explained that the document was shared with multiple users so that all the firm's employees could consult it as soon as it is updated by one of them. The facilitator concluded: "we can see that such a document takes little time to design, but then it saves time, we gain efficacy and credibility, you should be inspired by it!".

The standard for evaluating "best practices" is often the means–end ratio at the heart of the efficacy logic. In public-speaking training, "best practices" are above all "communication techniques" used by the interns during their performances and the subject of laudatory comments from facilitators, who invite the other trainees to draw inspiration from them. In fact, the facilitators use the performances of interns to identify the modalities for "communicating properly":

> OBSERVATION.– "Have you noticed? Repeating a term spoken by the other is a good springboard". "Stéphane conspicuously showed us the

importance of figures to convince the audience". "Marie gave us a beautiful demonstration of the use of different vocal colors".

The counterpart of "best practices" is "worst practices" that also participate, implicitly, in validating standards through their nonuse. The presentation of "worst practices" is an often-entertaining moment in training, which regularly arouses laughter from the interns.

The "worst practices" of trainees in public speaking, which are the source of amusement never, involve the trainees present, but, through micro-stories retold by facilitators, refer to those from former interns. For example, a facilitator told us that a participant had delivered a long and particularly boring performance where he retold the audience how he had almost drowned. According to the facilitator, as the narrator was alive and well to retell the story, there was no longer any suspense. This example enabled him to conclude that, to tell a good story, it is necessary to surprise the audience near the end.

In public speaking, "worst practices" are often undermined and caricatured by facilitators with a background in drama, encouraging laughter. Indeed, many facilitators imitate people who use repetitive gestures (such as touching their hair) or denounce discrepancies between the spoken utterances and the physical posture (e.g. declaring "I'm happy to see you" with a tense face) in order to show, through the "failed" illustration, the importance of body management and facial expressions when speaking in public.

In communications plan training, it is the "failed" advertisements that are the subject of amusement. For example, an advertisement, presented during one of the training courses, sparked many laughs among the interns. It was an advertisement for the restaurant brand *La Mie Câline* which depicted a man with a head in the shape of a sandwich. For the facilitator, this advertisement clearly embodied "a communication error". It enabled the facilitator to go into general terms by explaining the importance of "eliciting positive identification mechanisms in the target".

In her intervention in *grande école* A, one of the speakers, a former director of studies at Sofres, offered trainees a sequence entitled "How to fail your internal barometer in ten lessons", providing anonymized examples of surveys which were too long or biased. "Worst practices" are thus a reverse form of prescription: it involves showing "failures" and "errors" to be avoided.

In short, both the victorious example and the unfortunate example prove the recommendation's validity. For Schön, "reproducing an effective intervention amounts to facilitating the description of what I did in such a way as to be able to do it again in a situation comparable to the first one" (Schön 2011, p. 219). But, for the researcher, the problem with "what happens to good ideas" is that there is "a dominant approach to diffusion which involves formulating the principles and procedures associated with an innovation, with the goal of providing a training package that can be used for helping other practitioners replicate the good idea. But this approach appears most often as a mechanical and inadequate application of the 'package'" (Schön 2011, p. 219).

Ronan German also observes this generalization of "benchmarking" in the field of museum institutions. According to the scholar, this practice is characterized by its great plasticity and indifference to alteration processes (in the sense of "becoming other"), specific to any form of knowledge trivialization. In his view, "the desingularization required for the practice of mapping joins the decontextualization of the benchmarking practice and its total indifference to what constitutes the specificity of such or such mediations in the fields studied and explored in the search for best practices" (German 2017, p. 677).

The emphasis on "best practices" thus contributes to the decontextualization and generalization of singular experiences, exemplified for transitivity purposes. The primacy of the enunciation of standards, of the formulation of frameworks for taking contingencies into account, of the invitation to imitate the "best practices" therefore leads us to question the place of "creativity" in professional training.

### 3.4. Prescribing and standardizing "creativity"?

The efficacy imperative entails a need to elaborate measures to try to guarantee mastery over communication processes. These measures offered to trainees are diverse and take various forms and enunciations: "tools", "methods", "techniques", "best practices", etc. However, a new injunction is currently spreading in the world of work which, at first glance, seems hardly compatible with the prescription of "standard" procedures: it is the injunction to creativity. A term, widely used in training programs, is frequently summoned through this injunction: "the disruptive". It is also a communications leitmotif in large communication agencies and has been made visible in the publications of directors since the 1980s, especially by Dru (1997) who claims to be the "inventor" of this term. For the director of TBWA agency (who registered the term in 1992 as a trademark), "disruptive innovation is a breakthrough innovation, as opposed to incremental innovation, which simply optimizes what already exists".[10] Apart from the fact that it is dichotomous to oppose two categories of innovation instead of thinking of it as a polymorphous process, these discussions on the search for "disruptivity" are more largely involved in the creative injunction.

This notion of "creativity", its definitions, the socio-economic transformations it generates and the standards associated with it are, among others, invested by researchers who work on mutations in the cultural industries. This is the case of Bouquillion et al. for whom:

> The reference to the notion of creativity is present in the cultural industries and the communication industries, as well as in most other fields of activity. It constitutes an injunction which weighs on socio-economic actors and which is also taken up by public policy decision-makers (Bouquillion et al. 2015, p. 17).

In information and communication sciences, "creativity" is not considered as a state of affairs or a single process, but as a blend word, a nebula that encompasses complex phenomena, made up of injunctions and conceptions of culture and creation, whose mediations should be examined.

The theme for the *XXI Congrès de la Société française de l'information et de la communication* (SFSIC), held at the Maison des Sciences de l'Homme (MSH) Paris Nord, organized by the *Laboratoire des sciences de l'information et de la communication* (LabSIC) from 13 to 15, June 2018, was "Creation, creativity and mediations" and adopted a critical distancing from social and political injunctions from the very outset:

> Create! Be (all) creative! And, of course, be innovative! The calls for creation and creativity have become comminatory as "categorical imperatives", regardless of the sector of activity:

---

10. Dru J.-M., interviewed by Nora D. The concept of "disruption" explained by its creator. *Le Nouvel Observateur*, January 24, 2016.

the issue of innovation haunts all discourses, if not all practices, including info-communications, at work and in culture, in territories and research laboratories, in firms – ranging from CAC 40 companies to startups. Are these injunctions only a rhetoric to re-enchant the lives of individuals, life at work, the market, customer relationships? Between creation (which acts on the symbolic and social imaginary) and creativity (which implies a dynamic and agitates practices), what approaches does research in Information and Communication Sciences develop regarding the mediations instituted and organized across all of society's activities to encourage creation and creativity actions?[11]

Through the implementation of a seminar at the *Laboratoire d'excellence Industries culturelles et création artistique* (LabEx ICCA) entitled "Travail et créativité, créativité au travail : approche croisée à l'international"[12] or the 2014 ACFAS conference entitled "Injonction de créativité et création sous contrainte : parallèles entre secteur culturel et monde du travail à l'épreuve du numérique", Andonova et al. (2014) analyzed the way in which this injunction to creativity, initially present in the cultural and media industries, has extended to the entire work sphere. We are witnessing what Bouquillion et al. call an "industrialization of culture and […] a culturization of industry" (Bouquillion et al. 2013, p. 16). In the words of Andonova: "established as a social norm, in the space of two decades, the creative reference has become an omnipotent injunction in the corporate world" (Andonova 2015, p. 5). This can be considered both in terms of promises and paradoxes. According to the researcher:

> Invoked to introduce a marketing strategy, to get employees to adhere to the company's project, to promote the organization or to support a human resources policy, the creative reference is now part of the productive universe it attempts to re-enchant (Andonova 2015, p. 5).

---

11. First lines of the call for papers for the congress. See: https://www.sfsic.org/index.php/sfsic-infos-151/appels-%C3%A0-comm./3147-aac-congres-de-la-sfsic-2018.
12. See: https://icca.univ-paris13.fr/travail-et-creativite-creativite-au-travail-approche-croisee-a-linternational/.

Andonova has identified five promises behind the injunction to creativity in the corporate world: (1) the promise of performance at the service of the economy; (2) the promise of modernity linked to digital innovation; (3) the promise of cooperation; (4) the re-enchantment of the corporate world; and (5) the promise to elevate human potential.

For Andonova, "in the industrial company, the creative injunction takes the form of creative workshops and training in creativity management whose almost avowed goal is the search for efficacy and profits" (Andonova 2015, p. 7). Training in "creativity" increasingly makes part of educational offers in communication where "being creative" is considered as a transversal skill, especially in training offers relating to communication occupations. It is interesting to note that when I carried out a first study of prospectuses in 2016, there were only a few of them, whereas between 2016 and 2018, several training courses in "creativity" flourished, with a "New" stamp on them. I propose to analyze the presentation of offers relating to "creativity" in and through communication in the light of these five promises.

An index of the offers from eight professional training prospectuses makes it possible to analyze the reference made to creativity in professional training in communication seen as a transversal logic and in professional training for communicators. First, let us point out that two-thirds of the training courses that contain the term "creativity" in their title appeared between 2016 and 2018. This is therefore a fairly recent phenomenon in professional training. The offers containing the term "creativity" in their title are few (ten in the corpus analyzed) and mainly concern training in communication occupations, and more specifically, two main areas: graphic design and communication strategies.

The link between "creativity" and graphic design is perhaps the most obvious one, given the fact that designers are sometimes referred to as "creatives". "Proper communication" would therefore have to be original, "disruptive", enabling the firm to stand out from its competitors. As I have already emphasized in previous paragraphs regarding the association between "creativity" and communication strategies, we are witnessing an extension from marketing towards communication. Now, if we extend the indexing to all prospectuses, it appears that the reference to "creativity" is mostly present in management and in marketing training programs.

Even though the offers, which use the term "creativity" in their title, are only a few, the term is nonetheless present in the notices. In this regard, it is presented as a skill to be acquired in an ample variety of training programs.

Please note that some structures prefer the term "creativity", while others use the term "innovation". Let us try to find some explanations for these nuances. For example, in the prospectus from CSP (an organization that only offers training in communication as a transversal skill), there are 75 occurrences of the term "creativity", whereas the term "innovation" appears 12 times. This is related to the fact that the structure, whose slogan is "The art of training", frequently refers to the world of art, and in particular to live performances. They also offer a training course entitled, "how to communicate better orally through the clown approach", which promises to "reveal the clown in you to gain creativity and impact in your oral presentations". The notice focuses on the premise that a good clown is above all someone who knows how to adapt to the audience and play with emotions. The "professionality transfer" from these circus artists must allow trainees to "gain creativity" to "gain impact", "creativity" being thought of as an instrument at the service of language performativity.

In a broader sense, it seems that the products promoting offers in oral and written communication use the term "creativity" more often, whereas those aimed at communicators prefer the term "innovation". This could be explained by the fact that speaking is often associated with an art (oratory art, theatrical art, etc.), whereas the practices of communicators are apprehended as strategic actions that must either promote or give rise to innovation.

Another distinction relates to the types of structures. Although they both offer training in oral and written communication, *grandes écoles* use the term "innovation" more frequently. Could this be related to their academic status and the fact that innovation has been conceptualized more than "creativity"? This is a hypothesis. In contrast, another aspect can be mentioned: innovation is often associated with management. In concrete terms, both *grandes écoles* insist on the fact that they are aimed at executives, that is, at communications professionals who exert management functions.

For Andonova (2015, p. 8), "the attractiveness of the creative reference is due to its assimilation to innovation". While the adjectives "creative" and "innovative" are sometimes used synonymously in training notices (for qualifying original and impactful discourses or communication actions), the same does not apply to the noun forms "creativity" and "innovation". Let us note that while "creativity" can be mobilized as an asset for an individual (invited to "liberate" or "boost" "creativity"), innovation is either presented as a result, or as a collective process that can be "managed". For Alter, "change (for example a new technique) tends to focus on the "effects" of a transformation in the nature of relationships, relating them to a general-scope sociological theory. Innovation, for its part, aims to analyze the process which led to the implementation of the same transformation and integrates it into an at least partially economic perspective" (Alter 1996, p. 6). When the two terms are combined, "creativity" is presented as one of the elements of the innovative process, as one of its factors: it must elicit it, give birth to it.

In order to see how training programs promise to "develop the creativity" of trainees, let us take the example of one of the structures specializing in communication, through its course: "Developing creativity for a daring comms' strategy".

It is riveting to see that the training begins with the notion of a paradigm to address the "creative framework". We would be in the face of a new paradigm, that of "creativity". This adds to the previous development on the paradigm shift as an argumentative premise in short professional training. Announcing a radical change amounts to urging trainees to adapt to it, and the training program appears as a response to that necessity. "Creativity" is presented as something outside of the framework; hence, it is interesting to see that training promises techniques and procedures to learn how to get out from such framework. "Brainstorming" or "creative workshops" are unavoidable stages of the "creative process", which oscillates between "phases of divergence" and "phases of convergence". "Creativity" is presented as a game whose rules must be mastered, and one of the major rules is to know how to master and exploit this "creative liberation" for strategic purposes. We are quite far from a Promethean conception of creation.

"Design thinking", "strategic road mapping", " brainstorming" and the "creative process"[13] are all tools that the communicator must know how to use in order to harness "creativity" for the benefit of the firm's strategy. As discussed earlier, we find again this triple conception of the tool: its

---

13. Professionality in communication occupations also involves the use of an English language vocabulary.

pragmatic, hermeneutic and normative dimensions. These tools are also associated with experiential knowledge, such as "best practices" (examined in the preceding paragraphs). One of the specialized structures even offers a "Creative Learning Trip" presented as "an immersive journey, with guided tours of creative firms deploying an agility strategy at the service of innovation".

In the presentation video of this two-day training, the facilitator explains that this is a "new concept of training through experience and experimentation". The idea is to "visit a certain number of ecosystems in order to see what can be implemented within one's own structure [...] setting the firm in motion to adapt to today's changing world". Here, we see quite clearly how the creative reference works as a modernity imperative and that, in order to adapt to it, it is important to transfer "best practices" to the firm. This is in line with the previously mentioned analyses by Oger and Levoin, who showed how, within the framework of the awards to creativity in teaching, this is conceived as something that can be fit into reproducible frameworks.

If we take the five promises relating to "creativity" at the workplace proposed by Andonova, these are clearly found in the training programs studied (Andonova 2015, pp. 4–14). "Creativity" is closely linked to the digital and often found in the "Digital Transformation" products: it is part of a promise of modernity. "Creativity" particularly highlights the idea of cooperation, which produces a certain illusion of reciprocity and symmetry in the relationships between professional actors. Considered as a "liberation" in public speaking, "creativity" is presented as a self-fulfillment modality, as a way of being authentic to ourselves. In this, it promises a certain re-enchantment of the world of work. In the same vein, "creativity" is presented as contributing "to elevate human potential" (Andonova 2015, p. 11). This is evidenced by the verbs associated with the term ("to boost", "to develop", "to liberate"), whose link with "personal development" and the deployment of coaching are in no way trivial. Another training structure has partnered up with Dunod for the publication of its collection of training books and proposes a volume entitled *Les cinq clés pour être créatif au quotidien* (Coirault 2016), whose introduction reads:

> Constant change in the world we live requires us to reinvent ourselves every day. We are often unbeknownst creatives who cling to their skills. Yet creativity, curiosity and the exploration of divergent paths are vital for the group and the individual.

This creative dynamic allows us to achieve incomparable wellbeing and can increase our life expectancy.

Last but not least, "creativity" does not compete against economic efficacy but is, on the contrary, at its service. For Andonova, it is presented as a promise of growth:

> The advent of the "creative economy", based on innovation, creativity and knowledge, would be based on a new conception of culture, not only at the service of cultural industries but of economy in its entirety […]. Carrier of ideals of freedom, flexibility and autonomy, supposedly in favor of workers (in the cultural field and the industrial productive sector), the injunction to creativity is essentially limited to efficacy factors and the rationalization of production. Within firms, it is at the service managerial goals. Idealized, presented as an inevitable means of economic performance and as a competitive factor, it is part of an ideological plea which surely serves the managerial rhetoric (Andonova 2015, p. 7).

Thus, the reference to creativity no longer seems to be an injunction competing with the efficacy imperative, but rather one of the ways of accomplishing it. In his thesis, German also shows that the injunction to "creativity", which translates into "the permanent search for new talents and the regular renewal of forms" (German 2017, p. 263), is presented as a "firewall" against the constitutive uncertainty of communication, and more specifically, to the field of museum communication. Creativity is not seen as something that shakes up the established order but as something that completes it.

At first glance, we may believe creativity to be a counterpoint (or at least in dissonance with) an instrumental conception of communication, envisioned as a tool to be mastered in order to gain efficacy. Yet, it is quite the opposite: "creativity" is itself the subject of "techniques", "methodologies" and "procedures" supposed to guarantee its advent and optimization. Training in "creative" communication therefore seems to contribute to the standardization of creative processes. In this sense, it is a conception of "creativity as something abstract, cut off from its material and collective conditions of implementation" (Bouquillion et al. 2015, p. 22).

## 3.5. Debates on standards and the reflexivity of social actors

Despite the fact that, as shown throughout this chapter, training programs are a privileged place to enunciate standards and propose their application, they are also a place for discussing and debating said standards. Calling into question the efficacy imperative must not obscure the reflexivity of social actors. The insistence on the strategies of organizations, their offers, their promises and their mediation practices should not make us forget the heterogeneity of training experiences. The critical perspective does not imply an overhanging[14] viewpoint.

In field work, we come across social actors who do not share instrumental conceptions of communication. We also meet social actors who take a critical, sometimes disillusioned, look at the quest for efficacy which can lead to a loss of sense. We also meet social actors for whom knowledge is not an instrument to be mastered, but, on the contrary, the place of humility where we experience the world's complexity. Adopting a critical approach does not imply adopting an overhanging posture in relation to social actors. As Fassin points out, this involves shifting the critique:

> Locating it outside or beyond the choice which allegedly has to be made between unveiling and translation, between considering the agents as caught in an illusion subjecting them to a domination they are unaware of and affirming that they hold a truth about society, a truth the researcher only puts into form through analyses (Fassin 2009, p. 200).

For the anthropologist, the researcher is located on "a crest line", torn between commitment (not in the sense of activism but in the sense of a presence in the world) and distancing. We can therefore "affirm the need for a distanced view while recognizing the social intelligence of the actors" (Grignon 2020, p. 178). Distancing does not operate at the level of the actor but at other levels, in this case socio-political and socio-economic ones. No longer is it a question of adjustment with communication practitioners, but of choosing to introduce a dissonant, critical voice discerning what precisely is it that confronts professionals with an efficacy imperative which fails to leave enough room for reflection on the meaning of action and its value.

---

14. This questioning is particularly nourished by the exchanges I had at the "*Cultures de l'enquête*" seminar conducted by Le Marec since 2016.

The issue from the journal *Méthis* entitled "*Étendues de la réflexivité*", directed by Badir and Mouratidou, proposes to understand "the extent and diversity of its manifestations". In the introduction to the special issue, the coordinators emphasize that "while reflexivity is a concept used by most of the human and social sciences, it takes diverse forms depending on the disciplines and spans different questions in function of the objects studied" (Badir and Mouratidou 2012, p. 7). They then question the term's etymology and point out that the morphological and semantic constitution of "reflexivity" provides food for thought.

> While it is easy to define reflexivity as that which is reflexive, the quality of being reflexive concerns what exactly? Is it a reflection, like the bending of light and, by metaphorical extension, of the mind? (Badir and Mouratidou 2012, p. 8).

As for the prefix –re, for the authors it can be interpreted in two ways:

> Reflexivity could be considered as a form of return – to oneself, or to an object. Unless we dare to see – this would be the simplest extraction – the radical reflex. But how can we explain the meaning of reflexivity based on the reflex? The etymological study derives the three radicals from the same Latin verb, *reflectere*, to "bend again, make something turn." Two meanings emerge, one optical, the other intellectual, the second being, from the Latin period, a metaphorical extension of the first: "to turn one's mind towards" (Badir and Mouratidou 2012, p. 8).

Reflexivity as movement, as flexion, implies that the gaze changes its position. In this regard, the optical etymology pointed out by Mouratidou and Babou is heuristic, because it shows that it is not only a retrospective movement but also a change of perspective. Not only does this change of perspective invite us to question our place in research communication situations, but also to take a closer look at what may sometimes seem of the order of the ephemeral, the anecdotal and the aside. The inclusion of reflexivity at the core of the research process, as a permanent movement and not as a return to an accomplished journey, is of paramount importance for research ethics, respectful of the complexity of individuals and situations. However, this approach is particularly difficult to transcribe into the research text for several reasons.

It is easier to bring to the forefront the recurrences, standards, methods, procedures, of professional training than to integrate the gaps, the adjustments or even the oppositions – sometimes succinct and other times more in-depth – expressed in training programs. These reflective moments suspend, debate and even confront the standards and imperatives set out in training, first and foremost that of efficiency. But how can we grasp them outside the research experience? How can we put them into words along with the pattern of the research text, make them coherent, interpret them, without reducing their variety and scope and without decontextualizing them from the communication situations in which they are set?

The issue from the journal *Études de communication* entitled "*Questions de terrains*" raises these questions relating to the "back and forth between the distance in writing and the intimacy of experience" (Da Lage and Vandiedonck 2002, p. 8). In their introduction, Da Lage and Vandiedonck show the extent to which putting the research experience into written words is not self-evident:

> For the ethnologist, the question comes down to transforming the intimate and infinitesimal experience of an observer–participant into an authoritative textual narrative in/for modern Western culture. The researcher produces its authority through writing. Is any attempt to objectify an experience necessarily a betrayal? The question is no longer so much the articulation between theory and field as the restitution, the translation of field experience into scientific writing. [...] The researcher experiences in writing a back and forth movement between distancing and intimacy of experience. But this relationship undoubtedly varies depending on history or one's individual trajectory: the confrontation with otherness and the discovery, questioning of one's own practices, the response to the "chance" of an order [...]. In other words, does the researcher work "on", "with" or "for" its field? (Da Lage and Vandiedonck 2002, p. 10).

These remarks invite us to question the possible links between writing as a reconfiguration of meaning and the experience of research as an intersubjective experience. A first link involves not excluding ordinary communications (such as the exchanges during coffee breaks while attending the training) from the field of study and not considering the presence of the observer as a bias that should be erased in order to construct "scientific" knowledge. As Le Marec points out, the observables of research are above all communication situations (Le Marec 2002a), which must be taken into account. Back in the introduction, drawing on the works of Le Marec, I stressed the importance of reflexivity in research practice and its consubstantial nature with the elaboration of bodies of knowledge in the human and social sciences. This is why I tried – particularly through the inserts which punctuate this book – to develop reflexivity by questioning my posture, the strategies implemented to be able to observe training programs, my complex relationships with the actors involved in research, and more specifically, with facilitators, etc. Le Marec also explains that reflexivity is not unique to the researcher, but all social actors develop it. How can we account for these multiple and intersecting reflexivities in research writing?

In their chapter entitled *Des savoirs vivants de l'enquête à l'écriture de recherche* (Douyère and Le Marec 2014, pp. 117–140), the authors question what "is erased from research when it is expressed in the written form". For these authors, the standardization processes of scientific writing prioritize results over reflection on the methods for elaborating knowledge with the social actors involved in research. To do this, they suggest experimenting with other forms, notably narrative ones, which make the account of the encounter intelligible, "because the orientation given at the moment of the encounter is not a restriction or a bias, but a characteristic which will shed light on the results" (Douyère and Le Marec 2014, p. 129).

In a research practice, not only is it important to develop reflexivity in relation to the research object, but also to open ourselves up, to welcome, that of social actors. This seems even more important when the researcher observes communication practices. As Jeanneret points out,

> Communication is a reflective practice, not only for researchers but also for the subjects who implement it on a daily basis. Often left unexplained, their ordinary bodies of knowledge in communication are nonetheless a structuring reality (Jeanneret 2012, p. 21).

In an attempt to meet this requirement, I would say that what remains in my text from the reflexivity I perceived among the social actors of research is more fragments than an encompassing approach, something which I find unattainable.

Nevertheless, for these fragments to bring out some *ferments of reflexivity*, I assume my share of subjectivity in their selection and in their account through my research writing. I propose the term "ferments of reflexivity" mirroring the notion of "ferments of narrativity" developed by Philippe Marion. The ferment is a potential story that cannot be completed without the active contribution from the recipient. It is a fragment whose meaning is in some way suspended. For the researcher, this invites us to "differentiate the narrative, as an explicit and affirmed state, from the narrative as a possible dimension in view of a certain configuration of the object observed (whether this is a sign, a message or, more fundamentally, a medium). Narrativity would not only be a result, but would also contain a commissive dimension, that of a potential or a development" (Marion 1997, p. 88). The "ferment of reflexivity" is therefore a captured fragment, interpreted by the text's reader, who can see in it a reflection that reasons and resonates within. In a necessarily incomplete manner, I will report on some of these fragments which seem to contain ferments of reflexivity on the standards promoted within the framework of the professional training programs observed.

Inter-company training courses are presented as places for exchange between peers, moments, even short ones, for breaking away from everyday life at the firm. This is also an argument mentioned by those responsible for these offers. For the director of one of the structures specializing in communication:

INTERVIEW.– "Inter-company training is an opportunity to get your head out of your specialized sphere, to meet other employees from diverse worlds. It is very rewarding from a human point of view, it can encourage networking. Then, it is also a way of freeing oneself from the burdens of the corporate world, of having the feeling of being more in control, with greater leeway".

Not only do trainees exchange business cards and "best practices", but also their doubts, their questions and even their revolts in relation to their structures and the standards they set up. How can we grasp, or at least approach, the reflexivity of social actors involved in training? How can we "reflect the reflection on practices?" (Pineau 2013, p. 9). This is all the more difficult as reflexivity is not inserted in a pattern like training contents are, but can be quite fleeting and reveal itself in small remarks that may seem anodyne, is often played out on the "margins" of the training course (such as coffee breaks and lunch breaks), and is deployed along varied thematic axes.

First, training programs (and even more so, training in public speaking) are places of exposure, where we tell our own stories. It is not insignificant that at the beginning of training, facilitators all insist on the goodwill and confidentiality required for the smooth unfolding of the training. On this point, I actually found myself in a somewhat delicate situation. Before exploiting them for this research project, I deemed it important to send my observation reports to the facilitators who had welcomed me into their training. One of the facilitators reacted to my submission by being surprised to find in my text so many quotes from trainees and so many singular personal remarks. According to her, these quotes only had meaning for those who had experienced the training and writing them contravened the confidentiality rule stated during the training. I told her that she was right, that these quotes could not be decontextualized and had to be understood in the light of the communication situations in which they had been uttered, and that this was precisely one of the complex challenges of research work in my discipline. In my view, reproducing them did not seem to contravene the confidentiality requirement, insofar as in my text, I was planning to anonymize all of the interns' comments. The facilitator told me that we had to be careful not only to mention any names, but also to make sure that no one could be recognized by their working position or firm's name. The reflexivity of social actors is not only difficult to grasp in research writing but its treatment also poses questions which can be described as ethical.

Now, a distinction needs to be drawn between the account of personal experiences and reflexivity on said experiences. For example, in one of the speaking training courses I attended, an intern said that she had already followed a public-speaking training course, but that it had gone badly. The account was not reflective in itself, but the comment she made afterwards was. She explained that it was not "the training contents" which failed her, but the attitude of some of the interns, which she found malicious. This account includes elements of reflection on training as a specific communication situation where participants expose themselves to the gaze and possible criticism of other interns and clearly shows to what extent all learning is situated. Training is perceived not only as an unfolding of knowledge, but also as a complex social interaction, orchestrated by one or more facilitators and produced by all the exchanges within an ephemeral group.

Even though, as I have seen, when they are questioned about their expectations, interns mainly formulate them in terms of "practical" knowledge, "tools" and "methods". This does not necessarily mean that they do not express doubts regarding the standards prescribed in training. I also took part in debates on the feasibility of prescriptions made during training and more generally on the standards for "communicating properly". These scattered reactions from interns are of different natures. Some concern the realm of practical feasibility. For example, one participant found that the recommendations for preparing a speech took too long compared to the little time he had in his daily practice: "but is this only valid for big meetings? We don't have enough time to do this for every public speaking event". Another participant explained that he did not have the financial means to carry out the research prescribed for the diagnosis of the communications plan. Other remarks more fundamentally called into question the conceptions of communication which structure training courses. For example, several interns in public speaking training questioned the separation between form and content: "but how can we work on form without substance?". In strategic communication and planning, the subject around which debates focused the most concerns the standards for evaluating communication. I was particularly engaged in those debates.

The debates which implied a certain reflexivity on standards were especially present in the training course on strategic communication and planning, because as I have seen, these training programs crystallize standards on the professionality of communicators. If I take up the distinction made by Evetts (2003) between professionalism "from within" and professionalism "from above", we could say that above all, the debates crystallized the paradoxes between those two ways of defining and legitimizing the profession. In their conclusion to the book *L'injonction au professionnalisme*, Boussard et al. explain that professional actors are increasingly confronted with:

> Heterogeneous definitions of the work to be accomplished, differentiated conceptions of the missions to be carried out, competing points of view on what professional activity should be. This diversity can be thematized in the form of a disjunction between the definitions of work carried by those who perform it and those expressed by the actors in their environment (Boussard et al. 2010, p. 157).

Many interns shared their difficulties in having the right to participate in the reflection on the strategy of their organization, others pointed out the gap between the injunction to follow procedures and that of placing themselves "under permanent innovation", while others raised the fact that they were asked to use results indicators that did not seem relevant to them. Such debates contribute to fueling critical awareness of the social challenges underlying an activity. They also show to what extent, due to the instrumental conceptions of communication currently circulating, the communication occupations are particularly under tension. This is the observation made by Brulois and Charpentier when they point out the discomfort or even the dismay of internal communicators "torn between the obligations of reporting and their aspiration to devote more time to building connections and meaning within organizations" (Brulois and Charpentier 2014, p. 212). Blanc also uses this expression "torn" to describe another type of tension, relating to temporality:

> Communicators are torn between, on the one hand, a desire to carry out reasoned actions consistent with a long-term strategic aim and, on the other hand, an obligation to achieve short-term results inherent in management rationalization policies based on quantifiable indicators (Blanc 2014, p. 221).

Reflexivity practices involve not only a distancing from the knowledge and postures prescribed in professional training (and more broadly in the socio-economic world) but are themselves producers of knowledge. For Barbier:

> All of these developments actually have one thing in common: they presuppose intellectual activity on the part of trainees or learners on and from the actions or concrete situations in which they are engaged, for the purpose of producing new forms of knowledge and new skills (Barbier 1996, p. 3).

But does this knowledge stem from reflexivity in compliance with the efficacy imperative? For sure, absolutely not.

Bonnet et al., who worked on the training of nurses, clearly show that reflective practices can give rise to a critical vision of the institution and a greater desire to align an individual's own values with professional activity. This is particularly palpable in the nursing profession where conceptions of quality care clash with the imperatives of economic profitability. The authors say:

> An experienced facilitator alerted his colleagues: "we are training time bombs for the services". It is true that professionals

engaged in reflexivity can adopt a more "salient" posture, demand accountability and no longer be satisfied with barely being a performer, a simple worker at the service of a hierarchical or medical authority. But above all, in the name of an expertise whose contours they understand better, they may wish to harmonize their beliefs and values with their daily toil by taking a critical stance on the activity and in relation to the organization they work for (Bonnet et al. 2015, p. 185).

Although it can be reproduced in the research writing only through fragments which, I hope, nonetheless show their ferments, the critical reflexivity of social actors is not specifically engaged in the training programs studied. We could even say that sometimes it becomes a disruptive element which contradicts the rhetoric of guaranteed efficacy.

# 4

# Exemplification, Modeling and Memorization of Instrumented Bodies of Knowledge in Communication

The analysis of the forms of selection, hierarchization and legitimization of BOK in communication shows how short professional training programs in communication call upon bodies of knowledge heteronomous to Information and Communication Sciences, which reflects an instrumental approach to communication, driven by a quest for certainty.

## 4.1. Casuist mediation: the presumed efficacy of practical wisdom

In the introduction to their collective book entitled *Penser par cas*, Passeron and Revel (2005) argue that there are two major histories of case-based thinking: moral, legal and religious casuistry, and clinical approaches in the biological and psychological sciences.

> The moral casuistry of faults developed in the majority of established religions and philosophical moralities, in which the argument is conducted in reference to the authorities, is not the one implemented by the ethics commissions which nowadays seek the means of agreement on medical choices or in the field of genetic experimentation. The "casuistry" of ideal types of actions Max Weber spoke about to characterize the conceptual instrumentation of the comparative historian is neither that of

case studies in the first American sociology, nor that of the Chicago school (Passeron and Revel 2005, p. 17).

From the outset, the authors insist on the diversity of casuistry forms. A case is what happens, arises and raises questions. However, the methods for solving cases are different and do not all depend on the application of a principle.

The "casuist mediation" that I am investing is in line with moral casuistry, defined as the art of case resolution, a method applying a principle in practice. Used for the resolution of *casuum conscientiae*, casuistry is used by religions to study the way in which theological principles can be applied in concrete terms. Casuistry has been developed by the Protestant, Jewish (particularly in the Talmud) and Catholic religions. Back in the 16th century, in the Western world, it became the almost exclusive method of Catholic moral theology. "Cases of conscience" were included in syllabuses and taught using manuals. As I have explained in several publications (Seurrat 2016), the desire to develop concrete solutions for applying principles in practice, to propose to solve cases presented as exemplary, can be apprehended as a contemporary form of moral casuistry. Moral casuistry aims to order the ways in which the principle should be applied, to "make the rule applicable despite the constraints of the occasion" (Cariou 1993, p. 45). The cases treated serve as examples to be imitated under similar circumstances.

> The casuistry method solves the problems posed by concrete action by means of general principles and the study of similar cases. It is based on two principles: the validity of general laws as standards for particular action; the similarity of certain human actions, which makes it possible to transpose the laws of action from one to the other (Hurtubise 1993, p. 243).

Then, there is a shift from the particular to the general, through which the case becomes a generalizable principle of action. This "*étoprudence*" or "spiritual jurisprudence" (Hurtubise 1993, p. 278) aims to guide the practice of the confessor based on the resolution of cases deemed similar and established as action models.

Casuist mediation also has links with Evidence-Based Education, as developed by the "No Child Left Behind" program, launched in the United States in 2001 under the Bush administration. The goal of that program was to reference and to elevate to the rank of "educational method", practices recognized as the most effective. In addition, they were to be made visible on dedicated sites such as "what works".

> In what sense can Evidence-Based Education said to be industrial? This conception of pedagogy favors the use of problem-types, standard solutions, ready-made answers, on the basis of listed cases [...] It is not fortuitous for Evidence-Based Education to be inspired by the innovation introduced two decades earlier into medicine through the intensive use of "banked" cases to help in diagnose and treatment (Mœglin 2016, p. 30).

The case study approach is far from new in education and training. As Petit points out in his article devoted to the case-based approach:

> In another register, that of pedagogy, who has not heard of the tradition of case studies in business schools? The method, invented by the Harvard Business School between 1908 and 1920, invited students to explore at least two types of cases, typical specimen cases, representing the most frequent or extreme situations, instructive albeit rare ones, or a sample chosen at random, whose representative value was of a statistical nature. The former corresponded to cases constructed for the purposes of demonstration, while the latter were taken from real-life situations (Petit 2018, p. 141).

It should be noted that Petit makes a completely different use of case analysis. Depending on the researcher, the case study can be used as a research methodology provided that it is not guided by the search for recurrences, but by the identification of questions, each case should help to clarify:

> We do not put forward exemplary cases of regularities widely observed or illustrating a theory (the famous "school cases") nor exceptional cases for which we would be content to show how they deviate from the rule [...]. In other words, the cases we chose constitute opportunities to move back and forth from the real to the ideal or, rather, from the empirical to formalization (Petit 2018, p. 144).

As the case studies from business schools have a "professionalizing" intent, the cases treated in professional training have to encourage the emergence of "action knowledge".

> Traditionally assimilated to practical skills, hidden knowledge, experiential knowledge, informal knowledge, skills acquired in action, action knowledge or knowledge relating to the transformation of reality gives rise [...] to enunciation and formalization, which tends to strengthen their knowledge status and bring them closer to theoretical bodies of knowledge (Barbier 1996, p. 5).

In this, the casuist approach formalizes situations drawn from practice to establish them as action knowledge, as practical wisdom (*"savoirs prudentiels"*).

By using the expression *"savoirs prudentiels"*, I am drawing on the notion of *phronesis* developed by Aristotle in *Nicomachean Ethics* (Aristotle 1984) and analyzed by Jullien in his *Traité de l'efficacité* (Jullien 1996). The reader will note that "prudential" is the adjective associated with "prudence", the usual translation of the Greek *phronesis* in Latin languages, but which can also be translated as "practical wisdom" or "practical reason". Prudence is a faculty of discernment that enables decision-making. "It is thought to be the mark of a prudent man (a man of practical wisdom) to be able to deliberate well about what is good and expedient for himself (*Nicomachean Ethics*, VI, 5)" (Jullien 1996, p. 21). For Jullien, prudence is a logistical capacity which "fills the perceived need and whose principle is efficacy" (Jullien 1996, p. 22). On the other hand, by using the expression *"savoirs prudentiels"*, I am also referring to the notion of jurisprudence. "In Roman law, the expression *jurisprudence* designates the activity of juriconsults, the interpreters of the norm" (Melin-Soucramanien 2001, p. 199). In its contemporary legal sense:

> We will provide jurisprudence with a procedural definition, exclusive from any ontological assessment: the whole of processes which contribute to guaranteeing the unification of the interpretation of the law given by the courts. This definition leads us to seek jurisprudence, not in the sum of the decisions rendered by the courts, but in those rendered by the courts having the power to impose an interpretation to other courts (Serverin 2003, p. 73).

In the framework we are working on, in this case professional training, the intention is not to formulate a judgment in the legal sense of the term, but to learn how to make decisions based on other cases whose decision-making methods carry authority.

Two forms of casuistry should be differentiated: typical casuistry and "case scenario" casuistry.

> The case is what "falls" [*cadere*], either because it falls short of the prescribed behavioral standard: the case would then be the surprising and irreducible exception made to the norm, the mark of the norm's irregularity; or because it is so adequate that everyone agrees on what to do: the case would then be exemplary of the norm (Boarini 2005, p. 130).

The training courses studied use "typical configurations" more than "case scenarios": the typical configuration corresponds to usual situations in practice, the case is presented as representative of common situations; for their part, "case scenarios" are related to exceptional situations often described as "critical". This distinction often corresponds to the division of training into two levels. This can be seen, for example, in media training offers: level 1 proposes to master "normal" speaking situations in the media, whereas level 2 training offers exercises in more complex or "critical" situations.

This research project led me to refine my reflection on casuist mediation and to discover, in professional training, different modalities for implementing case studies. Here, I will establish three distinctions: the gap between "distant" cases and "proximity" cases; between the cases proposed by the facilitators and those resulting from the experience of trainees and finally, between one-off cases and assessment or "red thread" cases.

The first stage of the casuistic approach is to identify examples from experience which correspond to the goals set by the training program. The cases treated in the training in strategic communication and planning are all presented as "real" cases, whereas those "dramatized" in oral communication training are presented as simulations stemming from action frameworks different from those of trainees. I have already seen that the structure specializing in communication (which has developed "simulations" inspired in other universes such as those of *GIGN* experts, or airline pilots) vindicates the interest of this "transposition" of cases from one professional universe to another. The educational director of the structure also sees an opportunity for the development of this type of offer in augmented reality:

INTERVIEW.– "I think that the evolution of technology will make it possible to create simulations for absolutely crazy communication problems. The idea is really to trick the brain, to put it in specific environments on demand without there being any danger. We risk nothing and ensure that people, through case experience, find their own gaps in their know-how and look for these technologies, to test them. Just like pilots are trained in flight simulators".

This remark clearly shows the link between the three conceptions of mediation: digital technologies would allow for the "increased" deployment (instrumented mediation) of games (playful mediation) based on case studies (casuist mediation).

While the cases treated in public speaking training demonstrate a displacement, those discussed in strategic communication and planning are presented as being the closest to situations that professionals encounter in their daily activity. For this, facilitators insist on the fact that these cases are *recent* and drawn from *real* field experiences. The case must therefore be as close as possible to the daily concerns of trainees. Either these cases are presented as drawn from the experience of facilitators (from their experience as consultants or as communication managers) or the facilitators invite trainees to propose cases from their own activity. However, due to confidentiality reasons, among others, interns do not always contribute "concrete cases" from their organizations, despite the requests from facilitators. In one of the training courses I attended, the facilitator had planned half a study day for case studies contributed by interns. However, only one trainee in nine brought with her the communications plan she was working on. The facilitator was thus obliged to look for supplementary cases she had in stock on her computer to complete the training.

Finally, the cases treated can either be one-off, treated as a common thread or implemented as assessment cases. These three situations do not imply the same claim to generalization. While the one-off case is supposed to embody the resolution of a specific question, common thread cases and assessment cases must represent all the stages of training. The case chosen does not have exemplary value in itself. For Boarini, "the case is first and foremost the story of the case" (Boarini 2005, p. 139). The case cannot be reduced to a fact, but is made up of all the discourses which participate in retelling, problematizing, generalizing and solving it. The question then concerns the case's generalization modalities. It is precisely this question that is at the heart of the collective book *Penser par cas* (Passeron and Revel 2005). How can a singularity make room for a more general reasoning?

> In forms which have been quite diverse throughout the history of knowledge and know-how, "case-based thinking" reveals the logical particularities specific to any reasoning which, placed in front of an observable singularity, chooses to deepen its particular properties to base an argument of more general scope on their description, interpretation or evaluation (Passeron and Revel 2005, p. 285).

It seems that this ideal of the reproducibility of practices can conjure away the anxieties relating to the uncertainty of the professional world, and is part of a certain conception of communication practices, which is something that can be modeled according to a series of typical situations. For Berthelot-Guiet, this desire to master professional communication situations testifies to a "conception of communication as a sense-making process which can fit into analytical frameworks that are reproducible and comparable with one another" (Berthelot-Guiet 2005, p. 125). Communication situations are thus categorized into types, with similar mechanisms. Any negotiation, conflict, or meeting would have similarities that can be identified. As Jeanneret points out, "the development of bodies of knowledge in communication is historically linked to the development of projects for mastering the symbolic universe" (Jeanneret 2008, p. 41).

The cases are most often worked on from index cards distributed by the facilitators. These index cards serve both as a marker for interpretation (stating what questions to be asked) and enable a rise in generality by showing that the same framework should be able to be used for solving and planning actions in different frameworks. At the end of the study of each case, the facilitators reminded us of the usefulness of the index card, and the importance of not missing any stage for elaborating a communications strategy. For example, during the training course I attended at the multi-multi organization, three cases were proposed to take stock of the communications plan: the case of a distribution company, that of an aeronautics company and that of a car manufacturer. For each case, a paragraph of approximately 10 lines, starting with "You are the communications manager" announced the problem to be solved. For the mass distribution company, the challenge was to find "the right way" to turn employees into "ambassadors of sustainable development on a daily basis". In order to solve the case, trainees were invited to define "the communication goals" (without knowing the firm's context), "the targets", "the stakeholders" and "the actions which could make it possible to achieve said goals". After listening to the presentations from the different groups, the facilitator concluded on the importance of structuring the presentation in stages, of not forgetting any "stakeholders" and of setting realistic and measurable goals ("SMART"). The case serves as support for the rise in generality required for issuing recommendations.

---

**A red thread case:** *France Terre d'Asile*

During the training in strategic communication and planning I attended in *grande école* A, the facilitator explained to us that during the three-day training, we were going to work on a "red thread" case, in small groups. He then asked which interns were willing to propose their organization to be the subject of the red thread case. Two interns volunteered: the first worked for the interministerial mission to combat drugs, and the second one for *France Terre d'Asile*. For my part, I joined the *France Terre d'Asile*[1] group. At the end of each training session (two to three times a day), we were invited to meet with our group to work on an index card summarizing the points we had discussed during the session. It is interesting to note that the discussions within this group were especially fruitful because they called into question the validity of those patterns for reflecting on the particular situation of *France Terre d'Asile*. For example, there was a long discussion as to the relevance of talking about "targets" for referring to an organization advocating for the general interest, and about how to qualify "stakeholders". We also debated around the difficulty for a communications manager to deploy a communications strategy if they do not agree with the strategy supported by the direction.

Rather than a "rise in generality", the exchanges within my group operated as a "descent into singularity". Here, the term "descent" is not pejorative, but on the contrary, it conveys the idea that the regular exchanges that we had, through the mediation of the person working there, showed the difficulty of thinking about the communication of organizations within decontextualized frameworks which are nonetheless considered as reproducible.

---

**Box 4.1.** *Case example*

Exchanges regarding the strategic communication of this association led us to question, from a more political point of view, the tensions which could

---

1. Founded in 1970, *France Terre d'Asile* is a French association whose main purpose is to support asylum seekers and defend the right to asylum in France.

emerge between the convictions and the representations of the social role of the association by its employees, the managerial approach to communication and the complex bonds that this association maintains with political power. All things considered, this was truly a case study, not in the sense of the moral casuistry of problem solving for the purposes of building exemplarity but, as Petit points out, by the way in which this case crystallized questions, tensions which may be at work in other associations. The "descent into singularity" enabled "a rise in generality", not to typify the case but to highlight structuring problems.

Whether they are "lag" or "proximity", one-off or "red thread", the cases elaborated are expected to serve as models in professional situations with similar characteristics. The understanding of one case must enable the intelligibility of another. The challenge therefore concerns the reproducibility of practices and the standards governing them. The series of cases will help us argue on the importance of the norm and its communicational efficacy. However, exemplarity is not just an illustration of the norm; it is a complex construction which is also a reinvestment of the norm.

> The normative descriptive enunciation is considered in the light of its perlocutionary function: the enunciation of the typical case constructs the case, as it constructs any similar case that could occur in the future. [...] As a consequence, the case can no longer be illustrated *a priori* of the norm. It is necessarily a reformulation of the norm through the interpretation given to it by members placed in a difficult moral situation (Boarini 2005, p. 149).

Within organizations, it is also possible to see links between the generalization of "banked" cases and a growing trend toward industrial rationalization.

> The triplet case typification/formalization of methods for solving corresponding problems/acquisition and improvement of organizational and individual 'routines' designates a form of cognitive rationalization present in all professional services, either delivered individually or by large organizations. This is at work in the progressive constitution of the personal experience of individual professionals (Gadrey 1994, p. 174).

According to the author, this is expressed in a more systematic and formalized way in the case of large professional organizations whose rationalization logic is reinforced. In the training of their professionals, this leads them to favor the "identification of typified cases, methods and combinations of routines appropriate to the treatment of such cases. The question will obviously arise as to whether, pushed very far, cognitive rationalization and method formalization lead (or not) to an industrial standardization of the work of professionals hired by large organizations" (*id.*).

It is not because "typical" cases are developed and made visible that professional actors will therefore "apply" them systematically in their daily practices. The exchanges of my group around *France Terre d'Asile* were a convincing illustration of this.

The present use of casuistry in professional training can be understood as a practical wisdom mediation process which standardizes socio-professional practices; at the time, it shows that the validation of standards through case studies is not self-evident and that the case study can also be the framework for debates on the difficult application of pre-constructed schemes for thinking about communication.

While professional training particularly highlights knowledge derived from experience ("best practices"), it also involves knowledge presented as "theoretical". It is on these types of knowledge and their modes of presentation and legitimization that I will focus my remarks. As I will see in this chapter, "theory" in professional communication training has little to do with the theoretical approaches that we can mobilize in information and communication sciences and, more broadly, in human and social sciences. More than understanding the complexity of communication phenomena, BOK in communication whose modeling must enable memorization and ease of use, are part of a quest for certainty intended to conjure away the "cybernetics of the imperfect" (Jeanneret 2014, p. 11).

## 4.2. The order of "scholarly" discourses in professional training

As I saw above, "experience" bodies of knowledge play an important role in short professional training. The notices describing training offers all insist on the fact that training proposes "concrete examples", "practical cases", "situational scenarios", etc. However, professional training also highlights what they call "theory". Here, we will not draw a line between "theory" and "practice", but we will examine more closely what training courses call "theory". In this context, we will explore the order of discourses presented as "scholarly" in short professional communication training.

In *The Order of the Discourse*, Foucault posits "that in every society the production of discourse is simultaneously regulated, selected, organized and redistributed by a certain number of procedures whose role is to conjure away its power and its dangers, to master its chance events, to evade its heavy, formidable materiality" (Foucault 1971, p. 10). Examining the order of discourse leads to questioning the way in which knowledge "is put to work, valorized, distributed and in a sense attributed, in a society" (Foucault 1971, p. 19). As Jeanneret points out, "there is no sharing of knowledge which does not establish, explicitly or not, a sharing between bodies of knowledge" (Jeanneret 2005, p. 24). This implies rejecting an overhanging scientificity model, but instead, thinking about the place of "theory" in professional training in connection with the other types of enunciation circulating there, in connection with its specific aims and promises. In point of fact, "it would be naive to think that devices are by nature dedicated to the transmission of knowledge and that their integration into a strategy constitutes a perversion, in short, to believe that there are pure bodies of knowledge and instrumentalized bodies of knowledge" (Jeanneret 2014, p. 157).

The analysis of knowledge instrumentation processes (in the sense of becoming an instrument) is in line with research by Berthelot-Guiet on the use of certain semiotic bodies of knowledge (such as the semiotic square by Greimas) in the field of marketing (Berthelot-Guiet 2005). This perspective invites us to go beyond evaluative logic in order to understand the challenges of selecting, formatting and circulating bodies of knowledge considered as operational. As Moscovici has shown, social knowledge only exists when it is part of a materiality and when it is activated in social communications (Moscovici 1961). Understanding knowledge mediation in the context of training does not mean evaluating it in the light of a certain scientificity, but of trying to understand the regimes involved in its elaboration, circulation and appropriation.

Which bodies of knowledge are presented as "theoretical" in professional communication training programs, and what are the links established between "theoretical knowledge" and "academic knowledge"? The use of the term "theory" in training serves to implicitly qualify bodies of knowledge which do not result from professional experience but encompassing heterogeneous types of knowledge – academic or not – drawn from diverse theoretical frames. This is evidenced by the introductory remarks from various facilitators:

OBSERVATION.– "Let's start by laying out the stages of the communications plan, we will first see it from a theoretical and scholarly point of view, then we will tackle it more in concrete terms". "It's the academic summary that we find in the comms' books; but in real life it's a little different".

"Theory" is contemplated as opposed to practice, as something abstract. Furthermore, theory is defined by the fact of being published; by extension, all the "comms' books" would be representatives of this theory. Even if "theory" seems an unavoidable stage to subsequently legitimize practical knowledge, all the actors interviewed insist on the fact that it should not be abused, but that the right dosage should be found between "theory" and "practice".

For example, in the *Media Acting Guide* from the specialized structure (which is both the documentation provided on a USB key during training and a registered methodology owned by the firm), we can read: "*Learning by doing*, 80% practice + 20% theory = 100% efficacy!". For the structure's educational director, "in general, short training courses aim to contribute methodology. Theory is mainly the method and then there are mainly illustrations, examples, practical cases, activities".

If we consider theory as a set of concepts organized to produce conditions of intelligibility and methodology within a theoretical framework to operationalize it, the emphasis placed in training on "how to" implies that it is not the theoretical frameworks that are introduced and discussed. Indeed, it is not the theories but their *operating* methods which are presented and prescribed as the means for solving and controlling uncertainty in communication.

"Theoretical" knowledge serves not only as a premise and a guarantee for the "practical" knowledge provided in training but also as the place for enunciating the procedures that should be implemented to "master" communication. Invoking "theory" as a premise for allegedly legitimizing expert discourse is not specific to professional training. Regarding this subject, Morillon (who works on the relationships between researchers and communication practitioners) speaks of "the habit of certain practitioners who, with the goal of scientific endorsement, invoke somewhat imprecise or even hackneyed theories" (Morillon 2015, p.170).

For Jeanneret, "the question of knowledge arises at the same time in terms of the new construction of representations and in terms of legitimization of certain forms of knowledge in relation to others" (Jeanneret and Tardy 2005, p. 19). The bibliographies suggested in training and their commentary appear to be ideal moments for identifying the regularities of the order of "theoretical" discourse in short professional training.

The bibliographies, most of the time presented at the end of the training in case the participants wish to *take a step further* or *explore specific aspects*, are quite short (approximately 10 entries in general), and, when the facilitators discuss them, they often focus on the two or three *essential, unavoidable* or *particularly accessible* works. Then, it will not come as a surprise to find numerous practical guides in these bibliographies, some of which are published by training organizations. It is interesting to note that *La boîte à outils du responsable de communication* published by the multi-multi A organization is not only prescribed by the facilitators of this organization but also by the training programs from other structures. After these practical guides, the book which comes up the most is the *Communicator*. In training in strategic communication and planning (whose bibliographies are a little more extensive than in public speaking training programs), two authors, who work on the boundaries between academic and professional writing – who are also mentioned in ICS university training – are the most frequently cited: Libaert (2008, 2011) and Adary and Volatier (2016), whose writings are published by Dunod and who are also facilitators or "experts" in short training courses. When commenting on their bibliography, the facilitators emphasize the utilitarian, even performative, aspect of the recommended works:

OBSERVATION.– "This is the book that I prefer and that I recommend, because there are a lot of practical exercises, I have seen great results". "This book is a florilegium of captivating excerpts which can give you good ideas to hit the mark!". "I recommend two easy-to-read and inexpensive short books: *"Le procès de la communication"* by Philippe Wellhoff which has just been released and Wolton's little book *"Informer n'est pas communiquer"*. "Another good book is the one written by Assaël Adary on evaluation. If you read it, you will know how to make good evaluations of comms' actions". "I preferred to make a real selection rather than give you too long a list. If there's one book you absolutely must have, it's the Communicator. Thierry Libaert is an essential author in communication, in his works there is a good balance between method and practical examples. You don't have to read it from A to Z, but you can pick out what you find interesting. In these works, the digital is present in all the chapters. It is both methodical and above all concrete".

The publications become tools whose practical use predominates. In a similar manner to the kits, they are presented as adjuvants to practice: accessible and flexible adjuvants which should make it easier to grasp the concepts.

The public speaking training facilitator from *grande école* A nonetheless insists on the importance of discriminating information and appropriating the pieces of advice and prescriptions present in this type of book:

OBSERVATION.– "There are a lot of recipe books on oral communication. The drawback of recipe books is that they can make it seem like everything is useful for everyone in every context. But we have to find the piece of advice that suits us, sort it out".

It is also interesting to note that facilitators sometimes comment on the fact that few "academic" works are present in their bibliographies. A facilitator explains it in these terms:

OBSERVATION.– "There are plenty of academic works in communication, but they are somewhat soporific books. These works are a little too stratospheric, the focus is on conceptualization". "Despite their being intellectually riveting, what can we do with them? Not much ... Too bad".

The remarks made during this training reveal to what extent "academic" works are considered as the counter-model of professional training "needs". Such publications are deemed inapplicable, even useless. Such comments particularly struck me, and all the more, considering they were made in the context of training at a university structure.

Although all facilitators do not share this simplified and negative vision of university work, they often explain that there is little room for it in short training courses whose main goal is operational. As a former facilitator from multi-multi A organization points out:

INTERVIEW.– "Short training courses have a pragmatic intention. It would be suspicious if they weren't. You should not put too much emphasis on theoretical knowledge, which could be unwelcome. A friend who has written a thesis told me that he does not include this information in his facilitator resume, because it could work to his disadvantage. Short training does not particularly aim for reflection, because reflection makes you feel insecure".

Through this remark, the facilitator implies that there is no room for uncertainty in short training programs. The "theory" which corresponds to this order of discourse is the one claiming to combat such uncertainty, rather than the one seeking to make people think with it. This is demonstrated, for example, by the expectations of training organizations regarding the updating of their bibliography.

---

**Gift and counter-gift in research: the request to update bibliographies**

As I have already pointed out, my access to observing paying training courses was difficult for several reasons: this market is competitive and the structures could fear that my writings would harm their quest for authority; training takes place in small groups and as a participant, I occupied "a chair" (in training structures, they speak in terms of the number of chairs sold) which could not be sold and finally the fact that an observer could make the interns uncomfortable (knowing that I did not want to hide my status as a researcher working on the subject).

So, I had to find arguments, proposals as a *counter-gift* to remove such reticence and for the structures to accept me within their training programs, which did not work in all cases. For example, over two years I unsuccessfully tried to access training with specialist C. I offered the structure's managers a report on the training followed and then, if they wished, to have an exchange with me. I did not present this as a consulting service; there was no framework or precise goals determined upstream, but in certain cases, it still created an expectation for advice in terms of "improvement" to be made to the training offers.

---

**Box 4.2.** *Request to update bibliographies*

During my discussions with structure managers, line managers or even with facilitators after training, I often mentioned that I was surprised not to see information and communication sciences mentioned in these training courses and I shared my critical opinion regarding the recourse to other theories, particularly in experimental psychology, which I consider to be both reductive and outdated. I slipped from an approach oriented toward analysis (even criticism) to the formulation of judgments. It may seem that more than the criticism of reductionism that I made of these theories, it is their outdated character which most affected my interlocutors. As I will see later, most of the experiments in social psychology mentioned in training date from the 1960s. My interlocutors were interested in more "current" references. I explained to them that, despite its plural character, research in information and communication sciences does not produce this type of modeling. From that moment, apart from certain works on the analysis of enunciation, my proposals seemed to enter into dissonance with the order of discourse governed by the quest for certainty.

## 4.3. The quest for certainty and the scientistic relationship with knowledge

Training programs mainly aim to reduce uncertainty through the predictability of actions. For Bonnet and Galibert, organizations constantly face uncertainty and complexity:

> The concept of organization does not emerge unscathed from these analyses and this perspective. Its predictability, its mastery, its controlled efficacy, so sought after by a management which tries in this respect all strategies and means available, from quick wins to learn management, processes with forms of mutualization, now seem to be questioned in their very essence (Bonnet and Galibert 2016, p. 17).

This desire for action predictability makes it possible "to conjure away the complexity of practices" (Jeanneret 2008, p. 41). This undoubtedly has an impact on knowledge selection and presentation modalities. The quest for certainty appears as the horizon toward which these bodies of knowledge must tend; in other works, the promise they are expected to fulfill. While knowledge resulting from experience and the procedures proposed in training are the subject of debate and clearly show the critical reflexivity of social actors, "theoretical" knowledge remains, for its part, little questioned. On the other hand, the question of the theoretical (and ideological) frameworks in which they were produced is not debated, either.

In his book *The Quest of Certainty*, published in 1929, Dewey analyzes the place of the quest for certainty in the history of ideas. For the philosopher, "the quest for certainty is a quest for a peace which is assured, an object which is unqualified by risk and the shadow of fear which action casts" (Dewey 1929, p. 8). For Dewey, this quest responds to a need for security, in life as in thought:

> Perfect certainty is what man wants. It cannot be found by practical doing or making; these take effect in an uncertain future, and involve peril, the risk of misadventure, frustration and failure. Knowledge, on the other hand, is thought to be concerned with a region of being which is fixed in itself (Dewey 1929, p. 33).

Only theory can be certain, because uncertainty is what governs our daily lives. If we follow Dewey, we understand why the enunciation of certainty is promoted, crystallized, by the enunciation of "theory". For the author, this marks a shift from knowing as aesthetic enjoyment to knowing "as a means of secular control – that is, a method of purposefully introducing changes which will alter the direction of the course of events" (Dewey 1929, p. 100). This craving for mastery echoes the efficacy imperative, insofar as the enunciation of certainty seems to be a *sine qua non* condition for the deployment of the promise of guaranteed efficacy.

A type of media format that is currently popular and increasingly used in professional training illustrates the staging of certainty: the TED talks.

TED stands for "Technology, Entertainment and Design": a series of filmed conferences, organized internationally by "The Sapling Foundation" (an American nonprofit organization) and visible on the site www.ted.com. It is interesting to see that it is technology and entertainment that are highlighted in the name, rather than notions such as "findings" or "knowledge" (TED's slogan is "Ideas worth spreading"). In the title and slogan of TED, several aspects come up: the importance of seduction through entertainment; the ideal of sharing facilitated by digital technologies and the diffusionist model of knowledge. The speakers and conference themes are diverse, but the most viewed TED talks are those delivered by well-known personalities (entrepreneurs, politicians, artists, etc.). For example, we will find TED talks from Bill Clinton, Al Gore, the singer Bono or even Tim Berners-Lee. These videos have, of course, a promotional function for politicians, artists or business leaders who rely on these media formats to promote their ideas and actions and productions.

TED talks are characterized by their short format; they are assimilable to a *mise en abyme* of internships: the very short format (presenting itself as exhaustive) within the already abridged format. They are also characterized by their attractive and entertaining style. Speakers intervene on a stage, challenge the audience and use rhetorical "techniques" to the maximum.

Without claiming to have studied a representative corpus of TED talks, the six TED talks projected during the training courses I attended were staged as a show and shared the expression of certainty and the recourse to knowledge from so-called "hard" sciences. I will take the example of a TED talk which was broadcast at the conclusion of training in strategic communication and planning at *grande école* A. It was a 15-minute video entitled "How do great leaders inspire action?" by Simon Sinek[2], a British consultant, author of books on leadership and motivation. This video is built around a comparison between Apple's "epic" and that of Martin Luther King. Simon Sinek explains what, according to him, are the ingredients for a project's success. The starting point of the argument demonstrates a strong generalization, because the question does not come down to showing the differences between industrial and commercial success and a political vindication but highlighting the key to success for any type of action. The speaker calls out to the audience: "what is your cause, your belief, your difference?". For him, to be "inspiring", you must not talk about material reality but make people adhere to your values. He further elaborates that this is explained by biology and shows diagrams of the cerebral cortex (adding that the part of the brain which controls decisions is also the part which concerns beliefs). For the speaker, you have to talk about your beliefs. He shows the diagram of "the law of diffusion of innovation" and concludes: "what you buy proves what you believe, if your project resonates with the beliefs from the audience, you will succeed".

After watching this video, I explain to the facilitator that I do not agree with the video's content, that I find it too reductive and that I find it quite surprising to compare Apple and Martin Luther King. For the facilitator, this video is especially relevant in its connection to biology. "Researchers have shown that among Apple consumers, the same part of the brain is activated when we talk about Apple and about religion". The TED talk supports the main recommendation of training: "we need to shift towards aspirational communication".

---

2. See: https://www.ted.com/talks/simon_sinek_how_great_leaders_inspire_action?language=fr.

By promising to solve a question in approximately 15 minutes and being anchored in a logic of seduction, TED talks are a convincing example of media formats joining the promise for certainty. This seems to produce a certain type of relationship with "scholarly" knowledge which can be characterized as scientistic. In *Les problèmes théoriques de la vulgarisation scientifique*, Baudouin Jurdant explains that scientism is a certain type of social relationship with knowledge. An ideological posture in response to a social demand, scientism is an ideologically constructed attitude which assumes that "knowledge of the truth" is something achievable.

> The scientistic ideology emerges as a result of the movement generated by a contradiction towards its own resolution, whose essential idea is that knowledge of the truth is possible, no longer in the name of the divine guarantee invoked by Descartes, but in the name of SCIENCE as a singular entity (Jurdant 2009, p. 5).

> Sciences involve a *desire to know* detached from the ideological forms of demand (without which scientific "discovery" could not exist); ideology, on the other hand, is through which this desire is brought back to a social demand, both a requirement for meaning as a practical necessity (Jurdant 2009, p. 39).

Practical necessity and the quest for certainty seem to go hand in hand under the efficacy imperative which governs professional training.

For Tavernier, who works on the recourse to experts as a legitimizing dimension of the political process (and more specifically on the mediatization of expertise), expertise is oriented toward problem resolution, which leads to the production of an imaginary of "science" as a place for the enunciation of "truth" (Tavernier 2012a, pp. 87–109). For the researcher, scientism is not a particular property of science, but rather an attitude from the social and political body toward it. This is why a plural reading is preferable, triggered by situated analyses revealing the "diversity of arenas, actors and rhetorics which participate in scientism" (Tavernier 2012b, p. 12). Jacobi and Schiele also show that it is not the popularization of scientific research itself that leads to scientism, but the way in which scientific results and discourses are treated (Jacobi and Schiele 1988). For Roland Gori (interviewed by Tavernier), in this scientific relationship with knowledge, we find ourselves in a logic of inversion of the protocol for administering proof: "where the emergence of the result and signification produced as a result of such emergence make us forget the experimental protocol and in a broader sense (for human and social sciences), the problematization process which gave birth to these results" (Tavernier 2012c, p. 46). In professional communication training, this erasure of the problematization process and the methods which gave rise to the formalization of such and such explanatory or evaluative communication model is accentuated. This quest for certainty therefore leads to an over-determination of the claim to scientificity by models which are heteronomous to the social sciences.

### 4.4. The neuroscience, experimental psychology and management science triptych

This scientific expectation related to the quest for certainty favors certain types of "scholarly" bodies of knowledge over others. As previously mentioned, the distinction made by Berthelot within the "social sciences" between experimental reason and interpretive reason, between explanation and understanding, is heuristic for thinking about the order of "scholarly" discourses in professional training. The theoretical models invoked are more related to experimental reason and seek to explain, thereby relying on psychosocial experiments, neuroscience or management sciences.

Having an explanatory intention, these models are objectivist in that they aim to construct facts, "attestable and verifiable assertions, independent from the interpretations of each person". This objectification of the social sphere is often accompanied by a quantitative goal, since "only measurement makes it possible to identify strong structures" (Berthelot 2001, p. 218). This quest for certainty leads to taking life sciences as a standard of scientificity, which brings about a form of biologization of communication. For example, for the educational director of a specialized structure:

> INTERVIEW.– "We're going to talk to them about cortisol, oxytocin. It's interesting to frame interpersonal communication at the hormonal level, sometimes it helps to sort things out, to de-dramatize things. But we shouldn't open the door too much, because although it is an interesting subject (there are profiles of participants who are truly fond of it), this could quickly turn into a lecture on hormonal problems in interpersonal relationships. We are not going to talk about research that has been carried out on pheromones, albeit fascinating, due to time constraints and the

requirement for interns to end training better equipped than before they came, at some point we have to decide to shorten contents".

In the words of this educational director, we can clearly see to what extent communication is contemplated as a biological phenomenon. If life sciences are not particularly quoted in training, it is not for their lack of "validity", but because the short training does not leave enough time to fully deploy their knowledge.

In this same naturalizing vein, in public speaking training programs, NLP (Neurolinguistic Programming) has undisputed success. For one of the facilitators from the multi-multi A organization:

OBSERVATION.– "What NLP says is that, in our lives, we will experience events of the same nature. The repetition of these events will program me to react in a certain way to a certain type of event. NLP should help us change data in our personal software. In this programming and re-programming, language will play an essential role. If we program ourselves to fail, we will fail".

The facilitator then invited us to "experiment" with the method by first thinking of a happy memory and then associating it with a precise image, followed by a small gesture that can be done discreetly. "For it to work as a tool, you have to use it, put it in practice. It's absolutely brilliant, as soon as you undergo a stressful situation, you make your gesture and you will project yourself into this pleasant memory".

In order to argue the "method's" performativity, the facilitator insisted on the fact that they practice it on a daily basis:

OBSERVATION.– "I put it in practice before every theater performance or before every training session. And I really noticed a difference the few times I did not take the time to do it". "Let me briefly illustrate this tool's efficacy: I was just about to attend training at EDF, set at the 40th floor of a building and petrified by dizziness. As I knew this beforehand, prior to the event, I projected myself, using the positive visualization tool and I completed the training as if I had been on the ground floor, so powerful is this tool!". "All athletes use these tools to visualize their victory".

We see to what extent the "method's" enunciation is associated with the promise of guaranteed efficacy. Compared to software, individuals must know how to "reprogram" themselves in order to obtain the expected results. In the same vein as NLP, neuroscience currently seems to have greater visibility regarding the circulation of explanatory models of the social fact. Articulated with the social sciences, they seem to add to the promise of certainty those were lacking. Regarding this, we speak of a "cognitivist turn" in the social sciences. In its previous "Personal Development" line of products, *grande école* A offered until 2021 a short program entitled "Neurosciences and the social sciences: increasing individual and collective performance". The presentation of the internship was as follows:

> Neuroscience, articulated with social sciences, is leading to a managerial revolution. It provides new knowledge and new tools for acquiring fluidity in the face of uncertainty, the complexity of globalization, technologies, individuation and loss of meaning. It also helps to strengthen leadership.

It currently offers a training program entitled "Enriching leadership with neuroscience". The "cybernetics of the imperfect" (Jeanneret 2014) which characterizes all communication phenomena must give way to the cybernetics of the perfect.

In the public speaking training I attended at the multi-multi A organization, the introduction to the training course was based on Ned Herrmann's brain preference grid. Ned Herrmann (1922–1999) was an American psychological researcher and author specializing in creativity and teamwork. He developed the Whole Brain model and the HBDI tool (Herrmann Brain Dominance Instrument), which identify and categorize the thinking preferences of individuals. Herrmann worked for many years at General Electric (GE) in the United States, where he was training director. It was there that he was able to develop programs aimed at maintaining or increasing productivity, motivation and creativity in individuals. In *The Creative Brain* (1995), he developed the HBDI model. This grid, which assumes the idea that individuals can be divided depending on the areas of the brain they use the most, invites us to categorize individuals into four types – the factual, the conceptual, the methodical and the sensitive – and to adapt communication strategies to match this categorization. According to the facilitator, "what this diagram shows is that, in order to communicate better, we must vary the modes of communication to address all types of intelligence".

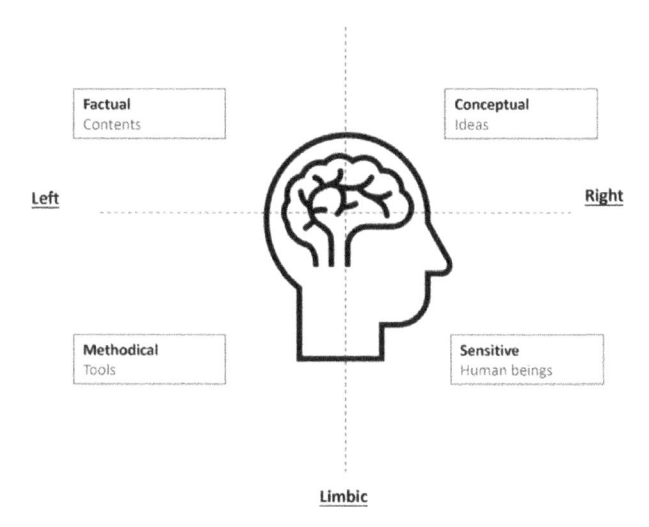

Instrumented Bodies of Knowledge in Communication 159

**Figure 4.1.** *Grid of the HBDI model (inspired by the teaching aids used at the multi-multi A organization). For a color version of this figure, see www.iste.co.uk/seurrat/mediation.zip*

The visual division of a simplified representation of a cortex into four zones which are supposed to correspond to four types of "cerebral preferences" illustrates the role of visual schematization among those who claim to master communication. As if they were similar phenomena, biological vocabulary ("cortical", "limbic") is automatically associated with qualifiers ("sensitive", "factual", "conceptual", "methodical"). These qualifiers should make it possible to identify the preferred methods for communicating effectively with each "type" of personality.

The facilitator then explained how to use this diagram in order to "improve communication and gain impact":

OBSERVATION.– "For the factual, you need to provide figures, facts, precision, results". "For the conceptual, we have to talk about meaning, goals, the future". "For the methodical, we emphasize stages, the process, instructions". "For the sensitive, we talk about the atmosphere, the relationship, we emphasize synergies". "Although subtle, it's terribly effective".

The correct identification of the category in which to place our interlocutor, combined with the implementation of an adapted argumentative strategy, supposedly guarantees the efficacy of communication. Certain training courses are also completely dedicated to the Ned Herrmann model. For example, a training organization offers a training program entitled "Convincing with the Ned Herrmann model". In the "Plus" section of the notice, the facilitator is described as holding a Herrmann certification. Besides, the participants will be able to have their brain preference profile diagnosed for normal situations and for stressful situations. We see to what extent certain "theoretical models" are designed, upstream, according to commodification logic and circulate thanks to labels and other certifications. In the case of Ned Herrmann's model, this was produced while he was working at General Electric and with an explicit objective of improving the productivity of individuals. By focusing on "four brain preferences", the model may not fully capture the diversity of thinking and working styles within a team. I would add that it does not take into account contexts or communication situations. In other words, the behavior and reactions of a person are not parameters that we can predict (or master) with this type of diagram. This example of the use of Ned Hermann's model in professional training undeniably illustrates the fact that the order of scholarly discourse in professional training is not that of research.

These models, borrowing from neuroscience, also coexist with the mention of other research papers, also aiming at naturalizing the social fact, inherited from experimental psychology. One of the most frequently cited research studies in public speaking training programs was authored by Mehrabian (Mehrabian and Ferris 1967 ; Mehrabian and Wiener 1967). Mehrabian is a professor emeritus of psychology at the University of California, Los Angeles (UCLA). At the end of the 1960s, he published the results of two experiments which aimed to study the role of facial expressions in the perception of empathy. For his first study, he asked subjects to listen to nine words (three positive, three neutral and three negative) pronounced with different tones (neutral, positive and negative). For Mehrabian, the nonverbal element is decisive in the perception of empathy (Mehrabian and Wiener 1967). By articulating the results of these two studies, he published figures on the shares that the verbal, the para-verbal and the nonverbal take in the attribution of the degree of empathy. According to the psychologist, 7% of communication is verbal, 38% is para-verbal and 55% is nonverbal.

In addition to the fact that it is possible to debate the methodology of these experiments and their claim to measure communication variables, these results have been widely generalized in the context of public speaking training. In point of fact, these figures are not used to specifically address empathy, but to qualify any communication situation. After briefly introducing Mehrabian's research, but above all, the experiment's results, a facilitator concluded: "this means that first we are seen, then we are heard and eventually we are listened to"; "this does not mean that we neglect the contents, the goal is 7%, but for the 7% to pass, we must remove barriers". In the introduction to training, the goal is to make trainees aware of the importance, even the primacy, of the nonverbal element in any interpersonal communication situation. Psychosocial experimentation seems to be the proof. For the educational director of one of the structures specializing in communication:

> it would be really interesting to recreate social psychology experiments here. Rather than sharing A. Mehrabian's results, we could recreate the experiment during training. It would be really interesting; it would allow us to always be experimenting.

The mastery of nonverbal communication is presented as an ability to adopt conscious, even reflex, behaviors to control our bodily postures and attitudes. Very popular in political communication, the use of nonverbal communication "techniques" claims to transmit a sort of gestures grammar. In his criticism of "communication gurus", Lardellier explains that they claim to

> "decode and decipher what our interlocutors express without their knowledge. But what they propose, above all, is to make communication effective. To this end, they set relations within a strategic, and even ballistic, perspective. Their ideological background, which follows the spirit of the times, is ostensibly liberal: we should now expect yield and profitability from social relations" (Lardellier 2008, p. 118).

In training courses dedicated to communication occupations, there is the same tendency toward mastering communication processes based on modeling promising to control communication strategies. In this context, it is not psychosocial experiments but management sciences that are most frequently evoked. Morillon also observes this supremacy of management sciences in his observations of the relationships between researchers and communication practitioners. For the researcher, the marketing model is omnipresent and structures the approach: "listening to demand, the analysis of needs, the strategy to be adopted, the support plan, the analysis of results and difficulties. Designed for action, it rationalizes and instrumentalizes communication intended to solve problems to achieve the organization's goals" (Morillon 2015, p. 169).

Even if part of research has emancipated from that approach, management sciences were born from a desire to create operational models for organizations. For Berry, who worked on their emergence, "the 1960s: we dreamt of management sciences, which were to decision-makers what ballistics was to artillerymen: an arsenal of concepts and methods enabling the desired goal to be achieved in an almost infallible manner" (Berry 1996, p. 43). However, for the author, such a dream was illusory, because "the postulate of the universality of laws and the transferability of solutions from one place to another cannot be retained, as solutions to management problems are local and ephemeral" (Berry 1996, p. 48). For the researcher, more than decision-making tools, scientific work must provide the means for developing reflection.

In the training in strategic communication and planning, we find a systematic recourse to modeling presented in *Mercator*, such as the "SWOT" model (standing for Strengths, Weaknesses, Opportunities, Threats), the "PESTEL" model for analyzing organizations around six poles (Political, Economic, Social, Technology, Ecology, Legislation), the "AIDA pyramid" (pyramid which defines the stages of a marketing strategy: attracting Attention, eliciting Interest, provoking Desire, inciting Action) or the "Kapferer prism". Certain forms of modeling are also the subject of short, dedicated training courses, for example, the "3 hours flat to analyze a situation using SWOT", proposed as an e-learning course. As it happens with modeling inherited from neuroscience or social psychology, the explanation of the "tool" is accompanied by the promise of performative efficacy:

OBSERVATION.– "PESTEL, a business school tool but which works very well in communication". "If there is one tool that should be used, it is SWOT: it is useful, effective and it is the best known, especially for your marketing director. SWOT is the tool *par excellence*". "SWOT is an excellent tool for summarizing the diagnosis and ensuring a rigorous approach".

A facilitator from *grande école* B school nevertheless insists on the fact that these "tools" must not be used mechanically: "a quick, seemingly effective SWOT can be completely useless. This does not involve simply ticking off stages, but experiencing them all in depth, not mechanically".

We can therefore see that even if similar models are used in educational structures which vindicate differentiating positions, the distinction is made in the way in which the model, described as an obligatory passage, is presented and in the qualification of its intended purpose of use. A necessary part of professional training in strategic communication and planning, SWOT has nonetheless been the subject of numerous criticisms, as evidenced by the literature review tackled by Porter (2001). This article challenges the traditional approach to SWOT analysis (Strengths, Weaknesses, Opportunities, Threats) and highlights that it tends to focus on static lists of internal and external factors, without actually guiding strategic decision-making. Porter suggests adopting a more dynamic and integrated approach, focusing on interactions, with a special emphasis on identifying linkages and potential synergies.

Presented as "specific to communication", the "Kapferer prism" is nevertheless also produced by a business school teacher. The analysis of brand identity proposed by Kapferer, professor at HEC, is based on the confrontation between the brand's substance or content, and its reflection (or projection) toward the consumer. This analysis assumes that it is possible to measure the gap between "perceived identity" and "desired identity".

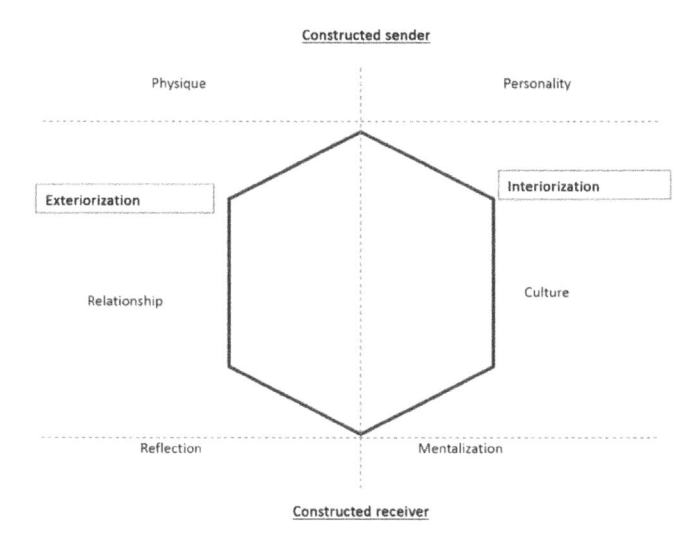

**Figure 4.2.** *Kapferer prism (inspired by the teaching aids of* grande école *A)*

This prism is a model of brand components according to Kapferer. For the latter, the brand is "a being of discourse" whose components must be known to be able to be mastered. According to the author, the physical is constituted by the "objective and salient characteristics which come to mind when we talk about the brand"; "personality" is how the brand talks about its products; the cultural universe corresponds to its values; "mentalization" is for Kapferer "the relationship that the consumer maintains with himself thanks to the brand" and finally, "reflection" is the image that the brand projects of its target. In this modeling (and in the two "poles": constructed sender and recipient), we can perceive links with the enunciation device as it was developed by Verón (1983, pp. 98–120). In addition, we can notice differences in what we could call "psychologization", and therefore, a certain brand naturalization. Even if this modeling has the merit of bringing to light the diversity of "components" (unlike other diagrams circulating during training which establish a binary opposition between "intended identity" and "perceived identity"), we also see that the desire to formalize all these disparate elements under one system contribute more to a desire for mastery, with an explanatory goal rather than a comprehensive one, as evidenced by the article's title: "*Maîtriser l'image de l'entreprise: le prisme d'identité*" (Kapferer 1998, pp. 76–83).

All these models have in common that they constitute "procedural knowledge", that is, sequences of "operations likely to lead to a given class of results" (Barbier 1996, p. 16). In this context, we can argue that certain theories seem more conducive to this schematization perceived as a guarantee of scientificity. As Berthelot-Guiet points out, "theories and models will be selected and over-represented because they have better operational propensities" (Berthelot-Guiet 2005, p. 28).

In training in communication occupations, management sciences offer tools for programming strategic action – here we also find the consequentialist logic of efficacy analyzed by Jullien. Those same tools are invoked to encourage trainees to systematically evaluate their communication actions (in a quantified manner), to measure the "ROI" (return on investment). For Lépine: "the approach to evaluating communication, as a management or strategic steering function, is part of the broader context of the managerial rationalization of organizations whose concrete practices are re-examined with regard to the standards which form their foundation" (Lépine 2014, p. 147). One of the structuring standards that appears in the evaluation is that of efficacy, and, to deploy models for mastering efficacy, we must rely on forms of certainty mediation.

In the words of Bouzon, who worked on advertising design models:

> If human and social sciences are called upon by designers, it is due to the efficacy of models "reduced" to the simplicity of type. The model is at the same time the tool for designing messages, the theoretical reference explaining consumer practices, and undoubtedly one of the factors of change in these practices (Bouzon 2006, p. 142).

We could say that management science models taught in training for communication occupations are both explanatory and injunctions to standardize communication practices in organizations.

Neuroscience, experimental psychology and management sciences may seem to involve different approaches, theoretical and methodological models. However, the search for coherence takes place on other levels: there is correspondence in the aim of mastery and, thereby, in the implementation of explanatory models for "communication".

German has identified this same triptych in communication consulting for museum institutions: the heterogeneous assembly of composite propositions on the epistemological level sharing one same goal – to master communication situations – "nonetheless serves to help it hold together and to make it operational and operating" (German 2017, p. 325).

"Scholarly" bodies of knowledge in communication relate to heteronomous models in the social sciences, and other spheres of discourse than academic works. Training "theory" is also the fruit of knowledge produced by communication agencies with an international dimension and by the training organizations themselves. As I will discuss in the following paragraphs, these "methods" mainly relate to mnemonics.

## 4.5. Theory and memorization: understanding versus mastering?

In his article on the scope and limitations of organizational communication models, Le Moënne (2006) differentiates "technico-practical" models from scientific models as intellectual devices. According to him, technico-practical models are similar to the seamstress's pattern that must be followed to comply with the standard, whereas scientific models are oriented toward the implementation of intelligibility conditions. However, he points out that this distinction is not always clearly stated:

> We can also wonder whether in the different uses of models there is not a confusion of logical levels between technico-practical models (developed in various ways with a view to guiding or anticipating action), and scientific or theoretical models, "simplified" intellectual devices presented as capable of testing certain hypotheses or certain aspects of a theory (Le Moënne 2006, p. 49).

This confusion between technico-practical models and scientific models seems to be at work in professional training, which includes both under the appellation as "theory".

We can distinguish three main types of production instances of technico-practical models presented in training courses: agency models; the models produced by training structures themselves (and presented as "registered methods"); and finally "authorless" models, a proliferation of mnemonic acronyms elaborated by unknown agents. Let us point out that the elaboration conditions of such models – as for the models in management sciences, neuroscience or social psychology seen above – are almost never explained.

As Grignon shows in his research work on the analysis of contemporary reconfigurations of communication expertise (Grignon 2020), to establish their legitimacy in a highly competitive market, communication agencies produce action and evaluation models intended to circulate as widely as possible. As Jeanneret emphasizes, "this explicit modeling work is generally carried out by collectives or professional agents" (Jeanneret 2014, p. 308). The best known in the field of marketing is the Boston Consulting Group (BCG), with its two-dimensional matrix for analyzing the firm's product portfolio.

Two agencies were repeatedly mentioned during the training on strategic communication and planning: Edelman and Occurrence (both specializing in communication evaluation).

On its website, the Edelman agency presents itself in these terms:

Edelman is the agency of Trust An integrated communications agency, Edelman advises and supports its clients in France and internationally by offering data-driven strategies and creative systems that create and fuel the trust of their stakeholders. With 6,000 employees distributed over 60 offices around the world, Edelman puts trust at the service of the reputation, transformation and growth of the largest brands, firms and organizations.

Its claim to produce BOK in communication is based both on its commercial success, particularly at an international scale, and its positioning as the agency incarnating "Trust". As for the communications research and consulting firm Occurrence, it was bought in 2022 by the *IFOP* group, a French leader in opinion research, to strengthen its offer in the evaluation of communication devices. It is fascinating to analyze how these communication agencies intervene in communication training and claim to produce modeling bodies of knowledge for the study of communication. The formalisms produced by the agencies are presented as authoritative knowledge, because they respond to the quest for certainty at the time they make it easy to grasp concepts. For example, the pyramid presented in two training courses delivered at the Edelman agency to reflect upon "the strategic role of influencers" is as follows:

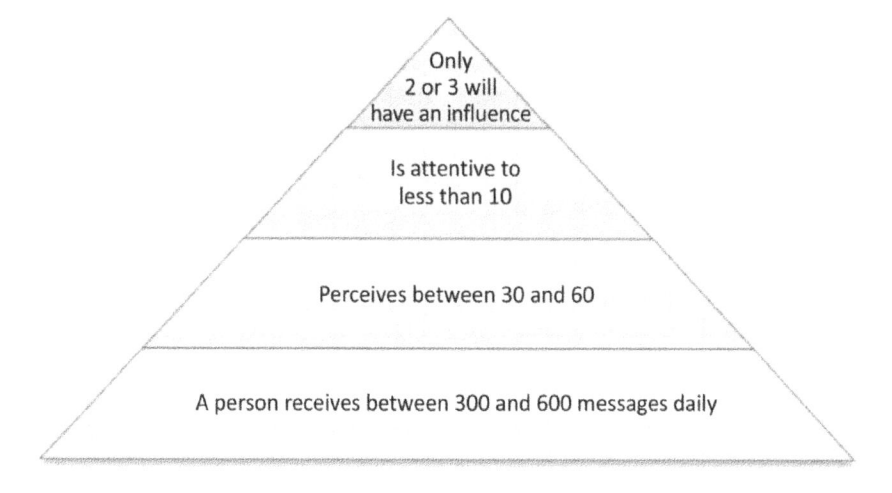

**Figure 4.3.** *Diagram inspired by the facilitator's drawing made during the training in strategic communication and planning at* grande école *B*

First of all, the agency's authority is associated with its notoriety: "you will find this Edelman study on the Web, it is a well-known communications agency". The way in which these figures were developed is never explained; confidence in them is posed as a prerequisite. They must make trainees aware of the importance of knowing how to address "the right people" and "in the right way" to ensure an amplified circulation of their messages. This shows to what extent the desire to master triviality is correlated with the elaboration of formalisms supposed to conjure away complexity. A certain number of formalisms also concern the evaluation of communication (such as those produced by the Occurrence agency). I will delve into these in the chapter dedicated to the question of evaluation.

Agency professionals offer their own training, or participate in the training of other structures to publicize their models. This aims to make them known to communications managers, to find new potential customers. The model must not only be considered in terms of knowledge configuration, but in its advertising function, as promotion for these agencies.

The training structures themselves also produce their own communication models, which enables them to present themselves not only as places for knowledge "transmission" but also as privileged spaces for producing it. For example, under its method registered at the *Institut national de la propriété industrielle (INPI)* and entitled "media-acting", the specialized structure proposes two associated methods: *OARIS* and *CHOC*. Although this method belongs to the firm, its president insists that it was born from the meeting between "a man with a background in dramatic art" and an academic: "In our DNA, there was the link with university research, because we worked with a researcher in social psychology, Jean-Claude Abric, at the Aix-Marseille research laboratory".

Abric (1994, 2008) was a professor of social psychology who founded the social psychology laboratory at the University of Aix-Marseille. His theory of the "central core" focuses on how to differentiate, in social representations, "central elements" from "peripheral elements". By knowing this history of the training structure, we understand why the psychosocial experiments of the 1980s–1990s hold an important place in its training programs.

During the two-day public speaking training course followed in this structure, the first day, led by an actor, was dedicated to the *OARIS* method and the second, led by a journalist, to the *CHOC* method. At first sight, we appreciate the importance of using acronyms to reinforce memory capacity.

*OARIS* is both a reading grid for public communication and a prescription grid for action. According to the facilitator:

OBSERVATION.– "What we call *OARIS* is kind of a checklist to make sure (from a behavioral point of view) you prove to the other person that you are talking to them. In fact, is the theory of communication which is at the heart of training. […] *OARIS* is theoretical in the sense that it is a framework for thought, it is therefore important to remember it".

In the educational document entitled "The media-acting guide" provided on a USB key, the "method" is introduced as follows:

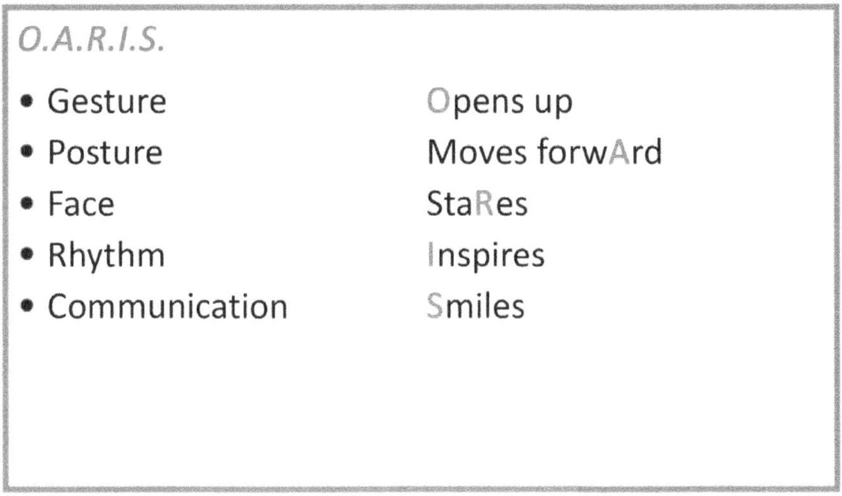

O.A.R.I.S.

- Gesture          Opens up
- Posture          Moves forwArd
- Face             StaRes
- Rhythm           Inspires
- Communication    Smiles

**Figure 4.4.** *OARIS method (inspired by the teaching aids from the specialized organization). For a color version of this figure, see www.iste.co.uk/seurrat/mediation.zip*

Presented as lists of actions to be performed in a certain order, *OARIS* appears as a procedure guaranteeing "the winning swing", that is, the performative efficacy of communication. The visual display of these slideshows embodies the claims of knowledge mediation: the question is to offer "simple", easily memorized knowledge, making it possible to reproduce chains of actions. The acronym's layout along a list with each of the letters in green color must enable the articulation between visualization and memorization. Centered on interpersonal communication and mainly on "nonverbal" communication, this method focuses on "the messenger" and is then associated with a second method, focusing on "the message": the *CHOC* method (taken from the French). This refers to the structuring distinction made in public speaking training between "form" and "content", between the skills of the actor and those of the journalist.

Also relating to a mnemonic acronym summarizing a list, the *CHOC* method is presented as a vector for the performative efficacy of communication. For the journalist–facilitator:

OBSERVATION.– "I'm going to teach you a simple but effective method, it comes down to 4 points: the *CHOC* method.

**Target ("*Cibler*")**: if for example we use the same language on *NRJ* and on *France Culture*, we will make a mistake, we have to know and adapt to our audience. The more we know who we are talking to, the more we change the way we communicate.

**Prioritize ("*Hiérarchiser*")**: what arguments do I have up my sleeve? In a scientific study, researchers demonstrated the notion of a tripod. Over four arguments, the listener gets lost. You have to make choices and accept them.

**Organize ("*Organiser*")**: once I have chosen my arguments, how do I organize them to make them impactful?

**Conclude ("*Conclure*")**: the introduction and conclusion are the strongest points. You have to know how to conclude in a powerful way".

Communication is not approached as a social phenomenon which transforms and produces value, but as an instrument that should be used as best as possible to guarantee the success of its ends. Procedures as lists of tasks to be performed in view of achieving a result are particularly appropriate to enter this mindset.

In its public speaking training, one of the multi-multi organizations offers a tool called the "magic lantern". The use of the term "magical" lets us foresee the performative dimension attributed to this formalism. The aim of the "tool" is presented in these terms by the facilitators: "to structure everything we have seen and not to forget anything, we are going to provide you with a tool: the magic lantern".

The tool has a double aim: the synthesis enabled by its graphic representation and memorization, the two going hand in hand.

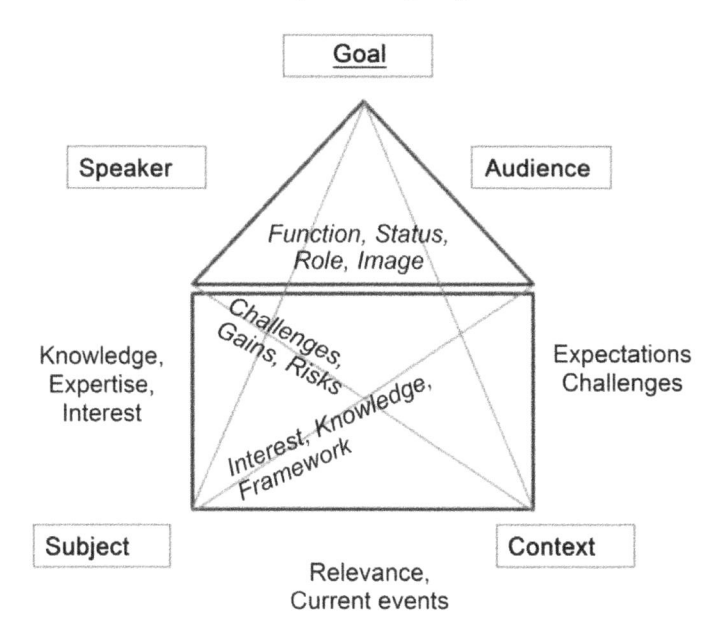

**Figure 4.5.** *"The magic lantern" tool (diagram inspired by the teaching aids from multi-multi A organization)*

Through the arrangement of thinking "in a system", this schematization must enable the arrangement of action following a procedure. Flattening all "communication parameters" would therefore allow us to break free from uncertainty and to gain mastery, that is, power. "Not to forget anything important" and "doing things in order" thus seem to be the two maxims guiding the enunciation of "theory" in professional training.

Mnemonic acronyms constitute a preponderant part of "theory" in training, whether in public speaking training or in strategic communication and planning. While in the cases of *OARIS* and *CHOC*, their origin is mentioned, the majority of cases are "authorless" enunciations, allegedly prominent "in books" or "manuals". An acronym comes up repeatedly in training in strategic communication and planning: the "SMART method".

A facilitator introduces it as follows: "To formulate good goals, we will use what comms' books call the SMART method".

They then project the text below:

| Communication goals should always be **SMART**<br>**S**: Specific<br>**M**: Measurable<br>**A**: Achievable<br>**R**: Realistic<br>**T**: Timed, hierarchized |
| --- |

**Box 4.3.** *SMART method (inspired by the teaching aids from the specialized organization)*

Although its origin is never mentioned in the training courses, we can note that "the SMART method" was introduced by George T. Doran in 1981 when he was president of Management Assistance Programs, a consulting firm based in Coeur d'Alene in the state of Idaho, in the United States. It is based on research by Peter F. Drucker, an American business management consultant. This approach makes it possible to formulate clear and precise goals by focusing on specific, measurable, achievable, relevant and temporal criteria. Let us emphasize that the use of the term "method" largely deviates from the use we can make of it in research. A method is actually a way of conceiving the approach we will implement to make a phenomenon intelligible. The goal here is not to understand communication, but to formalize it, and to format it following a constant concern for efficacy. We will find a florilegium of acronyms, a mixture of prescriptions and promises to master communication:

OBSERVATION.– "A message should always SHINE: Be Specific, Helpful, Immediately Interesting, New, Entertaining". "A message must always be SICAV: *Simple, Imagé, Court, Animé, Vivant*. (Simple, Pictorial, Short, Animated, Lively)". "To avoid loss, the message must be KISS: Keep It Short and Simple". "To avoid forgetting anything important, you need to go through the QQCOQP checklist".

Besides the fact that they demonstrate a reductive conception of communication whose efficacy would be guaranteed by a standardized factory of "messages", these acronyms, through mnemonic purposes, are there to create reflexes, automatisms. Even if they are also stated there, we notice a slight distancing from acronyms in the training in strategic communication and planning proposed at *grande école* A: "Beware, these checklists are a way of not forgetting anything, but they should not kill your creativity".

The intern is caught in a double, almost paradoxical injunction: to conform to procedures and standards, all the while remaining "creative".

All these thought formalisms, which are expected to produce a particular arrangement of action are above all writing formalisms. Taking up Mallarmé's expression "intellectual technologies" (Mallarmé 1945), which the poet uses to qualify the operation of classifying sciences[3], Jack Goody describes, as intellectual technologies, objects which make such classification possible, the ordering of bodies of knowledge. As Bazin observes in his preface, "this does not involve simple modes of presentation of knowledge, but formal matrices which partially determine contents" (Bazin 1979, p. 11). In these multiple formalisms prescribed in training, it is possible to identify matrices for determining contents and strategies, the goal being not to discuss them, but to assimilate them.

In his book *Mnémotechnologies*, Robert (2010) questions the relationships between intellectual technologies, memory and power. Through the use of the subtitle *"Pour une théorie générale critique des technologies intellectuelles"*, the researcher is in line with the work of Jack Goody. However, he wishes to emphasize a less explored dimension, that of memory and its political significance. Organized into four parts (a "general theory" then three "reasons" – graphic, classifying, simulating), the book shows to what extent different formalisms (models, tables, lists, maps, plans and especially computerized tools) organize our relationship to the world and to knowledge. For the author, memory is not only what fixes our relationship with the past, it is "a support for designing projects as well as for managing objects (which can be things, signs or human beings)" (Robert 2010, p. 26). In his chapter devoted to procedures and diagrams, he explains that the procedure is "a work of data recapitulation and organization and of operations capable of giving rise to an 'activation', to a making happen" (Robert 2010, p. 113). In this sense, the list, "starting with the simple

---

3. Mallarmé explains that he considers poetry as a science of language, since "all other sciences have found their denominator – what classifies them – in the intellectual technology equivalent to their classification" (Mallarmé 1945, p. 849).

shopping list we all make, summarizes a set of names/objects, often organizes them according to the rooms of the house (kitchen, bathroom, bedrooms, garage, etc.) and allows us to delegate this doing either to ourselves, or elsewhere and later, to someone else" (Robert 2010, p. 114). We can clearly see the link between writing formalism and prescription. Lists, so present in training, are both programs for the future (to be done when interns return to the firm) and ways of transmitting procedures and thought frameworks to others.

For Robert, we should differentiate "mnemotechnologies" from the "arts of memory" (Robert 2010, pp. 374–376). While the "arts of memory" as practiced in ancient rhetoric are methods for remembering the stages of a speech without having to write them down, "mnemotechnologies" are, on the contrary, inscriptions processes which rely on technologies to externalize memory. According to Robert, "while the arts of memory never remain indifferent to mnemotechnologies, mnemotechnologies are in no way the daughters of the arts of memory" (Robert 2010, p. 375). For the author,

> mnemotechnologies are, strictly speaking, intellectual technologies. The two expressions are therefore equivalent in my eyes, one insists more on the technical dimension of social memory, while the other emphasizes the socially constructed intellectual (architecture) aptitude. In both cases, they (often) give rise and (always) support a management activity in the broad sense (of numbers – human beings, things or signs –, of space, of time, of knowledge, etc.). In both cases, they are caught in an internal dynamic of construction of their regulatory tools (structured/structuring memory) and an external dynamic, an insertion into logistics with considerable political stakes (Robert 2010, p. 383).

In the training courses attended, the goal was not so much to provide technical equipment for externalizing memory but to transmit formalisms for thinking about communication. However, the distinction made by Robert between these two forms of memory is undoubtedly heuristic.

We can therefore see these two forms of relationship to memory in training: acronyms are in line with the "arts of memory" in that they are supports for memorizing a list of tasks, at the time they constitute "formal matrices" which determine thought about communication. Regarding schematic representations such as the "Kapferer prism" or the "magic lantern", these are graphic representations intended to be used by interns to formalize their approach (preparing for public speaking or reviewing a communication strategy) to "better master" communication, to "guarantee" the success of action. The order of discourse of "theory" does not involve conceptualizing the world in view of making it intelligible, but modeling it to make it graspable and conjure away uncertainty. In that sense, to master means to bring – even if this risks simplifying it – communication into a controllable "form". The question of "mastery" is not linked to that of comprehension, but to that of prediction. As Boltanski and Thévenot point out about "the industrial city": "it is in a *mastery* relationship that the state of what is great includes what is small. […]. The empire exercised only comes from the possibility of planning less complex actions, by integrating them into a larger overall plan" (Boltanski and Thévenot 1991, p. 259). Simplifying rather than exposing complexity is precisely the greatest surprise I had regarding the use of "theory" in short professional training.

---

**My astonishment at the place of "theory" in the training followed in two *grandes écoles***

When choosing the structures I was going to observe in terms of professional training, I opted for university structures (even though from an economic point of view, their weight is low in the market). That choice was guided by two reasons: the first was due to the fact that it allowed me to develop a reflection on professional training at university, and the second to the fact that I was applying, I could even say, I was hoping, that I could observe notable differences in the summoning of academic knowledge in training between private structures and university structures. That was not actually the case.

The training program I attended at *grande école* B was, in many respects, the one where the facilitator was the most virulent toward university knowledge (presented as useless and disconnected from reality), and where the prescription of mnemonic acronyms was the most developed. In no way am I generalizing these observations to all the training programs proposed at this *grande école*. As I was able to see, facilitators train for different structures and, as there was no co-construction of training content for inter-company training courses in this structure (the training's contents totally depended on the facilitator).

In broad terms, I could say that trainers were divided into two groups: on the one hand, teacher–researchers who explained during initial (or ongoing) training how different conceptual frameworks allow you to develop critical thinking about communication, and on the other hand, facilitators who prescribed models to better master it. This tension could also be felt within the same master's program.

The case of *grande école* A was a little different. First of all because one of the two training courses was provided by a university professor. However, social science knowledge was not necessarily invoked during that training. While the

> references and allusions made by the facilitator showed an anchoring in a literary culture, communication was presented as a series of techniques (more rhetorical than "nonverbal") rather than as a conceptual domain.
>
> I also had an exchange with two line managers from *grande école* A regarding the low visibility of social sciences in short courses. Among other things, they explained to me that they had to remove a training course called "The digital deciphered by the social sciences" from the prospectus because it did not work. According to them, this is mainly due to the expectations regarding the short format. They added that people who come for professional training are looking for and expect theoretical knowledge, whereas those who come for short training courses want "more directly operational" approaches.

**Box 4.4.** *Questioning the place of "theory" in training*

"Theory" in training can thus be understood as adhering to anticipatory narratives, "projecting their recipient into the future thanks to a methodical account" (Jeanneret 2014, p. 258). This methodical account, embodied by these writing and thought formalisms, can be understood as a "simulacrum"; in other words, "a reconstruction of the instances of communication itself" which is not based "on an observation of communication in action, but on a rationalization which makes it possible to optimize, on an imaginary scene, the way in which it is supposed to take place in a future enriched by professional expertise" (Jeanneret 2014, p. 258).

We can therefore call into question the relevance of these simulacra for training individuals who are increasingly asked to be "adaptable", "flexible" and "creative".

> The fact is that such a "method", whose constant and uniform application generates a sort of mechanical aptitude, is less and less adapted as one rises in the hierarchy of responsibilities and as one leaves the tactical plan for the strategy: the more we manage action as a whole, the greater the faculty of judgment, knowing how to appreciate the particularity of situations we call upon (Jullien 1996, p. 31).

The absence of anthropo-social sciences may be due to the fact that they do not cater to this order of discourse, and they do not comply with these models of scientificity exclusively based on certainty, predictability, mastery and control.

# 5

# Communication in the Face of Evaluation: Efficacy and Extension of the Managerial Model

An injunction made to communication professionals, evaluation guides the way actors act and think about their actions within organizations. Equipped and instrumented, it finally implies a fine-grained approach to mediations, in particular, the mediation of the computerized tools that give it substance.

I emphasized this idea: the communication occupations are increasingly under the control of models inherited from management sciences and marketing. Now, if there is one practice that is insistently prescribed in the managerial conception, it is evaluation. As I will show, the desire to evaluate and measure the "impact" of communication reflects an instrumental conception of communication to which many communication practitioners do not subscribe. Broadly speaking, this extension of the managerial regime has invited me to analyze how it contributes to unthinkable politics.

## 5.1. Evaluation and institutionalization of values

After questioning the links between efficacy and industrialization, efficacy and professionalization, and efficacy and mediation, the question of the links between evaluation and efficacy operates a synthesis of the three movements: the evaluation of mediation – mediation which itself prescribes methods for evaluating communication – is there to guarantee the trainees' professionalism gain. For Tallard, evaluation is accompanied by several challenges: the need for knowledge, (internal and external) control and legitimation; social actors have to show they are concerned about "the efficacy of the devices that they have elaborated[1]". I would also say that evaluation crystallizes conceptions (of "good training" and "good communication"), and through the circulation of evaluation formalisms, helps to institute them.

Evaluation is part of the logic of proof. For the efficacy imperative to be deployed, we must equip ourselves with the appropriate instruments to measure the adequacy between means and ends. Evaluation is also part of the logic of promotion, as it serves to make promises credible and tangible. Finally, evaluation is part of the prescriptive and controlling dimension: prescribing forms of evaluation amounts to prescribing ways of thinking about training and communication. Evaluation in this field of research takes place at a double level: training programs are evaluated, and at the same time they prescribe forms of evaluation of communication which are all forms of communication normalization.

The issue of evaluation leads me to question the growing place of managerial thought as a generalized mode of action (Marti 2015, p. 159), which aims to have the actors internalize performance and mastery standards. Evaluation appears not only as what will prove efficacy, but also as what will reinforce, provide tools and naturalize the efficacy imperative; rather than calling it into question, means are deployed to measure it. "Evaluation is central to the ideal of more effective management: it involves determining what serves as a sign of quality, measuring it, then evaluating this quality and recommending ways to improve it" (Waltzing 2017, p. 28).

How can we conceptualize the question of evaluation? For this, I will rely on the works of John Dewey, as well as those developed in Information and Communication Sciences by Julie Bouchard and Christine Barats, those developed in Educational Sciences by Guy Berger and Jacques Ardoino, and those on the reflections of Alain Desrosières on statistical reason.

---

1. Interview with Michèle Tallard. de Lescure, E. and Vezinatm N. (2017). L'élaboration des règles dans le domaine de la FPC, un mode de construction multi-acteurs. *Sociologies pratiques*, 35, 19.

In his *Theory of Valuation*, Dewey (1939) emphasizes that "evaluation" encompasses the idea of *valuation*, that is, value judgment. Values are central in Dewey's approach, because in collectives, they are not only "what values are held" but also "the means through which they are held" (Bidet et al. 2011, p. 12). The philosopher operates a shift from value as a fact to *evaluation* as an activity. For Dewey, evaluation points to the formation of judgment because it is in these *valuations* considered as facts or behaviors that we find observables:

> The same goes for value judgments: they have implicit propositional content. When we analyze them, we see that they refer both to an existing situation [...] and to a desirable situation that they help to set up by establishing a testable relationship between an end and the activities capable of achieving such end (Bidet et al. 2011, p. 15).

Thinking about the forms and functions of evaluation in our society allows us to question the institutionalization of modes of values. As Dewey explains, "to *cherish* is only a more or less systematic development of what is already present in the act of valuing" (Dewey 1939). The idea of value not only encompasses that of aiming, of wishing, but also that of praising, of mastering. The analysis of evaluation in and during training allows us to question values (what is valued), as well as the modes of control (what we seek to master).

Thinking about the forms of control implemented by evaluation should not, however, lead to having a uniform vision of the evaluation of and during professional training. As Berger and Ardoino (1985) clearly show, there are different ways of carrying out and thinking about evaluation, which invite us to distinguish between different epistemological and ideological groundings. The idea is not to be for or against evaluation, but to draw a distinction between evaluation as a dialectical process of analysis of complexity, and evaluation as control, subject to the logic of proof and the search for conformity.

Barats et al. (2018, pp. 11–23) distinguish five interrelated dimensions in evaluation:

– proceduralization, which corresponds to the development of rules and formal evaluation procedures;

– formalization, which involves the proliferation of written documents which delimit and format the evaluation;

– normalization, through bodies dedicated to the elaboration and dissemination of evaluation standards;

– standardization, involving the production of numerical indicators and their automation;

– publicization of the evaluation processes and results.

These five interrelated dimensions are heuristic not only for thinking about the evaluation of organizations and training programs themselves, but also for evaluating the communication prescribed by those same training courses. The overlapping of those dimensions makes it possible to consider evaluation as a socio-political and socio-economic phenomenon, as well as an organized arrangement of scriptural processes. As we will see in the following pages, evaluation is a procedure based on a certain number of documents falling within a more or less industrialized logic. In this framework, specialized bodies emerge, either for the evaluation of training programs or for the evaluation of communication. This normalization of certain ways of *referring to* and *performing* the evaluation contributes not only to the standardization of practices, but also to the ways of thinking about training and communication. While evaluation is a way of building "values and influence" (Patrin-Leclère and Seurrat 2015, p. 37) over social phenomena (in this case, knowledge mediation and communication), it is also a way of establishing its authority, of publicizing and legitimizing its role as a structuring actor of *triviality*.

In training and, more broadly, in the service economy, evaluation seems to be a necessary step to maintain and strengthen our position in relation to competitors. According to Mayère, in the service economy, it reflects "the transition from a means-oriented obligation to a results obligation" (Mayère 1993, pp. 53–59). For this researcher, "from a legal perspective, services are only subject to a means obligation (with some exceptions), regarding specific points, such as security for architects, or protection of shareholders" (Mayère 1993, pp. 53–59). For Mayère, if the results obligation is delimited for services, this is because the objective elements that it is based on are only partial, or even, inexistent. In fact, the service provider does not master an essential component of the service's successful delivery: participation and engagement from the customer. As a result, there is a shift, or a certain equating, between the guarantee of results and control over service quality.

> In services, even more than in the manufacturing industry, quality management is similar to risk management: a particular risk, conditioned by customer behavior, and which must be avoided by maximizing the chances of a fruitful collaboration. When we are dealing with complex services, such as training, this risk is linked to the diversity of customers/users (Mayère 1993, pp. 53–59).

The words of Mayère allow us to better understand the difficulties and challenges of evaluating training, and also explain why we often speak of the "quality process". Now, which components characterize quality in training? It is not so much the trainee's learning that we seek to evaluate, but the presumed "impact" of training on the firm's economic activity. For Delamotte, the theory of human capital elaborated in the 1960s illustrates the neoclassical theories of rational behavior according to which "the employee seeks to increase productivity, and therefore remuneration, with the help of training" (Delamotte 1993, p. 63). The researcher asserts that the term "investment training" has gradually shifted from the individual in the work collective to the corporate world.

> Training now seems to be integrated into the firm's specific policy which expects results. An analysis of the genesis of training practices reveals that training contents are increasingly linked to economic factors, such as the organization of the mode of production in which business development thrives (Delamotte 1993, p. 64).

This viewpoint is also shared by Léné: in the theory of human capital, education is considered as an investment the individual makes with a view to constituting productive capital (Léné 2005, pp. 91–103).

The presentation of their "quality system" is a necessary part of prospectuses, especially for large training organizations. In its prospectuses and various brochures, one of the multi-multi organizations calls this "the wow effect". As explained on their website: "The Wow effect!" (The Whao, Waoh or Wow effect) is widely documented on the Web. Initially used in relation to product marketing, it also applies to the relationship with the customer. To elicit astonishment, admiration, gratitude and enthusiasm in the customer: that is its challenge".

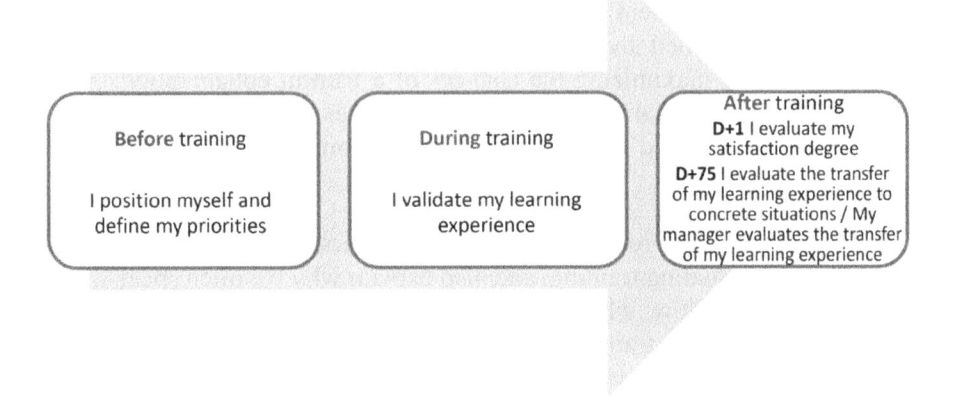

Before training

I position myself and define my priorities

During training

I validate my learning experience

After training
D+1 I evaluate my satisfaction degree
D+75 I evaluate the transfer of my learning experience to concrete situations / My manager evaluates the transfer of my learning experience

**Figure 5.1.** *Showcasing the quality system (inspired by the prospectus from a multi-multi A organization). For a color version of this figure, see www.iste.co.uk/seurrat/mediation.zip*

Evaluation is not only presented as what measures "impact", but is also supposed to "reinforce" it. In this, evaluation is endowed with double power: that of objectifying, measuring and making reality commensurable, as well as acting on it. This action, illustrated using the arrows in the diagram above, is presented as a temporal *continuum* that ignores the plurality of social, communicational and professional situations in which training is undertaken. The evaluation figures are supposed to reveal the performativity of training.

> What lies at the heart of these methods is the question of the effects of certain variables over others. This question only finds meaning in a perspective of action and transformation of the world. What must be done to achieve this goal? The variable summarizes an aim (a social indicator, a convergence criterion set by a treaty), or a means of action of general scope. The variable is designed to be written on a dial on the action man's dashboard (Desrosières 2001, p. 124).

The very end of the "hot" questionnaire sent by the multi-multi A organization (where interns are asked whether they wish to have the questionnaire sent to their manager), is illustrative of this double power conferred on the evaluation, of this conception of evaluation as the preferred tool of instrumental reason:

> We suggest that you ask your manager the same questions you have just answered. This evaluation will be confidential and will not be shared with anyone within your firm. It will give you an outside perspective on the first visible effects of training and fuel the discussion with your manager on possible additional actions to maximize its impact.

To begin with, we can object that the questionnaire method does not apprehend the ways in which training may have impacted the trainee, but its opinion, or at least, what is declared. Furthermore, as a line manager explains, since its transmission depends on the intern's decision, the evaluation by means of a questionnaire intended to "collect" the manager's opinion (which is no less declarative than that of the trainee) is always positive.

INTERVIEW.– "For the cold evaluation, we suggest they get closer to their n+1 to take stock. They may agree or disagree. If they say yes, we contact the manager to find out whether the intern is satisfied. Most of the time, if the employee agrees to contact the manager, it is because the manager is satisfied. Those who let us contact their manager are sure of themselves".

This illustrates the way in which quantitative research through questionnaires is perceived, as an "objective" modality for analyzing reality, despite the fact that questionnaires can only capture representations, judgments made in a context in which interns must value themselves. If the intern responds that the training did not enable them to acquire the targeted skills, this can be considered as a failure, which can also be attributed to them.

As Desrosières and Kott point out, statistics is seen as a valuable objectification tool, but its expected function is to provide relevant results. "The verb *to quantify* is used in a broad sense: it expresses and brings into existence in a numerical form what was previously only expressed through words, not numbers" (Desrosières and Kott 2005, p. 3). For these authors, it is important to define and differentiate to verbs *to quantify* and *to measure* because they are often used synonymously.

The idea of measurement, inspired by the natural sciences, assumes that something real can be 'measured', using realistic metrology. In the case of the social sciences, the immoderate use of the term 'measure' is misleading, shadowing the conventions of quantification. The verb *to quantify*, in its active form (to make a number), implies that there is a series of prior conventions, negotiations, compromises, translations, inscriptions, coding and calculations leading to the setting in numbers (Desrosières and Kott 2005, p. 3).

For these authors, it is necessary to break down the quantification process into two stages: the conventions which guide quantification and measurement. Quantification is not understood as a simple sampling operation, but as a socially and cognitively creative activity. "This not only provides a reflection of the world (usual methodological point of view), but transforms it, by reconfiguring it in a different manner" (Desrosières and Kott 2005, p. 4).

Presented as "neutral" and enabling "performance steering", statistics from training evaluations fully fit into this conception, in the belief that "training effects" may be objectified, as in natural sciences. This does not mean, however, that the "direct" observation of practices would be a more "objective" method, although it shows in what ways the method is associated with the promise of certainty, a promise which contributes to measurement and therefore, to the mastery of complex situations which are nevertheless unsuitable for this type of formalization.

Wanting to measure the "effect" of training on the productivity of interns reflects a fairly deterministic conception of educational mediation. The idea of evaluating the "impact" of an advertisement is a fiction (Berthelot-Guiet 2013), and so is measuring the "productive impact" of training (a fortiori, short, "[non]technical" training). This seems to be a pitfall related to the idea of measuring "effects", an assumption which is nonetheless present in many fields of activity (the media, public systems, managerial policies, etc.).

> The effect is too simply causal and too purely explanatory, excessively produced and too finite, to be able to account for the efficacy at work; its concept is both too dull and too narrow: too dissociated from the overall procedure which made it happen, too flatly result-oriented; it is still too spectacular and

demonstrative (to the point of being able to appear so, as when there is a blatant intention to produce an effect, in music as in poetry, or when we speak of a "nice effect": such effect is too theatrical and technical). In contrast, and closer to its verbal origin (*efficere*: to ensure that), to *effect* (to cause, to bring about) involves an operational dimension, it is what leads to it and makes it effective: it is the effect *in progress* (Jullien 1996, p. 189).

Please note that the processual, gradual, evolving and multidimensional dimension of efficacy cannot be apprehended by devices claiming to isolate variables so as to better measure them.

Even if the evaluation is active, this does not mean that its effects can be guaranteed. Although I was unable to collect the results of the evaluations of the training courses I attended (which clearly shows the extent to which evaluation is a sensitive and strategic subject for organizations), the analysis of questionnaire formalisms makes it possible to discern the standards and conceptions of "quality" at work, a shift from the evaluation of "training effects" to the collection and valorization of trainee satisfaction.

According to Ardoino and Berger (1985), marked by the objectivist illusion, the economic concern for performance pushes us to reduce the evaluative approach to the simple construction of a few standardized indicators.

## 5.2. Evaluation and (willing) (temporary) suspension of reflexivity

The issue of evaluation leads me to question the growing place of managerial thought as a generalized mode of action (Marti 2015, p. 159), which aims to have the actors internalize performance and mastery standards. Evaluation appears not only as what will prove efficacy, but also as what will reinforce, provide tools and naturalize the efficacy imperative; rather than calling it into question, means are deployed to measure it. "Evaluation is central to the ideal of a more effective management: it involves determining what serves as a sign of quality, measuring it, then evaluating such quality and recommending ways to improve it" (Waltzing 2017, p. 28).

As I have seen throughout this text, the prescriptive dimension is central in professional training. Now, if there is a particularly prescribed practice, it is evaluation. In this aspect, the two main types of training analyzed in this research project – communication training seen as a transversal skill and training destined to communication professionals – stand out. In training in public speaking or media training, the evaluation is structured on two levels: following the instructions from facilitators, interns evaluate the performances of each intern, something which is supposed to help them learn how to better evaluate themselves. This contributes to building *valuation* modalities of "good, anchored communication", as I discussed earlier, following a rhetorical efficacy conception. Even when framed by interpretative guidelines, the practice evaluating communication rarely appeals to quantified indicators and is less subject to formalisms than the evaluation of communicative actions from communication professionals.

In strategic communication and planning training, evaluation is oriented towards producing "data", "quantified indicators", the underlying belief being "what cannot be measured cannot be improved".

For Lépine, who has been working on the evaluation of communication for several years, the question of measuring and evaluating communication activities is old, as evidenced by the first articles on advertising efficacy published in the *Cahiers de la publicité*, in the 1960s. For the researcher, this approach is part of a broader context involving the managerial rationality of organizations.

> [These] standards of thought and action which underlie the evaluation approaches of communication professionals have been partially stabilized by borrowing the conceptualizations of management sciences since the mid-1980s in France, while the contributions from Information and Communication Sciences seem to have difficulty finding their place in the reflection and practices of communicators (Lépine 2013, p. 148).

In this conception, the evaluation is always oriented towards the search for economic efficacy, as shown by the descriptions of the offers entitled "Evaluating the efficacy of your communication actions", proposed by all the training organizations which have dedicated lines of products in communication occupations.

The presentation notice for the internship offer "Evaluating your marketing and communication actions" from a multi-multi A organization clearly illustrates the challenges and standards associated with the evaluation of communication.

The training is divided into five stages:

– getting your marketing/communication plan under control;

– choosing your indicators;

– creating your dashboard;

– steering your actions;

– exploiting results effectively.

In the detail of each of these stages, the semantic fields of control, measurement and its indicators are omnipresent. We will find, for example, tasks such as: "Defining your KPIs[2] depending on the nature of goals: notoriety, acquisition, interaction, satisfaction, conversion, etc.", "Defining SMART objectives", "Creating a dashboard". This training offer shows the pre-eminence of marketing models applied to communication and the recurring articulation between measurement, control and the certainty ideal.

By taking up the dimensions identified by Bouchard and Barats, evaluation appears as part of a procedural logic whereby evaluation must be "systematized". This systematization is made possible through the use of instruments and evaluation tools (presented in the form of "essential toolboxes") that the professional must use in order to formalize and standardize the approach. Presented as an essential means for "rationalizing investment choices", evaluation also contributes to the standardization of the professional's action. Diverse as they may be, actions must fit into the procedure's boxes and metrics. Finally, as it happens in the evaluation of training offers, evaluation is above all a mode of publicizing action presented as an essential means for "supporting one's actions in front of one's management". Evaluation also crystallizes the quest for certainty, which was developed in the previous chapter. In the rhetoric of certainty, numbers, "data" and metrics are presented as neutral and reliable management instruments. In the words of Martin-Juchat, who has worked on the place of strategic thinking in communication as seen by agencies, "the

---

2. The acronym KPI stands for key performance indicator.

statistics produced by audience measurement tools (media awareness monitoring, image barometer, etc.) are widely acclaimed as a means for judging the results of a communication policy" (Lépine 2014, p. 58).

As Desrosières explains, "a specter haunts the work of the statistician, that of the reality of the object whose measurements he exhibits. The production and circulation of this work's results cannot be freed from a realistic aim, inspired by the rhetoric of scientific metrology" (Desrosières 1995, p. 23). What is the reality of "communication"? It is not possible to answer this question if we consider communication as a composite, nondeterministic phenomenon governed by the *cybernetics of the imperfect*. Still, this nonresponse fits in poorly with the desire for mastery which governs the efficacy imperative. To banish this uncertainty, it is then necessary to produce devices that will make communication an instrument whose effects can be measured.

As highlighted above, the evaluation of communication in public speaking training is not, at the moment, specifically the subject of metrics. I am purposely using the words "at the moment", because certain actors propose to equip researchers working on communication and training organizations with "neurological sensors" to "measure" the brain activity of a person during an oral presentation. During the 2018 Congress of the International Communication Association (ICA) held in Prague, I was approached by a structure offering this type of equipment. Created in 2005, Imotions[3] is an American company that relies on research in neuroscience (in partnership with Harvard's neuroscience department) offering equipment (sensors and software) enabling the analysis of facial expressions. The structure compares facial expressions from an image database and equips researchers and practitioners with sensors so that they can record the brain "data" of the subjects observed. Its promise lies in the technique's ability to reveal the mechanisms of human behavior, to classify and quantify them.

Currently, in French public speaking training, the evaluation of communication is mainly implemented through a series of interpretative markings (Boutin et al. 2014, pp. 101–129), which correspond to the enunciation of criteria (such as *OARIS* and *CHOC* methods from the specialized structure analyzed in the previous chapter), which guide the evaluation of communication. "Good communication" is communication

---

3. See: www.imotions.com.

that makes good use of this repertoire of techniques. "Communication techniques" are used both to format communication and to evaluate it. As discussed earlier, according to this interpretation frame, logic is structured: separating the criteria for evaluating "content" from the criteria for evaluating "form". This does not mean, however, that training in public speaking or media are not at all grappling with the idea of a quantified evaluation of the "impacts" of speaking in public. For example, during the media training attended as part of "the experts" site, the facilitator explained:

OBSERVATION.– "The first question, before speaking in media, concerns the goal. This goal must be concrete and measurable". "For example, if I talk about experts, my goal will be measured in the number of registrations on the site". "You must translate your goal into something measurable, otherwise you cannot evaluate the impact of your public presentation. If I take the example of the experts site, it can be the number of clicks, the increase in journalists who contact experts, the recruitment of experts, the number of tweets. We must be able to translate this into concrete goals". "For female researchers, this could be the number of times you are cited".

We see that the passage from communication as a social phenomenon to figures supposed to measure its impact is seen, not as a process transforming qualitative questions into numerical indicators, but in terms of translation (as if the social world could be transposed without alteration into metrics). The evaluation of communication is correlated with the idea of measuring its "effects", its "impact". Steering away from this ballistic conception of "impact" has been a desire supported by our discipline for several years, but this posture struggles to circulate more widely. Miège (2003, pp. 113–121) rightly explains that the question of influence was one of the first, if not the first question to have been taken into consideration by researchers and theorists of communication and the media. Made visible by American research embracing the "empirico-functionalist" current, this perspective suitably matched the stimulus-response behaviorist model by Watson.

For Miège, even if they were subsequently criticized in a number of scientific writings, the success of these theories, which (without necessarily being cited) continues to guide the understanding of communication and media, is linked to social demand.

> Whether they accept it or regret it, whether they seek it or consider it unfortunate, researchers and theorists must face the

facts: when it comes to media, the interference between theoretical development and response to "social demands" is not avoidable, and (more than for other areas of social action) the authors' proposals remain marked with the seal of normativity; functionalists, post-functionalists and critics in any case share this same concern (Miège 2003, p. 116).

In professional training, this production of result indicators intended to prove the efficacy of communication is presented as being part of a "social demand" (or more precisely, a request from managers), and appears as an imperative to legitimize the communication function within organizations. This was commented on by one of the facilitators:

OBSERVATION.– "Communication is not a cheerleading and coloring function, it is a strategic function whose impact we must be able to evaluate". "A function worthy of the name must be able to measure its ROI with KPIs and with a DASHBOARD". "Communication should not be an expense, but an investment". "One has to be able to prove what communication is useful for". "The communication function must become a GPS function, and a GPS needs a map and precise indicators to find its way on the map".

Whether encrypted or not, these methods for evaluating communication were hotly debated in the professional training courses I attended. This will not come as a surprise given the fact that evaluation crystallizes the standards prescribed during training. As I emphasized at the end of the second chapter, questioning the efficacy imperative must not make us lose sight of the ordinary reflexivity of social actors on communication. This is particularly true regarding evaluation. Many participants in public speaking training report that it is difficult to evaluate public speaking in different contexts with different goals according to the same criteria. Others point out that it is not easy to evaluate "content" and "form" separately. Furthermore, in training in strategic communication and planning, interns express their doubts with regard to measurement instruments and share their discomfort in the face of the injunction to evaluate everything through numbers. For Lépine, "the evaluation of communication performance does not go smoothly and forces the professional to de-instrumentalize expertise to reframe it reflexively, risking becoming a performance technician" (Lépine 2013, pp. 70–89). This is demonstrated, for example, by the remark of one intern: "The problem in my organization is that they want everything to be measurable, we are obliged to express ourselves in terms of ROI, even if something is not measurable".

Through these remarks, interns express that they are fully aware that these forms of evaluation reduce the complexity of communication. Paradoxically, they will *cope with* it and *play the game* of evaluation. In my opinion, this illustrates what I would call a (willing) (temporary) suspension of critical reflexivity. Coleridge (1817), writer and critic of the early 19th century, explains that the "*willing suspension of disbelief*" is a mental operation by which a reader agrees, for a time, to believe in a story, even when they know that it is fictional. Here I do not use the term "disbelief" which is more suited to fictional frameworks, because it seems to me that it is not disbelief that is suspended, but rather critical reflexivity, the return to ourselves, to our own practice. If I speak of "critical reflexivity", it is to propose a junction between reflexivity and critical distance. The connection between reflexivity and critical distance may seem paradoxical if we consider that reflexivity is a process of coming closer to ourselves and critical distance, a distancing process.

Kuhn (2019) explores the concept of critical thinking as a discursive practice. Kuhn highlights that critical thinking is more than an individual skill, it is a dialogic practice that individuals engage in and attach themselves to. She emphasizes that critical thinking initially manifests interactively, then in an implicitly internalized form with the other. This dynamic conception of critical thinking is suitably articulated with the conception of reflexivity elaborated above (and based on the work of Le Marec).

In my opinion, "critical reflexivity" is characterized both by an analytical return to our own practices and postures, and by a second movement, understanding how these are placed, positioning ourselves in relation to others and participating in social, economic and political life. This complementarity between reflexivity and critical distance was highlighted in an article by Grenier (2015), in which he argued that implementing reflexivity within educational activities can significantly contribute to the educational goals of critical pedagogy.

Why would professional actors be led to suspend their critical reflexivity? To the "suspension of critical reflexivity", I add between brackets the terms "willing" and "temporary", because this suspension is more or less constrained, and the tolerance limit for coping with standards we do not adhere to depends on each individual.

Why do actors follow standards they do not necessarily believe in? I find it would be too simple to suggest that actors have no choice, no matter how strong injunctions may be. This suspension may also be tactical, perceived as necessary to gain action power.

---

**A tactical use of the willing suspension of reflexivity**

During training in strategic communication and planning, one of the speakers, specializing in the evaluation of communication, presented several indicators including Equipub, which proposes to convert articles published about a brand or a firm. A debate was sparked with the participants on the difference between advertising and editorial content. How can an article on a blog be assimilated to an advertisement? The intervener developed a critical discourse regarding this indicator. According to the intervener, we wanted to schematically translate communication into financial data, which is an error, because such a figure does not correspond to reality. For the intervener, this practice is dangerous in that it gives the media the impression that their articles are assimilable to advertising, which opens the door to corruption and confusion between management and editorial roles. He then gave the example of an agency which also invented the "credibility coefficient", which despite being widely used, is false, according to him.

Through these remarks, the intervener not only kept a critical distance, but also engaged in an ethical questioning regarding the production of this type of indicator. However, he concluded his remarks by telling interns: "let me give you a cynical piece of advice, use it in survival mode if you are asked for numbers, but remember that it is false".

This indicates a shift from the question of belief in the reliability of indicators towards the choice to make tactical use of them. Coping with evaluation instruments does not necessarily imply believing in them, but rather knowing how to use them to gain action power.

---

**Box 5.1.** *The willing suspension of reflexivity*

The main goal of the generalized practice of evaluating communication is to give credibility to the communication function, even if the actors directly concerned do not necessarily believe in its veracity. As Lépine et al. explain:

> To justify the financial, human and material investments made by organizations in the development of communication activities, professionals must account for the profits and advantages presumed to result from such investments. The evaluation of communication actions, as well as the methods and tools for measuring their efficacy are central questions in the dynamic for legitimizing the professionalization of communicators (Lépine et al. 2014, p. 142).

The methods and tools for measuring the efficacy of communication are crucial elements for training in communication occupations; they are oriented towards the production of metrics, a production which is reinforced by the use of computerized devices.

### 5.3. Metrics and quantitativist reduction

Evaluation as a procedure is the subject of writing formalisms which clearly highlight the instrumental and logistical conceptions of communication. In this context, as I have already pointed out based on the work of Gardey, sheets are "most often preformatted documents which lead to the restriction and standardization of information transmitted at each stage of a procedure" (Gardey 2008, p. 162).

We witness a reversal: instead of measuring in order to understand, we seek to comprehend what can be measured by operating shifts, flattening the complexity of the social sphere, behind the presumed objectivity of metrics.

If we take the example of an "action-measure sheet" prescribed in one of the training courses in strategic communication and planning, we perceive how the writing formalism produces a thought formalism, marked by a managerial conception of communication.

| Action-Measure Sheet ||
|---|---|
| Action Title: ||
| Date<br>Place | Person in charge |
| Targets | Coordinates |
| Budget ||
| Objective of communication ||
| Basic goals (numbers if possible) | Measuring tools | Results observed |
| 1 |||
| 2 |||
| 3 |||
| 4 |||
| Measuring device ||
| Measuring tools | Remarks |
| Sample | Date | Place |
| Planned budget | Real budget |
| Assessment of the action ||
| Highlights ||
| Difficulties encountered ||
| What needs to be renewed/what can be improved ||

**Table 5.1.** *Action-measure sheet (inspired by the teachings aids from the multi-multi A organization)*

This "action-measure sheet" is a good example of the formalization, in a writing framework, of the consequentialist logic at work behind the efficacy imperative. "Measuring tools" serve as means to judge the plan's suitability (built around quantified goals) for its achievement (the results observed). The sheet must make it possible to formalize the plan and clearly show the outcome expected from the programmed action. It translates the willingness to master, to control in order to "bring means and goals into exact conformity, without doing too much or not enough" (Jullien 1996, p. 67). The sheet is oriented by the logic of proof. It is necessary to be able to demonstrate through a "measuring device" (whose numerical indicators are central) that we can prove the efficacy of the communication and isolate variables as bearers of success. The repetition of the same writing framework as a pattern for successful action contributes to standardizing practices around managerial thought: any budget spent must be justified in relation to the goals set and the results obtained. As Lépine explains, "the goal of measuring these forms of communication makes part of a strictly economic justification: to demonstrate the profitability of the actions undertaken" (Lépine 2013, p. 152).

That goal does not merely involve thinking about the outcome of an action, but about the action in its entirety. All interveners insist on the fact that the programming of measurement must take place upstream, at the stage where communication goals are defined. Ultimately, it is not a question of focusing on what can be measured in an action, but of thinking, upstream, about the action as a method for producing and collecting "objective data".

This tendency to produce instruments intended to isolate the "effects" of communication and to argue that only figures can enter into the logic of proof of well-spent budgets is reinforced by the growing use of software intended to produce metrics on web activities. As Martin-Juchat explains, the pressure for evaluating communication actions has increased over the last 10 years because of shareholders who expect results in terms of corporate visibility in the public sphere.

> From a political viewpoint, the shift towards communication being evaluated through the amount of transactions implemented in the media sphere was possible thanks to IT, which can produce audience statistics, referencing and discursive occurrences. In this regard, the notion of e-reputation associated with the development of digital relationship management tools (so-called social networks) is the symptom of the success of cybernetic thinking dating from the 1940s, which reflects upon communication in terms of transactional efficacy, rather that content quality (Martin-Juchat 2015, p. 67).

A great number of examples of prescriptions in the training in strategic communication and planning illustrate these points. Facilitators and interveners stress the importance of "knowing how to account for our own actions on the web" and teach interns the means to do so. This involves the implementation of different categories of indicators. For an agency director specializing in communication evaluation, and participating in several training structures, "when we talk about efficacy, we talk about impact, so we need to know from the outset the impact on whom". According to that director, the first step is the definition and proper knowledge of the targets. Once we have set our targets, we must question the effect we are looking for on this audience and finally define the indicators for evaluating such an effect.

For the facilitator, it is necessary to differentiate cognitive effects (accompanying the transformation of opinions, making people understand, making people adhere) from conative effects (the transformation of behaviors and attitudes). Then, we must define the thresholds we set to judge whether an action has been successful or not. "A HR manager has an accident rate, he knows whether it is good or bad. And if we have a 0.5 engagement rate on a web campaign, is that good?" He explains that the problem is that not everyone measures the engagement rate in the same way: some measure by the number of *likes*, others the numbers of *shares*, and there are now all the pictograms offered on Facebook. What value should we give them? Besides, what is a favorable article? For this intervener, we must "create a culture of measurement, of reasoned and realistic measurement", which demands establishing reliable indicators. He then presented four families of indicators: resource indicators (time/budget), activity indicators (number and type of actions), audience indicators (number of visitors, engagement rate) and impact indicators (satisfaction, image).

According to another intervener, the most difficult indicators to put in place are audience and impact indicators. This has to be carefully considered upstream:

> OBSERVATION.– "The time we spend doing this, we gain to the power of 10 in efficacy". "And if you don't have the budget to be able to measure every time, act as if you were going to do so when you are planning your action, your action will be significantly more efficient".

The issue of the generalization of evaluation metrics does not only raise the question of the methods governing them (namely, indicator "reliability"), but more broadly, that of the conceptions of communication that these practices establish. As Jeanneret points out, "any computer modeling carries a project of transformation of communication processes, whose nature and extent in no way constitute a fixed grammar" (Jeanneret and Tardy 2005, p. 195). As Mœglin explains, this transformation of communication processes brings about "the tendential reduction of the creative activity to the production of traces, as rudimentary as they may be (number of *likes*, elementary notations, simple manifestations of a geolocalized presence, etc.) […]. And this reduction reinforces the closed circuit diagram of circulation in its pure state" (Mœglin 2015, p. 60).

Grignon further explains this transformation of social and symbolic practices into indicators which can only apprehend semiotized gestures (clicks, shares, posts, etc.). In his analysis of the architext (Grignon 2016) and uses of Google Analytics (architext which is widely recommended in training and the subject of dedicated training), he shows that the signs displayed by Google Analytics can only reflect the uses made, "although it is not what the index directly reveals that the analyst is interested in. There is always more. Behind the textualized reading, the analyst tries to perceive the reader" (Grignon 2015, p. 30). The figure is not there to qualify what it can really measure (the number of clicks, for example), but its claim is greater: there is a conversion of semiotized gestures into reveals of the meaning of social activities; the number of clicks makes it possible to apprehend engagement rates, the number (not the content) of comments, the interest rates, etc. In that sense, "the compilation of gestures from website users enables us to visualize a set of individuals, to shape types of practices, to reconstruct enunciation, to infer actor strategies… It promises access to new, quantified, organized and schematized knowledge about social and cultural phenomena" (Grignon 2015, p. 32). Grignon explains that these "traced" and counted uses are considered as revealing of the "performance" of the website observed. The actors who recommend these evaluations "see in the development of new quantification tools the possible advent of more effective and rigorous communication, with effects that can be reduced to a set of statistical formulas" (Grignon 2015, p. 40).

The interveners in the training courses observed nonetheless insisted on the fact that "measurement must be reasonable", and that "communication cannot do everything". One of the interveners during the training at *grande école* A explained that we must differentiate audience from effect. According to her, the desired effect is to encourage certain behavior or to change mentalities, whereas, on the web, we only measure the interest aroused. However, this shift from number of "clicks" to the notion of interest or engagement is not called into question.

As Desrosières explains, if critical reflexivity seems so difficult to marry with metrics requisitions, this may owe to the fact that a complete explanation of their mode of construction and their content would risk ruining their argumentative efficacy, not only because it would 'reveal' conventions or approximations unsuspected by the user, but quite simply due to 'economic' reasons relating to the course of exchanges, debates, demonstrations in which these statistical arguments find their place (Desrosières 2008, p. 145).

The evaluation instruments prescribed in training courses intended for communication professionals clearly show the extent to which the logic of the "return on investment" is predominant and contributes to transforming communication phenomena into variables that can be isolated, measured and compared for the purposes of controlling uncertainty. Here we find the reflections proposed in the second chapter of this book, on the asymmetrical relationship between the communication function and the marketing function in most organizations. As Lépine has cleverly observed, communication professionals are faced with the injunction to implement "indicators consistent with the quantitative logic for measuring efficacy, inscribed in the tradition of classical and rationalist models developed by the management sciences" (Lépine 2013, p. 149).

## 5.4. Knowledge about communication and managerial regime

Evaluation through measurement is endowed with objectification power. This is demonstrated by the words of the facilitator, for whom measurement is crucial to be able to make trade-offs: "you need data to be able to create objectification"; "it's the problem of subjectivity that drags us down". The question does not involve coping with the complexity of any communication process, but of conjuring it away. We can therefore reflect on the reasons for this quest. They are largely due to the fact that the uncertainty constituting any communication process thwarts managerial reason. "What cannot be measured cannot be improved": this statement from one of the facilitators sharply embodies the role given to evaluation in management logic.

Evaluation is at the heart of the logic for verifying "successful" actions and is presented, in a systemic approach, as an essential step in the *quality circuit* which should foster *permanent improvement*. In training programs, this is demonstrated by the regular recourse to the "Deming wheel".

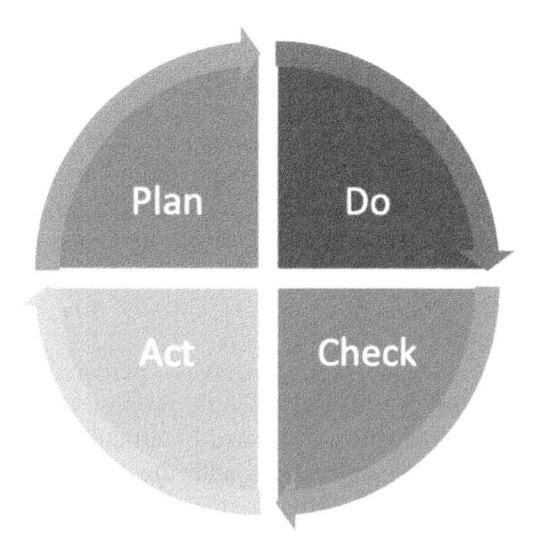

**Figure 5.2.** *PDCA (Plan-Do-Check-Act) cycle (diagram inspired by the teaching aids from grande école B). For a color version of this figure, see www.iste.co.uk/seurrat/mediation.zip*

Also called the "PDCA cycle", this modeling of the four recurring steps (Plan-Do-Check-Act) to perform any action was formalized by Deming (1986), an American statistician. Management consultant and professor of statistics at New York University, he produced his model after observing Japanese companies for several years. Used as a framework for a certain number of certification devices – for example, the ISO 9001 standards – this system is presented as "bringing simplicity into the organization's complexity" (Chardonnet and Thibaudon 2003, p. 60).

This modeling is mainly presented as a fractal device: "in a PDCA we can include other PDCAs inserted in each of the parts, like 'nesting dolls'" (Chardonnet and Thibaudon 2003, p. 50). More than an instrument for supporting action, this modeling has a far greater claim: it is supposed to make it possible to think about the firm in its entirety: "applicable to all levels of the firm where everyone should consider themselves as a small driving wheel and feel like the carrier of the whole firm for the implementation of the firm's major goals" (Chardonnet and Thibaudon 2003, p. 55).

When presenting this modeling during training in *grande école* A, the facilitator explained:

OBSERVATION.– "Measurement and planning are always combined. There is no improvement without measurement and planning. The doctor always starts with the diagnosis (measurement) and then proceeds with the prescription (planning)". He concluded: "It's simple and dates back to the 1950s. The problem is that for a long-time communication wanted to escape this".

This conception of medical diagnosis perceived as a reliable measurement is interesting, because we could propose another conception – that of hermeneutics – gradually constructed by articulating the interpretation of symptoms and having a conversation with the patient. As the intervener emphasized, if communication seems to "resist" this type of modeling, it is precisely because bringing it into this framework amounts to putting aside the creative and uncertain dynamic of triviality. The "Deming wheel" seems to properly illustrate the claim from managerial thought to prescribe, not only ways of doing things, but also ways of thinking about action within organizations, and this through the imposition of cyclical gestures.

In the *Petit bréviaire des idées reçues en management*, Pesqueux (2008) devotes a chapter to deconstructing and uncovering the ideology underlying Deming's wheel model. According to him, the theme of permanent improvement is recurrent in managerial ideology and a systematic reference is made to Deming and his metaphor of the "wheel". For the author, the "process" approach inherent in it – but which nonetheless dates from the 1950s – is so dominant that it was retained as the basis for the ISO 9000 standard in the early 2000s. For Pesqueux (2008, p .5), "agent psychology is limited to obedience, insofar as the contributions from the instrument (and not only the principles) are taken for granted and considered as the programmer of their behavior". Furthermore, he also emphasizes that this model is imbued with a conception of certainty, in that it presents itself as "an infallible procedure". He links this conception of certainty with a conception of efficacy, "measured as a result of the gap between the ideal model and the fruits of direct action on the world" (p. 7). It is interesting to note that in order to show that this conception of efficacy is cultural, Pesqueux also draws on the thought about efficacy from Jullien.

The work of Boussard (2008, p. 84), which focuses on the sociology of management, arrives at this observation: "the managerial logo has become hegemonic". For the researcher, management has become an indisputable modality for governing any form of collective action: "it is the international standard, the model with which everyone seeks to align" (Boussard 2008, p. 80). For Boussard, the managerial ideal is constructed according to three principles: mastery, performance and rationality. We can therefore detect close links between industrialist thought and the managerial logic. In the second part of her book, the researcher warns that we must not neglect the existing gaps between the prescription of managerial logic and the "real behavior" of organizations. Just as the prescriptions made in communication training studied for this research project cannot give rise to strict and systematic application, the managerial logo encounters, if not opposition, at least some forms of resistance or adjustment.

This observation of the hegemonic aim of managerial thought, which meets the plurality of practices of actors and institutions, is shared by a certain number of researchers in Information and Communication Sciences, who have already been quoted in the previous pages. These researchers work on different subjects, with varying research perspectives, which reveals the interest in bringing these approaches together.

Several researchers who work on organizational communication (in particular, Martin-Juchat and Lépine) question the growing predominance of marketing models and practices applied to communication and show how this managerial logic produces difficulties for the professional actors of communication, who struggle to find their place within organizations and think about their role. Grignon's work on communication expertise shows the interest in exploring the devices which equip this managerial thought. Marti's work is oriented from the perspective of analysis of market mediations and shows the way in which the "semiotic management" of brands is elaborated. Finally, German's thesis clearly shows that this managerial thought does not only apply to private firms, but also affects the configuration practices of museum institutions, among others.

Finally, the work of Robert questions the links between IT and the managerization of society.

> Managerization refers to a logic of the management system withdrawing into itself: there is no longer any exteriority. It then becomes what I call a tool of truth. It closes the conditions for discussion, the very possibility of discussing. At the risk of becoming structuring, opposition arises between the

managerization logic and that of democracy. It would be wrong to believe that one is political while the other is not. These are two different political logics, in competition with one another and, contrary to what we like to say, the second one seems less inherent in Information and Communication Technologies (ICTs) and the digital world than the first one. In other words, ICTs are less likely to reconfigure the space of democracy than to work on its logic in depth on the basis of managerization (Robert 2018, p. 293).

By presenting itself as relying on trustworthy "data", rigorous procedures and control instruments, the strength of managerization claims to neutralize conflict, by passing off measurement devices which are not devoid of political conceptions as simple "tools" for improvement.

These research works, so diverse in terms of postures, objects and methods of analysis, clearly show how strongly the question of the extension of the managerial model can become a structuring axis for research in Information and Communication Sciences. But managerization is not an external object that the researcher analyzes: the teacher–researcher is confronted with it on a daily basis. If communication professionals find themselves in an uncomfortable position with regard to the extension of managerial rationality, we can say that teacher–researchers (and, more broadly, all university staff) can also feel immersed in such discomfort.

# Conclusion

# Elements for a Sociopolitics of Bodies of Knowledge in Communication

Instrumentalization under the efficacy criterion turns knowledge mediation into a functional resource; under the power criterion, it engages symbolic operativeness to reserve force; under the value criterion, it exploits the force of representation for the benefit of hegemony (Jeanneret 2014, p. 158).

As I was able to see, the conceptions of professionalism particularly raise questions with regard to communication occupations. Indeed, they are crossed by paradoxical injunctions and must increasingly prove their legitimacy, by aligning themselves with managerial standards.

If I take up the quote from Jeanneret placed at the opening of this conclusion, knowledge mediation in professional communication training is presented as "a functional resource" which must respond to a need: the quest for greater professional efficacy among trainees. As I have seen (and even more markedly for training in communication occupations), this quest for efficacy is a quest for power, an attempt to "reserve strength" to establish our authority. Under the guise of practical knowledge, the "useful", the "operational", the production and visibility of certain values in communication are at stake. These representations benefit a certain hegemony which sees in communication a series of techniques and procedures to be mastered, a component which could be isolated, as well as logistics to be evaluated, whose "impact" must be measurable. As Jeanneret points out, "the development of BOK in communication is historically linked to the development of projects for mastering the symbolic universe"

(Jeanneret 2014, p. 41). Bodies of knowledge mediated in short professional training are considered as tools at the service of the quest for efficacy. These training systems can be understood as places of choice, valorization, distribution and attribution of bodies of knowledge (Foucault 1969) and the values associated with them.

This book should contribute to understanding the trivialization of instrumental conceptions of communication in organizations. In the quest for efficacy, more than comprehending the complexity of communication phenomena, the question involves being convinced of our power to act through and upon communication. The communicational claims of training programs are built upon a "how to" which must attribute a communicative "power to do", which allegedly confers social power.

The goal of this book is not to make a radical critique of the efficacy imperative, but to question its primacy, to disclose how it contributes to erasing values other than economic ones. The focus on the means contributes to putting aside the question of the ends, to abandoning controversies, divergences of conceptions in favor of a managerial logic which neutralizes[1] conflict. While the field of professional training practices seems to be a heuristic field of research for investigating questions that affect our society, I believe that this research also raises broader questions. This is evidenced by the links that I was able to highlight thanks to the multiple works of young researchers which do not focus on professional training but on expertise in agencies (Grignon 2020), museum communication (German 2017), managerial communication (Allein 2017), professional journals (Abid-Dalençon 2022), etc. Here, I will address some questions that this book seems to have opened up.

The first is part of the work carried out by researchers from the RESIPROC network on the professionalization of communicators and deals with problems relating to the recognition of these professions. Training courses for communicators are presented as places for strengthening this professionalism in tension, as adjuvants to reinforce the imperatives which govern their professionality. Communication professionals are expected to become involved in the firm's "strategy" at the time communication is

---

1. In his course at the *Collège de France* on the "Neutral", Roland Barthes indicated that "neutral is any inflection which avoids or thwarts the paradigmatic, oppositional structure of meaning, and therefore aims at the suspension of the conflicting data of discourse" (Barthes 1978, p. 31).

reduced to the level of a logistical tool which leans on marketing. On the other hand, the question of the conceptions of professionality in communication occupations also raises that of the place left to the social bond under managerial logic. As Lépine et al. point out in the conclusion of the book *Acteurs de la communication des entreprises et organisations, pratiques et perspectives*:

> "what is left of the social bond and the creation of meaning in organizations when the action is structured towards a purpose – economic performance – integrating a promise of social progress which constitutes a belief contemporaries have amply decomposed, but we ask communicators to perpetuate?" (Lépine et al. 2014, p. 230).

In my opinion, a vivid question arises as to the modalities according to which we think about university training in information and communication sciences. How and to what extent can we articulate the requirement for professionalization and the concern for people and the complexity of social situations?

While this research project highlighted the conceptions of "effective" knowledge mediation, I was also able to see to what extent the conceptions of mediation and those of communication are interdependent. As Jeanneret stresses, "the claims formulated by the various professional actors and in the texts of professionalists are never completely autonomous in relation to the conceptions of communication which circulate in the media and in larger mediation instances (teaching, public debates, cinema, etc.)" (Jeanneret 2014, p. 312). This invites us to articulate the epistemological questions which drive our discipline with the consideration of the conceptions of communication which circulate in our society and which structure a number of social intervention devices. This engages our responsibilities as researchers and teachers taking part in the development, circulation and operationalization of knowledge in communication. As Berthelot emphasizes:

> "questioning the conditions of scientificity of these disciplines involves not only analyzing their knowledge system with regard to 'higher' normative criteria, but symmetrically calling into question these criteria in their grounds and their legitimacy and transforming these normative injunctions into objects of analysis" (Berthelot 2001, p. 250).

This leads me to a larger reflection: what is the production of knowledge in the social sciences supposed to bring to society, on the way in which knowledge "is put to work, valorized, distributed, and in a sense attributed, in a society?" (Foucault 1971, p. 19). I was able to see that, within the framework of the efficacy imperative, the goal is less to understand than to know how to master, less to know how to think than to know how to manage, less to think about frameworks than to conform to them. It therefore appears that the efficacy imperative contributes to reinforcing what I propose to call the (willing) (temporary) suspension of critical reflexivity. This *order of discourse* is not, however, the only one. I was able to observe, through various remarks from interns and also during different collaboration experiences with professional actors, that there is a demand, an expectation, a concern for the complexity and most importantly, a reflexivity among actors. As Le Marec observes, "in the field, the researcher cannot master the meaning of communication situations, which involve actors other than the researcher, and whose overall sense cannot be claimed by only one of the parties" (Le Marec 2002a, p. 19). This implies reflection on the places, modalities, frameworks and forms of valorization through which we can contribute to developing these reflexive exchanges between researchers in the human and social sciences and professional actors.

In an article from *Cahiers du numérique*, Morillon et al. (2018) postulate:

> "that an epistemological tension is likely to explain, at least in part, this situation: while practitioners are looking for predictive and functionalist models, researchers, from a distanced and comprehensive perspective, favor interactionist and constructivist epistemologies, sometimes against a critical posture backdrop".

They then suggest thinking about "the opportunities for adopting constitutive approaches in order to reduce this tension" (Morillon et al. 2018, p. 156). For these authors, on the one hand, there are not many "institutionalized interfaces" for researchers and communication practitioners to meet and, on the other hand, the "socio-economic pressure tends to decrease the time spent in firms on activities deemed not immediately productive" (Morillon et al. 2018, p. 157). This joins the questioning of this book on what the efficacy imperative does to the knowledge mediation in communication: it allows us to sort between knowledge judged to be operational in a logic of productivity and knowledge deemed ineffective. However, according to these researchers, this is above all related to an epistemological tension due to antagonistic conceptions of communication:

the search for predictive models based on a functionalist conception does not get along with the "multidimensional explanatory models" from anthropo-social sciences. Researchers then seek to identify approaches that may help reduce such tension.

I share this desire to intensify the links between researchers and communication practitioners, because these links are questioned not only in their modalities but also in their aims. Gryspeerdt (2004) observes that in our discipline, there is a "gap" between researchers and practitioners, a gap which is not only due to the fact that our approaches do not correspond to an instrumental conception of communication, but also because researchers have certain conceptions – sometimes even radical ones – of the corporate world. Social representations are therefore not only those of practitioners in relation to researchers, but also those of researchers toward economic actors.

The involvement of researchers in the field, as in the context of "action research" or "research and development" (R&D), enables researchers to experiment with aspects having remained unknown to them until then. For example, during our ManEGe R&D program (Labelle and Seurrat 2012), Labelle and I faced the difficulty of implementing, within the constraints relating to the coding of *gameplay* of a *serious game*, the plural conceptions of the debate on the energy sector which we desired to "bring into play". In the corpus analysis of *serious games*, we highlighted the mechanistic conceptions of the social relationships at work in these devices. By participating, in conjunction with players in the sector, in the manufacturing of a device, we found it challenging to integrate the complexity we wished to maintain with the code mechanics. As Grignon (2020) explains looking back on his thesis experience in the corporate world:

> It was by being subjected to annual evaluations myself that I understood the logic of competition between teams and employees. It is by multiplying "roles" that I grasped the image and reputation games that prevail in this type of structure. It was by increasing the number of late nights at work that I was able to experience professional solidarity. It was by being subject to the systematic monitoring of activities that I was able to grasp the determinants of practices which I observed with a sometimes-ironic distance, or the tricks that enable consultants to respond to the contradictory injunctions made upon them... Placing oneself "in the shoes" of the actors does not amount to speaking at their place or speaking for them. It is seeking to

understand what one's individual experience can reveal from the field investigated, without making it an emblem of the situations experienced by everyone.

However, the approaches proposed by Morillon et al. (2018) to "reduce this tension" seem to relate to a certain conception of information and communication sciences which can be questioned. These researchers put forward approaches referring to *Organizational Communication* theories (Putnam and Nicotera 2009) and the so-called *Communicative Constitution of Organizations* (Ashcraft et al. 2009). In these approaches, "attention is paid to the way in which the members of the organization act and express themselves, produce, negotiate and accept the rules of the organizational 'game' in a dynamic field of constraints" (Morillon et al. 2018, p. 163). Although presented as multidimensional, these approaches seem to be particularly anchored in an interactionist model which fails to take into account the question of mediations (which are not only social and organizational). In addition, they are anchored in a "comprehensive" approach and hardly raise sociopolitical questions (in particular, those relating to conceptions of communication).

Wishing to "solve misunderstandings" (Morillon et al. 2018, p. 161) may imply that there are adjustments or negotiations to be made instead of encouraging a substantive debate on sociopolitical conceptions of communication. For these authors, "the adoption of approaches satisfying research and practice issues could contribute to the recognition, legitimization and visibility of the discipline across various scientific, professional and social spaces" (Morillon et al. 2018, p. 173). As the authors point out, there are more and more practitioners

> "confronted with the dynamism of contexts, the networked fragmentation of organizations, the diversity and qualifications of actors, as well as the 'crisis' of the mechanistic paradigm and the relative efficacy of predictive models, which seek new ways of thinking and apprehending their practices. To improve the 'factory' of their activities, to obtain a detailed analysis of significant phenomena, to open up perspectives of thought and action, they are gradually interested in other approaches and multidimensional explanatory models, sometimes critical ones" (Morillon et al. 2018, p. 162).

However, it is precisely the aim of improving the "factory" of their activities which is not called into question. The activity is not questioned in terms of its meaning and purpose; optimization is always the horizon of thought.

This tendency to emphasize optimization to the detriment of reflection on purposes seems to be reinforced by the increasing digitalization of professional training. Although it grants access to professional training for a larger number of interns, it also has two main limitations which engage both our relationship to knowledge and our relationship to others. The first concerns the growing use of online modules, which mainly leads to an increasingly strong modularization of "brick" content. Modularization, which means that the time frames within the same training program are increasingly reduced, also leads to a stronger division (and isolation) of bodies of knowledge, and to the primacy of schematic knowledge, which is better suited to mediation in short temporalities. The second limitation concerns the place of socialization, peer learning and the dialogical dimension of critical reflexivity. The "individualization" of remote training can lead to the trainee's isolation. Our research has shown that professional training interns particularly appreciate sociability and informal exchanges, and that critical reflexivity, a source of emancipatory knowledge, is the fruit of these exchanges. Finally, the recent development of training using content generation tools based on artificial intelligence (AI) shows that it is not a question of analyzing these technological transformations from a distance and reflecting on the ends we associate with these new means, but of learning to master them with a view to delegating tasks and reducing the time taken to accomplish them. As Andler (2023) shows, human intelligence cannot be reduced to a sum of capabilities and to the resolution of problems, even complex ones.

# References

Abid-Dalençon, A. (2022). Genèse et métamorphoses de la presse professionnelle en communication. PhD Thesis, Université Paris Sorbonne, Paris.

Abric, J.-C. (1994). *Pratiques sociales et représentations*. PUF, Paris.

Abric, J.-C. (2008). *Psychologie de la communication : théories et méthodes*. Armand Colin, Paris.

Adary, A. and Volatier, B. (2016). *Évaluer vos actions de communication. Mesurer pour gagner en efficacité*, 2nd edition. Dunod, Paris.

Allein, M. (2017). Les enjeux symboliques et organisationnels de la communication portée par les managers : sens, consensus et dissensus dans la communication managériale. PhD Thesis, Université Paris Sorbonne Celsa, Paris.

Alter, N. (1996). *Sociologie de l'entreprise et de l'innovation*. PUF, Paris.

Amossy, R. (2010). *La présentation de soi. Ethos et identité verbale*. PUF, Paris.

Andler D. (2023). *Intelligence artificielle, intelligence humaine : la double énigme*. Gallimard, Paris.

Andonova, Y. (2015). Approche critique des injonctions à la créativité : relations entre secteur culturel et monde du travail industriel, introduction au supplément. *Les enjeux de l'information et de la communication*, 16/3B, 5–15.

Andonova, Y., Kogan, A.-F., Wilhelm, C. (eds) (2014). Injonction de créativité et création sous contrainte : parallèles entre secteur culturel et monde du travail à l'épreuve du numérique. In *82ème Congrès de l'ACFAS*, 12–16 May. Université Concordia, Montreal [Online]. Available at: https://pastel.hal.science/SSG/hal-03664813v1.

Ardoino, J. and Berger, G. (1985). *D'une évaluation en miettes à une évaluation en actes. Le cas des universités*. Andsha, Paris.

Aristotle (1984). *The Complete Works of Aristotle*, Barnes, J. (ed.). Princeton University Press, Princeton.

Aristotle (1999). *Nicomachean Ethics*, Ross, W.D. (trans). Batoche Books Ltd., Kitchener.

Aristotle (2014). *Œuvres complètes*, Pellegrin, P. (ed.). Flammarion, Paris.

Ashcraft, K.L., Kuhn, T.R., Cooren, F. (2009). Constitutional amendements: 'Materializing' organizational communication. *The Academy of Management Annals*, 3(1), 1–48.

Aubert, N. (2006). *Hyperformance et combustion de soi*. S.E.R, Paris.

Audebrand, F. and Matuszak, C. (2008). Le sens de la médiation. *Les cahiers dynamiques*, 42, 67–69.

Austin, J.L. (1962). *How to Do Things with Words*. Clarendon Press, Oxford.

Badir, S. and Mouratidou, E. (eds) (2012). Introduction. In *MethIS : étendues de la réflexivité*, volume 3. Presses Universitaires de Liège, Liège.

Barats, C., Bouchard, J., Haakenstad, A. (eds) (2018). *Faire et dire l'évaluation. L'enseignement supérieur et la recherche conquis par la performance*. Presses des Mines, Paris.

Barbier, J.-M. (ed.) (1996). *Savoirs théoriques et savoirs d'action*. PUF, Paris.

Barbier, J.-M., Bourgeois, E., Chapelle, G., Ruano-Borbolan, J.-C. (eds) (2009). *Encyclopédie de la formation*. PUF, Paris.

Barth, F. (1969). *Ethnic Groups and Boundaries. The Social Organization of Culture Difference*. Waveland Press, Bergan.

Barthélémy-Ruiz, C. (2011). Jeux et détours en pédagogie. *Actualité de la formation permanente,* 224–225.

Barthes, R. (1978). *Le Neutre. Cours au Collège de France*. Le Seuil, Paris.

Bautier, R. (1994). *De la rhétorique à la communication*. Presses universitaires de Grenoble, Grenoble.

Bazin, J. (1979). Avant-propos. In *La raison graphique. La domestication de la pensée sauvage*, Goody, J. (ed.). Éditions de Minuit, Paris.

Berry, M. (1996). Savoir théorique et gestion. In *Savoirs théoriques et savoirs d'action*, Barbier, J.-M. (ed.). PUF, Paris.

Berry, V. (2008). Pong à World of Warcraft : construction et circulation de la culture (vidéo) ludique. In *La ronde des jeux et des jouets*, Brougère, G. (ed.). Autrement, Paris.

Berthelot, J.-M. (2001). *Épistémologie des sciences sociales.* PUF, Paris.

Berthelot, P. (2006). Les SIC à l'épreuve de la logique du CIFRE. Le cas d'une convention en agence de design. In *Questionner les pratiques d'information et de communication. Agir professionnel et agir social. Actes du 15ᵉ Congrès des sciences de l'information et de la communication*, 10–12 May. Université de Bordeaux, Bordeaux.

Berthelot-Guiet, K. (2005). Instrumentalisations de la sémiotique. *Études de communication*, 27. doi: 10.4000/edc.148.

Berthelot-Guiet, K. (2013). *Paroles de pub. La vie triviale de la publicité.* Éditions Non Standard, Le Havre.

Berthelot-Guiet, K. (2015). *Analyser les discours publicitaires.* Armand Colin, Paris.

Berthelot-Guiet, K. and Boutaud, J.-M. (eds) (2014). *Sémiotique mode d'emploi.* Éditions Le Bord de l'eau, Bordeaux.

Bidet, A., Quéré, L., Truc, G. (2011). Introduction. In *La formation des valeurs*, Dewey, J. (ed.). La Découverte, Paris.

Blanc, G. (2014). Débat et controverse autour des résultats de recherche entre universitaires et professionnels. In *Acteurs de la communication des entreprises et organisations, pratiques et perspectives*, Lépine, V., Martin-Juchat, F., Millet-Fourrier, C. (eds). Presses universitaires de Grenoble, Grenoble.

Boarini, S. (2005). Collection, comparaison, concertation. Le traitement du cas, de la casuistique moderne aux conférences de consensus. In *Penser par cas*, Passeron, J.-C. and Revel, J. (eds). Éditions de l'EHESS, Paris.

Bobbitt, J.F. (1913). Some general principles of management applied to the problems of city-school systems. In *Twelfth Yearbook of the National Society for the Study of Education*, National Society for the Study of Education (ed.). Nabu Press, New York.

Boltanski, L. (2009). *De la critique. Précis de sociologie de l'émancipation.* Gallimard, Paris.

Boltanski, L. and Chiapello, E. (1999). *Le nouvel esprit du capitalisme.* Gallimard, Paris.

Boltanski, L. and Thévenot, L. (1991). *De la justification. Les économies de la grandeur.* Gallimard, Paris.

Bonnet, J. (2015). L'intelligence du social dans les organisations. *Communication et organisation*, 47, 63–74.

Bonnet, J. and Galibert, O. (eds) (2016). Organisations et savoirs : quelles médiations ? *Communication et organisation*, 49, 5–17.

Bonnet, J., Bonnet, R., Viard, P. (2015). L'analyse de la pratique en formation infirmière. Vers une "clinique du sens". *Communication et organisation*, 47, 177–188.

Bouchard, J. (2017). Academic media ranking and the configurations of values in higher education: A sociotechnical history of a co-production in France. Between the media, state and higher education (1976–1989). *Higher Education*, 73, 947–962.

Bougnoux, D. (1991). *La communication par la bande*. La Découverte, Paris.

Bougnoux, D. (1995). *La communication contre l'information*. Hachette, Paris.

Bouquillion, P., Miège, B., Mœglin, P. (2013). *L'industrialisation des biens symboliques : les industries créatives en regard des industries culturelles*. Presses universitaires de Grenoble, Grenoble.

Bouquillion, P., Miège, B., Mœglin, P. (2015). Industries du contenu et industries de la communication. Contribution à une déconstruction de la notion de créativité. *Les enjeux de l'information et de la communication*, 16/3B [Online]. Available at: https://lesenjeux.univ-grenoble-alpes.fr/wp-content/uploads/2018/12/01-2015B-Bouquillon-Miege-Moeglin.pdf.

Bourdoncle, R. and Demailly, L. (eds) (1998). *Les professions de l'éducation et de la formation*. Presses Universitaires du Septentrion, Villeneuve d'Ascq.

Boure, R. (ed.) (2002). *Les origines des sciences de l'information et de la communication. Regards croisés*. Presses Universitaires du Septentrion, Villeneuve d'Ascq.

Boussard, V. (2008). *Sociologie de la gestion. Les faiseurs de performance*. Belin, Paris.

Boussard V., Demazière, D., Milburn, P. (eds) (2010). *L'injonction au professionnalisme. Analyses d'une dynamique plurielle*. Presses Universitaires de Rennes, Rennes.

Boutin, P., Candel, E., Escande, P., Gomez, G., Seurrat, A. (2014). "Le sens, c'est par là…". Manipulations ordinaires des productions médiatiques. In *Sémiotique mode d'emploi*, Berthelot-Guiet, K. and Boutaud, J.-M. (eds). Éditions Le Bord de l'Eau, Bordeaux.

Bouzon, A. (2002). Expertise et communication en conception de produits innovants. *Questions de communication*, 2, 47–56.

Bouzon, A. (2006). Modèles et conception publicitaire. Des pratiques incertaines, entre bricolage et braconnage, MSH Aquitaine. *Communication et organisation*, 30, 126–146.

Brougère, G. (2005). *Jouer/Apprendre*. Éditions Economica, Paris.

Brougère, G. (ed.) (2015). *Penser le jeu*. Éditions du Nouveau Monde, Paris.

Bruillard, E. (2011). Discours généraux sur les TIC en éducation : beaucoup de slogans peu étayés, en quête de débats. *Epinet* [Online] Available at: http://www.epi.asso.fr/revue/articles/a1110e.htm

Brulois, V. and Charpentier, J.-M. (2014). La communication interne au défi du social. In *Acteurs de la communication des entreprises et organisations, pratiques et perspectives*, Lépine, V., Juchat, F., Millet-Fourrier, M. (eds). Presses universitaires de Grenoble, Grenoble.

Brulois, V., Carignan, M.E., David, M., Errecart, A. (2016). Avant-propos. In *Dynamiques de professionnalisation en communication : entre ruptures et continuités, prescription et émancipation*, 4, 5–22. UCLouvain, Louvain.

Bullich, V. (2011). Le droit d'auteur en regard de la théorie des industries culturelles. *Les enjeux de l'information et de la communication*, 12/1, 51–68.

Bullich, V. (2018). La plateformisation de la formation. *Distance et médiations des savoirs*, 21 [Online]. Available at: https://journals.openedition.org/dms/2096.

Cariou, P. (1993). *Pascal et la casuistique*. PUF, Paris.

Carré, P. (2004). Bandura : une psychologie pour le XXI$^e$ siècle ? *Savoirs*, 5, 9–50.

Carré, P. (2016). L'apprenance : des dispositions aux situations. *Éducation permanente*, 207, 7–24.

Chardonnet, A. and Thibaudon, D. (2003). *Le guide du PDCA de Deming. Progrès continu et management*. Éditions d'Organisation, Paris.

Charlier, B., Deschryver, N., Peraya, D. (2006). Apprendre en présence et à distance. Une définition des dispositifs hybrides. *Distances et savoirs*, 4, 469–496.

Choppin, A. (1992). *Manuels scolaires : histoire et actualité*. Hachette Éducation, Paris.

Coirault, Y. (2016). *Les 5 clés pour être créatif au quotidien*. Dunod, Paris.

Coleridge, S.T. (1817). *Biographia Literaria*, Nigel Leask (ed.). J.M. Dent, London.

Combès, Y. (1993). Rationalisation de la formation : le lien social en question. *Études de communication*, 14, 37–50. doi: 10.4000/edc.2724.

Coriat, B. and Weinstein, O. (1995). *Les nouvelles théories de l'entreprise*. Livre de Poche, Paris.

Da Lage, E. and Vandiedonck, D. (eds) (2002). Questions de terrains. *Études de communication*, 25. doi: 10.4000/edc.92.

Dadoy, M. (1986). À la recherche de la notion de professionnalité. *Cahier du plan de construction*, 1, 137–148.

Darbellay, F. (ed.) (2012). *La circulation des savoirs. Interdisciplinarité, concepts nomades, analogies, métaphores*. Peter Lang, Bern.

Davallon, J. (2004). La médiation : la communication en procès ? *Médiation et information*, 19, 162–193.

Dayan, J.-L. and Eksl, J. (2007). À quoi sert la formation professionnelle continue ? *La note de veille*, 62, 13–18.

De La Broise, P. and Morillon, L. (2014). Des pratiques aux formations professionnelles, les liaisons dangereuses du marketing et de la communication ? In *Acteurs de la communication des entreprises et organisations, pratiques et perspectives*, Lépine, V., Martin-Juchat, F., Millet-Fourrier, C. (eds). Presses universitaires de Grenoble, Grenoble.

De Lescure, E. (2017). Apprendre à travailler à tout âge, pour qui et pour quoi ? *Sociologies pratiques*, 35, 1–7.

De Tressac, G. (1996). Savoirs, compétences et travail. In *Savoirs théoriques et savoirs d'action*, Barbier, J.-M. (ed.). PUF, Paris.

Delamotte, É. (1993). La formation comme lieu d'une industrialisation. *Les enjeux*, 14, 61–71 [Online]. Available at: http://journals.openedition.org/edc/2726.

Delamotte, É. (1998). De la professionnalisation à l'industrialisation. In *L'industrialisation de la formation. État de la question*, Mœglin, P. (ed.). CNDP, Paris.

Delmas, C. (2011). *Sociologie de l'expertise*. La Découverte, Paris.

Deming, W.E., (1986). *Out of the Crisis: Quality, Productivity, and Competitive Position*. Cambridge University Press, Cambridge.

Despres-Lonnet, M. (2000). Contribution à la conception d'interfaces de consultation de bases de données iconographiques. PhD Thesis, Université Lille 3, Lille.

Desrosières, A. (1995). Classer et mesurer : les deux faces de l'argument statistique. *Réseaux*, 13(71), 11–29.

Desrosières, A. (2001). Entre réalisme métrologique et conventions d'équivalence : les ambiguïtés de la sociologie quantitative. *Genèses*, 43, 112–127.

Desrosières, A. (2008). *L'argument statistique. Pour une sociologie historique de la quantification.* Presses de l'École des Mines, Paris.

Desrosières, A. and Kott, S. (2005). Quantifier. *Genèses*, 58, 2–7.

Dewey, J. (1929). *The Quest for Certainty: A Study of the Relation of Knowledge and Action.* G.P. Putnam's Sons, New York.

Dewey, J. (1939). Theory of valuation. In *The Later Works of John Dewey 1925–1953*, volume 1, Boydston, J.A. (ed.). Southern Illinois University Press, Carbondale.

Dewey, J. (2011) *La formation des valeurs*, Truc, G. and Bidet, A. (trans). La Découverte, Paris.

Domenget, J.-C. (2016). La professionnalisation des référenceurs aux prises avec le changement permanent. *Cahiers du RESIPROC*, 4, 25–41.

Douyère, D. and Le Marec, J. (2014). Des savoirs vivants de l'enquête à l'écriture de recherche. In *Méthodes de recherche sur l'information et la communication, regards croisés*, Bourdeloie, H. and Douyère, D. (eds). Mare & Martin, Paris.

Dru, J.-M. (1997). *Disruption : briser les conventions et redessiner le marché.* Village Mondial, Paris.

Dubar, C. (2015). *La formation professionnelle continue*, 6th edition. La Découverte, Paris.

Ducrot, O. (1984). *Le dire et le dit.* Éditions de Minuit, Paris.

Erenberg, A. (1994). *Le culte de la performance.* Calmann-Lévy, Paris.

Evetts, J. (2003). Explaining the construction of professionalism in the military: History, concept and theories. *Revue française de sociologie*, 4, 759–776.

Fassin, E. (2009). Une science sociale critique peut-elle être utile ? *Revue Tracés*, 9, 199–211.

Fichez, E. (1993). Du "marketing de la formation" : naturalisation, genèse et enjeux d'une notion. *Études de communication*, 14, 107–122.

Fichez, E. (1998). Industrialisation contre médiation. In *Industrialisation de la formation : état de la question*, Mœglin, P. (ed.). CNDP, Paris.

Flahault, F. (1978). *La parole intermédiaire.* Le Seuil, Paris.

Flamant, N. (2005). Observer, analyser, restituer. Conditions et contradictions de l'enquête ethnologique en entreprise. *Terrain*, 44, 137–152.

Foucault, M. (1969). *The Archeology of Knowledge*. Pantheon Books, New York.

Foucault, M. (1971). *The Order of Discourse*, McLeod, I. (trans). The Anarchist Library [Online]. Available at: https://theanarchistlibrary.org/library/michel-foucault-the-order-of-discourse.

Fournier, M. (2016). Formation en Europe : les principaux modèles. *De la formation au projet de vie*, 41, 61–69.

Gadea, C. and Olivesi, S. (eds) (2016). *Professions et professionnels de la communication*. Octarès Éditions, Toulouse.

Gadrey, J. (1994). La modernisation des services professionnels. Rationalisation industrielle ou rationalisation professionnelle ? *Revue française de sociologie*, 35–2, 163–195.

Gardey, D. (2008). *Écrire, calculer, classer. Comment une révolution de papier a transformé les sociétés contemporaines (1800–1940)*. La Découverte, Paris.

Gautron J. (ed.) (2003). *Le guide du benchmarking*. Éditions de l'Organisation, Paris.

German, R. (2017). L'intervention des médias informatisés dans le continuum de la médiation patrimoniale. D'une écriture des pratiques de visite à une pratique des écritures de médiation. PhD Thesis, Celsa Paris Sorbonne, Paris.

Goffman, E. (1959). *The Presentation of Self in Everyday Life*. Anchor Books, New York.

Goody, J. (1977). *The Domestication of the Savage Mind*. Cambridge University Press, Cambridge.

Grenier F. (2016). How can reflexivity inform critical pedagogies? Insights from the theory versus practice debate. *International Studies Perspectives*, 17(2), 154–172.

Grignon, T. (2015). L'expertise communicationnelle au prisme de ses instruments. L'exemple de Google Analytics. *Communication et professionnalisation*, 3, 23–47.

Grignon, T. (2016). Quand Google fait école. Une prétention pédagogique en question. *Communication & langages*, 188, 123–139.

Grignon, T. (2020). Contribution à l'analyse des reconfigurations contemporaines de l'expertise communicationnelle : prétentions, prédilections, savoirs, instruments. PhD Thesis, Université Paris Sorbonne Celsa, Paris.

Gryspeerdt, A. (2004). Relations publiques et recherche en communication. *Hermès*, 38, 148–154.

Guénée, P. (2017). La place des entreprises médias dans la formation des journalistes. *Chercheurs & journalistes*, 80 [Online]. Available at: https://www.cnmj.fr/wp-content/uploads/La-place-des-entreprises-medias-ds-formation-des-journalistes_web_planches.pdf.

Habermas, J. (1973). *La technique et la science comme idéologie*. Gallimard, Paris.

Habermas, J. (1987). *Toward a Rational Society*. Polity Press, Cambridge.

Herrmann, N. (1989). La mesure des dominances cérébrales. *Communication & langages*, 80, 52–72.

Herrmann, N. (1995). *The Creative Brain*. Quebecor Printing Book Group, Montreal.

Hurtubise, P. (1993). *La casuistique dans tous ses états*. Novalis, Montreal.

Jacob, C. (ed.) (2007). *Les lieux de savoir. Espaces et communautés*, volume 1. Albin Michel, Paris.

Jacobi, D. and Schiele, B. (eds) (1988). *Vulgariser la science. Le procès de l'ignorance*. Champ Vallon, Paris.

Jaillet, A. (1998). *La rhétorique de l'expert. Analyse de discours de consultants en entreprise*. L'Harmattan, Paris.

Jeanneret, Y. (2004). Le partage des savoirs entre métamorphose des médias et poétique des discours. In *Médiation et représentation des savoirs*, Metzger, J.-P. (ed.). L'Harmattan, Paris.

Jeanneret, Y. (2008). *Penser la trivialité : la vie triviale des êtres culturels*. Éditions Hermès-Lavoisier, Paris.

Jeanneret, Y. (2012). Le statut des savoirs ordinaires dans l'analyse des pratiques de communication. *MethIS*, 3, 21–50.

Jeanneret, Y. (2014). *Critique de la trivialité. Les médiations de la communication, enjeu de pouvoir*. Éditions Non Standard, Le Havre.

Jeanneret, Y. (2017). *Existe-il (vraiment) des technologies de l'information et de la communication ?* Presses Universitaires du Septentrion, Villeneuve d'Ascq.

Jeanneret, Y. and Tardy, C. (eds) (2005). Métamorphoses médiatiques, pratiques d'écriture et médiation des savoirs. Final Research Report, CELSA - Sorbonne Université, Paris.

Jézéquel, B. and Gérard, P. (2016). *La boîte à outils du responsable communication*, 3rd edition. Dunod, Paris.

Joly, P.B. (2015). Le régime des promesses technoscientifiques. In *Pourquoi tant de promesses*, Audétat, M. (ed.). Hermann, Paris.

Jullien, F. (1996). *Traité de l'efficacité*. Grasset, Paris.

Jurdant, B. (2009). *Les problèmes théoriques de la vulgarisation scientifique*. Éditions des archives contemporaines, Lyon.

Kapferer, J.-N. (1998). Maîtriser l'image de l'entreprise : le prisme d'identité. *Revue française de gestion*, 71, 76–83.

Kerbrat-Orecchioni, C. (2001). *Les actes de langage dans le discours*. Nathan, Paris.

Kuhn, T. (1996). *The Structure of Scientific Revolutions*. University of Chicago Press, Chicago.

Kuhn, D. (2019). Critical thinking as discourse. *Human Development*, 62(3), 146–164.

Labelle, S. and Seurrat, A. (2012). Médiations ludiques et activités d'apprentissage : réflexions à partir d'une expérience de conception d'un serious game. *RIHM*, 13(1) [Online]. Available at: http://europia.org/RIHM/V13N1/RIHM13(1)1-Edito.pdf.

Labelle, S. and Seurrat, A. (2014). Jouer pour être. *La Vie des idées* [Online]. Available at: http://www.laviedesidees.fr/Jouer-pour-etre-recrute.html.

Lambert, F. (2007). *L'écriture en recherche*. Parcours Éditions, Cannes.

Lambert F. (2013). *Je sais bien mais quand même. Essai pour une sémiotique des images et de la croyance*. Éditions Non Standard, Le Havre.

Laot, F. and De Lescure, E. (2006). Formateur d'adultes. Entre fonction et métier. *Recherche et formation*, 53, 7–9.

Lardellier P. (2008). "Arrêtez de décoder !" Une généalogie critique des pseudosciences du "décodage non verbal". *Communication & langages*, 155, 115–131.

Latour, B. (1990). Quand les anges deviennent de bien mauvais messagers. *Terrain*, 14, 76–91.

Laville, F. (2000). La cognition située. Une nouvelle approche de la rationalité limitée. *Revue économique*, 51(6), 1301–1333.

Le Bouëdec, A. (2016). La construction d'un discours organisationnel par le Message Management. Étude de cas du travail mené par une agence de conseil en communication. *Revue française des sciences de l'information et de la communication*, 9. doi: 10.4000/rfsic.2250.

Le Bouëdec, A. and Douyère, D. (2016). *Prise de parole en public et professionnalisation de la communication. Dynamiques de professionnalisation en communication : entre ruptures et continuités, prescription et émancipation.* UCLouvain, Louvain.

Le Marec, J. (2002a) Situations de communication dans la pratique de recherche : du terrain aux composites. *Études de communication*, 25, 15–40.

Le Marec, J. (2002b). *Ce que le terrain fait aux concepts : vers une théorie des composites.* Université Paris 7, Paris.

Le Marec, J. (2006). Les musées et bibliothèques comme espaces culturels de formation. *Savoirs*, 11, 9–38.

Le Moënne, C. (2006). Quelques remarques sur la portée et les limites des modèles de communication organisationnelle. *Communication et organisation*, 30, 48–76.

Lecomte, J. (2004). Les applications du sentiment d'efficacité personnelle. *Savoirs*, 2004(5), 59–90.

Léné, A. (2005). L'éducation, la formation et l'économie de la connaissance : approches économiques. *Éducation et sociétés*, 15, 91–103.

Lépine, V. (2013). L'évaluation de la communication : représentations et enjeux pour les professionnels. *Communication & professionnalisation*, 1, 70–89.

Lépine, V. (2014). La communication : questions d'évaluation et de mesures. In *Acteurs de la communication des entreprises et organisations, pratiques et perspectives*, Lépine, V., Martin-Juchat, F., Millet-Fourrier, C. (eds). Presses universitaires de Grenoble, Grenoble.

Lépine, V. and David, M. (2014). *Pratiques et réflexions autour des dispositifs d'apprentissage et de formation des communicateurs.* UCLouvain, Louvain.

Lépine, V., Martin-Juchat, F., Millet-Fourrier, C. (eds) (2014). *Acteurs de la communication des entreprises et organisations, pratiques et perspectives.* Presses universitaires de Grenoble, Grenoble.

Levine R., Locke C., Weinberger D. (2000). *The Cluetrain Manifesto: The End of Business as Usual.* Perseus, Cambridge.

Levoin, X. and Oger, C. (2012). Prix de créativité dans l'enseignement. "Bonnes pratiques" et modèle diffusionniste. *Communication & langages*, 173, 113–128.

Libaert, T. (2008). *Le plan de communication.* Dunod, Paris.

Libaert, T. (2011). *Les tableaux de bord de la communication.* Dunod, Paris.

Mallarmé, S. (1945). Diptyque. In *Œuvres complètes*. Gallimard, Paris.

Marion, P. (1997). Narratologie médiatique et médiagénie des récits. *Recherches en Communication*, 7, 61–87.

Marion, P. (2003). Médiagénies de la polémique. Les images "contre" : de la caricature à la cybercontestation. *Recherches en communication*, 20, 127–143.

Marti, C. (2015). De la gestion sémiotique à la prétention sociale des marques. Une analyse communicationnelle des pratiques du marketing. HDR, CELSA – Sorbonne Université, Paris.

Marti, C. and Seurrat, A. (2018). Kits de marques et médiation des savoirs : prétentions communicationnelles et reconfigurations médiatiques. *Les enjeux de l'information et de la communication*, 19/3B, 33–46.

Martin-Juchat, F. (2014). La place de la pensée stratégique en communication au sein des entreprises vue par les agences. In *Acteurs de la communication des entreprises et organisations, pratiques et perspectives*, Lépine, V., Martin-Juchat, F., Millet-Fourrier, C. (eds). Presses universitaires de Grenoble, Grenoble.

Maury, Y. and Kovacs, S. (2014). Étudier la part de l'humain dans les savoirs : les sciences de l'information et de la communication au défi de l'anthropologie des savoirs. *Études de communication*, 42, 15–28.

Mayère, A. (1993). Point de vue d'une économiste sur les services de formation (entretien avec Delamotte, É.). *Études de communication*, 14, 53–59.

McDonald, S. (2005). Studying actions in context: A qualitative shadowing method for organizational research. *Qualitative Research*, 5, 455–473.

Mehrabian, A. and Ferris, SR. (1967). Inference of attitudes from nonverbal communication in two channels. *Journal of Consulting Psychology*, 31(3), 248–252.

Mehrabian, A. and Wiener, M. (1967). Decoding of inconsistent communications. *Journal of Personality and Social Psychology*, 6(1), 109–114.

Melin-Soucramanien, F. (2001). La notion de jurisprudence du conseil constitutionnel. In *La pratique constitutionnelle en France et en Espagne*, Laroff, D. and Ramire, M. (eds). Presses Universitaires de Bordeaux, Bordeaux.

Miège, B. (2003). Une question à dépasser : celle de l'influence de la télévision et des médias de masse. In *La télévision et ses influences*, Fourquet, M.-P. and Courbet, D. (eds). De Boeck Supérieur, Louvain-la-Neuve.

Miège, B. (2004). *L'information-communication, objet de connaissance*. De Boeck, Brussels.

Miège, B. (2012). La circulation des savoirs et l'édification des sciences de l'information – communication. In *La circulation des savoirs. Interdisciplinarité, concepts nomades, analogies, métaphores*, Darbellay, F. (ed.). Peter Lang, Paris.

Moatti A. (2012). Le numérique, adjectif substantivé. *Le débat*, 170, 133–137.

Mœglin, P. (ed.) (1998). *L'industrialisation de la formation. État de la question*. CNDP, Paris.

Mœglin, P. (2005). *Outils et médias éducatifs : une approche communicationnelle*. Presses universitaires de Grenoble, Grenoble.

Mœglin, P. (2010). Industries culturelles et médiatiques : propositions pour une approche historiographique. Document, LabSIC – Paris 13, Paris. [Online]. Available at: http://observatoire-omic.fr/fr/art/411/industries-culturelles-et-mediatiques-propositions-pour-une-approche-historiographique.html

Mœglin, P. (2012). Une théorie pour penser les industries culturelles et informationnelles ? *Revue française des sciences de l'information et de la communication*, 1 [Online]. Available at: https://journals.openedition.org/rfsic/130.

Mœglin, P. (2015). Pour une économie politique de la création. De la trivialité à la créativité. *Communication & langages*, 185, 49–66.

Mœglin, P. (ed.) (2016). *Industrialiser l'éducation. Anthologie commentée (1913–2012)*. Presses Universitaires de Vincennes, Vincennes.

Mœglin, P. and Petit, L. (2016). Jacques Piveteau. Comme la production industrielle, le système scolaire ? In *Industrialiser l'éducation. Anthologie commentée (1913–2012)*, Mœglin, P. (ed.). Presses Universitaires de Vincennes, Saint-Denis.

Molinié, G. (2007). Rhétorique et herméneutique. *Dix-septième siècle*, 236, 433–434.

Monte, M. and Oger, C. (eds) (2015). Discours d'autorité : des discours sans éclat(s) ? *Mots*, 107 [Online]. Available at: https://journals.openedition.org/mots/21844.

Morillon, L. (2015). Rencontres de praticiens et de chercheurs en communication des organisations, des hybridations plurielles. *Les enjeux de l'information et de la communication*, 16/3A [Online]. Available at: http://lesenjeux.u-grenoble3.fr.

Morillon, L., Grosjean, S., Lambotte, F. (2018). Tension épistémologique en sciences dc l'information et de la communication. Regards croisés sur la communication organisationnelle. *Cahiers du numérique*, 15, 155–178.

Moscovici, S. (1961). *La psychanalyse, son image et son public*. PUF, Paris.

Müller, B. (2009). Les lieux de savoir : un entretien avec Christian Jacob. *Genèses*, 76, 116–136.

Née, E., Oger, C., Sitri, F. (2017). Le rapport : opérativité d'un genre hétérogène. *Mots. Les langages du politique*, 114, 9–24.

Oger, C. (2013). Fondements et formes de l'autorité en discours. HDR Thesis, CELSA - Sorbonne Université, Paris.

Parlier, M. and Ulmann, A.-L. (2013). Réflexivité et pratiques professionnelle : construire l'expérience. *Éducation permanente*, 196, 5–158.

Passeron, J.-C. and Revel, J. (eds) (2005). *Penser par cas*. Éditions de l'EHESS, Paris.

Patrin-Leclère, V. (2011). La communication revisitée par la conversation. *Communication & langages*, 169, 15–22.

Patrin-Leclère, V. and Seurrat, A. (2015). Rencontre d'Yves Jeanneret avec la rédaction d'*Esprit* suivie d'une interview de Jean-Maxence Granier. *Communication & langages*, 185, 37–48.

Pesqueux, Y. (2008). Planifier, agir, contrôler : voilà la recette du progrès continu. In *Petit bréviaire des idées reçues en management*. La Découverte, Paris.

Petit, L. (2013). À la recherche d'indices de changements paradigmatiques en éducation. HDR Thesis, Université Paris 7, Paris.

Petit, L. (2018). Revisiter l'approche par cas en sciences de l'information et de la communication. *Les cahiers du numérique*, 15, 139–154.

Pineau, G. (2013). Les réflexions sur les pratiques au cœur du tournant réflexif. *Éducation permanente*, 196, 9–24.

Porter, M.E. (2001). "The Limitations of SWOT Analysis: A Critical Review" by Michael E. Porter. *Journal of Marketing Theory and Practice*, 9(2), 54–69.

Putnam, LL. and Nicotera, AM. (2009). *Building Theories of Organization: The Constitutive Role of Communication*. Routledge, New York.

Rabatel, A. (2004). L'effacement énonciatif dans les discours rapportés et ses effets pragmatiques. *Langages*, 156, 3–17.

Reboul, A. (1992). Le paradoxe du mensonge dans la théorie des actes de langage. *Cahiers de linguistique française*, 13, 125–147.

Robert, P. (2010). *Mnémotechnologies*. Éditions Hermès-Lavoisier, Paris.

Robert, P. (2014). Les logiques politiques des TIC, les TIC, entre impensé, glissement de la prérogative politique et gestionnarisation. *RFSIC*, 5 [Online]. Available at: https://journals.openedition.org/rfsic/1046.

Robert, P. (ed.) (2017). *L'impensé numérique*. Éditions des archives contemporaines, Paris.

Robert, P. (2018). Penser la raison politique du numérique. *Cahiers de la SFSIC*, 14 [Online]. Available at: https://cahiers.sfsic.org/sfsic/index.php?id=293.

Santelmann, P. (2004). *De l'efficacité en formation continue*. Liaisons, Paris.

Schön, D. (2011). À la recherche d'une nouvelle épistémologie de la pratique et de ce qu'elle implique pour l'éducation des adultes. In *Savoirs théoriques et savoirs d'action*, Barbier, J.-M. (ed.). PUF, Paris.

Searle, J.R. (1969). *Speech Acts: An Essay in the Philosophy of Language*. Cambridge University Press, Cambridge.

Serverin, E. (2003). Les divergences de la jurisprudence comme objet de recherche. In *Les divergences de jurisprudence*, Angel, P. and Rivier, M.-C. (eds). Presses universitaires de Saint-Étienne, Saint-Étienne.

Seurrat, A. (2005). La construction de l'exemplarité. Légitimation, mise en forme et en circulation de "bonnes pratiques" en gestion de "la diversité" dans l'entreprise. Master's Thesis, CELSA - Sorbonne Université, Paris.

Seurrat, A. (2009). Les médias en kits pour promouvoir "la diversité". PhD Thesis, CELSA - Sorbonne Université, Paris [Online]. Available at: http://www.e-sorbonne.fr/sites/www.e-sorbonne.fr/files/theses/THESE-SEURRAT.pdf.

Seurrat A. (2010). Les médias en kits pour promouvoir "la diversité". *Les enjeux de l'information et de la communication*, 11/1, 160–169 [Online]. Available at: http://w3.ugrenoble3.fr/les_enjeux/2010/Seurrat/home.h.

Seurrat, A. (2011). Les bonnes pratiques en gestion de la diversité dans les entreprises In *Gestion des entreprises. Nouvelles compétences sociales et défis interculturels*, Benguerna, M. (ed.). Éditions Cread, Rennes.

Seurrat, A. (ed.) (2014). *Écrire un mémoire en sciences de l'information et de la communication : récits de cas, démarches et méthodes*. Presses Sorbonne Nouvelle, Paris.

Seurrat, A. (2015). Mesurer la diversité dans les médias ? Le cas du baromètre du CSA. In *La médiatisation de l'évaluation*, Bouchard, J., Candel, E., Cardy, H., Gomez-Mejia, G. (eds). Peter Lang, Paris.

Seurrat, A. (2016). Casuistique et médiation des savoirs dans la formation professionnelle. *Communication & organisation*, 49, 21–31.

Souchier, E. (2004). Mémoires – outils – langages. Vers une "société du texte" ? *Communication & langages*, 139, 41–52.

Soulé, B. (2007). Observation participante ou participation observante ? Usages et justifications de la notion de participation observante en sciences sociales. *Recherches qualitatives*, 27, 127–140.

Soulez, G. (2004). Rhétorique, public et "manipulation". *Hermès*, 38, 89–95.

Tallard, M. (2017). L'élaboration des règles dans le domaine de la FPC, un mode de construction multi-acteurs. *Sociologies pratiques*, 35, 19.

Tavernier, A. (2009). Rhétoriques journalistiques de médiatisation. La co-construction de l'expertise. *Questions de communication*, 19, 71–96.

Tavernier, A. (2012a). Vous pouvez répéter la réponse ? L'expertise scientifique au risque de la certitude. *MEI: Scientisme(s) & communication*, 35, 101–127.

Tavernier, A. (2012b). Introduction. *MEI: Scientisme(s) & communication*, 35, 9–21.

Tavernier, A. (2012c). De la normalisation des savoirs à l'imposture scientifique : détours de l'idéologie scientiste. Entretien avec Roland Gori. *MEI: Scientisme(s) & communication*, 35, 45–53.

Teisserenc, F. (2012). *Le Sophiste de Platon*. PUF, Paris.

Tindale, C. (2009). L'argumentation rhétorique et le problème de l'auditoire complexe. *Argumentation et analyse du discours*, 2 [Online]. Available at: https://journals.openedition.org/aad/493.

Treem, J. and Leonardi, P. (eds) (2016). *Expertise, Communication and Organizing*. Oxford University Press, Oxford.

Tremblay, G. (1998). Une approche pertinente ? In *L'industrialisation de la formation. État de la question*, Mœglin, P. (ed.). CNDP, Paris.

Tremblay, G. and Paquelin, D. (2016). Harold A. Innis. Un doyen contre les dérives de l'industrialisation. In *Industrialiser l'éducation*, Mœglin, P. (ed.). Presses Universitaires de Vincennes, Saint-Denis.

Trépos, J.-Y. (1996). *La sociologie de l'expertise*. PUF, Paris.

Verón, E. (1983). Il est là, je le vois, il me parle. *Communications*, 38, 98–120.

Waltzing, A. (2017). NPM y es-tu ? France, Pays-Bas, Allemagne années 1980. In *Faire et dire l'évaluation. L'enseignement supérieur et la recherche conquis par la performance*, Barats, C. and Bouchard, J. (eds). Presses des Mines, Paris.

Watzlawick, P., Beavin Bavelas, J., Jackson, D. (2011). *Pragmatics of Human Communication*. WW Norton, New York.

Weber, M. (1959). *Le savant et le politique*, Freund, J. (trans). Plon, Paris.

Weber, M. (2004). *The Vocation Lectures.* Hackett Publishing, Indianapolis.

Weiss, D. (1983). Du concept de professionnalité dans les relations industrielles italiennes. *Relations industrielles*, 38, 2. doi: 10.7202/029357ar.

Wittorski, R. (2005). Les relations entre formation et travail, et la professionnalisation. HDR Thesis, Université Paris 13, Villetaneuse.

Wittorski, R. (2009). À propos de la professionnalisation. In *Encyclopédie de la formation*, Barbier, J.-M., Bourgeois, E., Chapelle, G., Ruano-Borbolan, J.-C. (eds). PUF, Paris.

Wolton, D. (2009). *Informer n'est pas communiquer.* Éditions du CNRS, Paris.

# Index

## A, B

asynchronous, 40
authority, 7, 8, 10–14, 17, 29
best practice(s), 65, 66

## C, D

casuistry *see also* casuist, 137, 138, 140–142, 145, 146
certainty, 137, 146, 152–156, 158, 164, 167, 176
claim(s), 99–102, 104, 107, 108
creativity, 99, 117, 118, 120–127
critical distance, 191, 192
digitalization, 11, 17, 38, 44

## E, F

efficacy *see also* effective, 1, 8, 11, 12, 18, 20, 22, 23, 26, 29–31, 35, 37, 39, 41–43, 47, 52–55, 57, 58, 61, 65, 69–71, 73–84, 87, 88, 99, 100, 103, 105, 107, 109, 110, 113, 114, 116–120, 122, 126–129, 135, 137, 139, 140, 145, 148, 152, 153, 155, 157, 159–162, 164, 165, 169, 170, 172, 177, 178, 184–186, 188, 190, 193–198, 200
evaluation(s) *see also* evaluate, 177–193, 195–198

expertise *see also* expert, 4, 10–12, 14–17, 20, 22, 24, 26, 36, 38–40, 51, 57–62, 66, 67, 74, 76, 77, 79, 83, 85
formalism(s), 167, 168, 170, 173, 174, 176

## H, I

hierarchization, 137
industrial *see also* industrialization, 13, 33–37, 40
instrument *see also* instrumentalization, 147, 170

## L, M

legitimacy *see also* legitimization *or* legitimize, 1, 7, 8, 17, 40, 53, 137, 146, 149, 166
manager *see also* management, 177, 178, 181, 183, 185–187, 192, 195, 196, 198–201
mediation(s), 26–37, 42–45, 47–49, 137, 138, 141, 142, 144, 146, 147, 159, 164, 169, 177, 180, 182, 184, 199, 201
memorization, 146, 165, 170, 171
metrics *see also* measurement, 184, 187–190, 193, 195–198, 200, 202
model(s) *see also* modeling, 146, 147, 150, 152, 153, 156, 158–168, 173, 175, 176

## P, R

paradigm(s), 88–93, 95, 96
prescription(s) *see also* prescribe, 107–111, 115, 116, 119, 120, 133
procedure *see also* procedural, 99, 102, 110, 114, 115, 119, 120, 125, 127, 129, 134
professionalization *see also* professionality, 57, 59, 62, 64, 67, 68, 79, 80, 82, 84, 85, 88
promise(s), 8, 16, 22, 26, 30, 31, 33, 37, 40, 41, 44, 49, 54, 55
reflexivity, 99, 127–135, 185, 190–192, 197
rhetoric, 59, 71–75, 79, 86, 96

## S, T, V

skill(s), 59, 60, 62–68, 70, 77–82, 84–86
standard(s) *see also* standardization, 99, 107, 108, 110, 115, 118, 120, 121, 127, 129–133, 178, 180, 185–187, 190, 192, 193, 199–201
synchronous, 25
tool(s), 100, 103, 105–107, 109, 111, 113, 125, 127
triviality, 27
value *see also* valorization, 177, 179, 180, 183, 185, 196